The Economics of Sin

The Economics of Sin

Rational Choice or No Choice At All?

Samuel Cameron

Reader in Economics
University of Bradford, UK

Edward Elgar
Cheltenham, UK • Northampton, MA, USA

Published by
Edward Elgar Publishing Limited
Glensanda House
Montpellier Parade
Cheltenham
Glos GL50 1UA
UK

Edward Elgar Publishing, Inc.
136 West Street
Suite 202
Northampton
Massachusetts 01060
USA

A catalogue record for this book
is available from the British Library

Library of Congress Cataloguing in Publication Data

Cameron, Samuel.
    The economics of sin : rational choice or no choice at all?/Samuel Cameron.
      p. cm.
    Includes index.
    1. Economics—Moral and ethical aspects. I. Title.

    HB72.C36 2003
    174'.4—dc21   2002027146

ISBN 1 84064 867 8

Typeset by Cambrian Typesetters, Frimley, Surrey
Printed and bound in Great Britain by Biddles Ltd, *www.biddles.co.uk*

Contents

List of figures

List of tables

Acknowledgements

Thanks to the following individuals for commenting on some of the following or otherwise contributing to its formation: Alan Collins, Frances Hutchinson, John Sedgwick, Iain Smith.

PART I

1. Introduction

There is no Sin except stupidity.
Oscar Wilde

What has economics got to do with sin or indeed vice versa? These are the questions typically asked in connection with the present endeavour. A bold initial step could be taken, from a religious point of view, by saying that economics, as defined, endorses sin by dint of its stress on individual selfishness. In the formative days of professional economics much energy was expended fending off just such criticism from humanist critics such as Charles Dickens, John Ruskin and Thomas Carlyle. The battle may ultimately have led to the formulation of the optimality conditions of welfare economics, in the early part of the twentieth century, although the answers were to be found in seminal form in Adam Smith's monumental *Wealth of Nations* in 1776 when economics (or political economy as it was known) was still viewed as very much a branch of moral philosophy. The defences against this crude attack on the virtue of economics have grown in recent times, but many of them may have slipped from the view of the workaday economist besieged by the flood of research materials available and narrowed by the inevitable specialization attendant on ordering the discipline as a progressive positivistic enterprise with intensively cultivated sub-fields.

A more pragmatic response is that there are many activities, which significant segments of the population consider to be sinful, generating large amounts of revenue. For those who consider this activity to be the source of negative externalities it would be possible to go on to argue that standard measures of national income might well be adjusted to give a truer measure of the wealth of the nation. I do not propose to do this in the present work, which will sit firmly on the fence in the matter of quantitatively based advocacy with regard to sin. There are no cost–benefit analyses of sin, *in toto*, backed up with simulations and regressions, to be found in this book. Looking at the national wealth measure issue from the other side, it is possible that some would argue that attaching the sin label to essentially harmless activities is a severe drag on output and efficiency. For a start, in anticipation of Chapter 6, it is tempting to ask the reader by what percentage they would expect the national output to shrink if no one ever told a lie. A more concrete recent example of production barriers from ideas of sinning is the case of Sunday trading in the UK. Only comparatively recently has this become widespread. There were many intermittent moves to instate it, but these were met by constant objections that Sunday, being the Sabbath, was a day of rest and therefore should be 'kept sacred'. A very brutal economic logic was battering against this convention, viz. if the country bans trading on a seventh of the available time then it may be foregoing large economic gains, albeit individuals might simply choose to reallocate their time out of the previously condoned time zones.

A related link of sin to revenue generation is through the taxation of activity deemed to be sinful. This idea of sumptuary taxation can be linked to the notion of preventing excess and waste in a developing economy by taxing areas that may be detrimental to development potential. This is a straightforward efficiency argument derived from the belief that externalities are generated in the areas marked down for extra taxation. For example, the wealthy may expend their income in 'frivolous' consumption as opposed to savings that could be channelled into investment. The specifically sinful feature in this situation is the notion of waste, which is considered in Chapter 4. The more direct sumptuary tax argument is clearly stated in the 1892 textbook by Irish public finance economist, C.F. Bastable (p. 455): 'The last important influence that affects the selection of the objects of indirect taxation is the desire to discourage certain forms of outlay that are regarded as pernicious, or to take the mildest view, not promotive of economic or other virtues. This idea which lies at the root of all sumptuary taxes, is represented in modern Finance by the treatment of intoxicating drinks and tobacco.'

Although alcohol and tobacco have been taxed in almost all places, at some time or other, sumptuary taxes have extended to other less obvious items: for example in the reign of Catherine II in Russia, there was a tax on playing cards [Ryan (1999, p. 328)]. The sumptuary tax is justified partly on grounds of revenue transfer, but also in the hope of deterrence of sinning. In addition, it may signify a transfer of the concept of penance, from the expression of emotional energy into an economic form where the discharge of failure is through the medium of money.

This line of thinking is prone to heat up considerably, beyond a mild view, if we extend it to such things as prostitution, pornography and cocaine (see Chapters 8 and 10). Does it still seem quite reasonable to use a 'virtuous sin tax', i.e. imposing taxation to transfer income from the less virtuous to the more deserving when we bring those activities into the discussion?

Another reason for economists to be interested in sin is that its presence may overthrow some of the conventional wisdom on policy measures. Specifically, if sin is a public 'bad' then one might come to the conclusion that it would be best supplied under conditions of monopoly rather than the usually favoured market structure of perfect competition. This line of reasoning was hinted at by Schelling (1971) and taken to its limit by Buchanan (1973) in the context of organized crime. The key proposition is the very elementary one that profit-maximizing monopolists will seek to optimize by providing lower quantities at higher prices than their competitive equivalents. There are, of course, many caveats that could be made around this sweeping conclusion. Waiving those for the moment, one faces the conclusion, which Buchanan himself found rather unpalatable, that maybe the state should actively encourage monopolistic structures in sin industries rather than just tolerate them passively. Active promotion could of course be combined with a sumptuary tax policy or even state provision of the monopoly with potentially consequent redistribution of some of the profits to less sinful individuals. This policy package does resemble the way in which gambling has been treated in many places, where publicly owned or franchised bodies have usurped market provision generally in the form of a lottery.

Turning to perhaps the most obvious answer to our opening question, one derived from the empire building geist of the Becker/Chicago school in economics, we might say that economics analyses human choices under scarcity regardless of whether explicit movement of money or operation of markets is involved. Therefore, as engaging in anything seen to be sin is an act of choice, it can be subject to the logic of choice in the economic model. Movements of money and the machinations of markets simply represent the formation of institutions which are collective goods that enhance individual welfare. Churches, families, charities and so on are simply alternative means of doing this. They are not a species of supra-rational emanation which must be taken as given or delegated to some expert from another discipline for inspection. Thus economics becomes an analysis of how institutions form from the collective attempt to maximize utility. A useful definition of an institution from the viewpoint of conventional economics (rather than the largely marginalized American tradition of the 'old' 'Institutional Economics') is provided by Gifford (1999):

> . . . shared intentionality, shared expectations and belief systems that they entail represent a mental public good. One of the interesting aspects of this good is that it does not wear out with use in fact, it is strengthened by use, and it wears out, that is, is diminished or destroyed, with misuse or nonuse. Private or public individuals that misuse or exploit the system by behaving opportunistically impose two sorts of externalities on others. The first externality is imposed on an individual directly when another reneges on an obligation to her, the second is that the institution as a whole is weakened by individual misuse.

Whilst sin is not an institution *per se*, it is a feature which many institutions may seek to regulate due to an ontological belief in its existence, and/or use as a rhetorical ploy to manipulate behaviour. Chapters 2 and 3 will deal with the

formation of overt institutions in the form of organizations and the associated
matter of the evolution of norms and conventions. Before this, we need to
explore more fully the notion of individual rational choice: this takes up the
early part of Chapter 2, but first some preliminaries on the kind of territory we
are entering.

One may consider that, of the list of goods and services in the economy,
some fall into the category of sinful and others do not, with it being a straightforward process to analyse the choice between them in terms of relative prices.
This is the 'sin as an implicit tax approach', presuming that the individual feels
a sensation of negative utility flowing from guilt. A more complex version is
to treat sin as an abstract factor in the individual's production of satisfaction,
as opposed to a mere influence on the preference ordering of other goods.
Thus it becomes part of the human capital stock along with the various types
posited in Becker & Murphy's (1988) model of rational addiction. In technical terms the sin is separable from the goods rather than being embodied in
them, although we could have both types present simultaneously. I shall call
the abstract type 'generalized sin' to distinguish it from the more obvious
particularized sin case of an example such as the following: a young sport-
loving, and unwaveringly religious, boy grows up in a religious faith that
strictly denies the playing of sport on Saturday, yet he lives in a community
where the total utility of sport participation is greater on Saturday than any
other day. Thus, he is strongly incentivized to play on the 'wrong' day of the
week. Whether or not he does so comes down to a straightforward cost–
benefit calculation, trading off the gain from the sin versus the loss in terms of
internal guilt or anguish plus specific punishment costs (such as denial of other
goods) if detected. In this example there is a sinful commodity, albeit one
composed of an otherwise sin-free commodity, and an inappropriate time
zone. There is no satisfaction from sin *per se* in this case: the sin is simply a
negative consequence of a positive act no different from the hangover felt by
an areligious drunkard with no regrets for any negative effects of his/her
actions on others. The sin inheres in the goods or commodities. The obvious
case of abstract sin can be found in a strict religion with a pessimistic world
view, for example, where the individual feels a personal sense of guilt that is
invariant with respect to economic activities. Say they felt that their particular
sinful weakness was greed, such that they felt a sense of 'being greedy' attendant on the desire for even the most frugal consumption level, then their utility function would be shifted down compared with other people.

Generalized and specific sin can, of course, therefore have the unusual
feature of being a 'negative' form of capital. That is, it will have the capital-
like property of being a stock at a point in time, which may have a rate of
depreciation, but it will yield a flow of disutility over time, in that individuals
will be worse off than they would have been if they could have chosen to have

a sin-free preference set. In more prosaic terms, the case just cited refers to the individual who has acquired a stock of sin through investment in them by those of a religious disposition assuming that they are not simply manifesting some kind of neurosis of low self-esteem arising from other sources. One should caution that this depends heavily on the type of religion, a point we will return to in Chapter 3.

Further reflection shows that generalized sin is not unambiguously defined as a source of utility. That is, working within the confines of a given taste pattern, an individual may actually enjoy abstract sinning at certain times, even though suffering also ensues from the specific individual acts of sinful consumption. If we pursue the capital analogy (or metaphor) in conjunction with the assumption of rational choice, it follows that individuals may make investments which accelerate or reduce the depreciation rate of sin capital. If the sin capital has a simple direct relationship with adherence to religion then the investment decision involves deliberately manipulating one's own beliefs. Sin capital might also be subject to exogenous unplanned stochastic shocks: for example someone who moves to a new area because of a job may find an unanticipated increase in the cost of maintaining their sin capital from religious observance.

Whilst specific versus generalized sin is a fine distinction that can be made to do some work in terms of theoretical model-making, it is not capable of being deduced from revealed preference. In terms of the bread and butter economics of the demand curve, the presence of either form of sin is unlikely to alter the direction of its expected price and income relationship. What may well occur at the individual level are instabilities and irregularities such as 'binge' consumption where demand peaks radically and then falls near to zero. The likelihood of such things may differ depending on the precise specification of how sin enters the utility function. As the generalized sin notion is driving us in the direction of considering individuals to be in conflict with themselves rather than the owners of a unified set of preferences, we take up the attempts to extend choice into the area of 'meta-preferences' and self-command in Chapter 2.

Beyond the question of individual choice analysed in isolation, there is a growing literature on the economic analysis of group behaviour in terms of adherence to conventions, customs, norms or the manifestation of faddish, or fashion following, behaviour which may prove to be useful in analysing the emergence of 'sin' as a generally accepted term for certain activities. If the person is choosing a good or activity from the sin basket then it will have the implicit tax, mentioned above, in terms of their own feelings of guilt plus any feelings of shame or stigma from the disapproval of others [cp. Drago (1995)] which has to be added on as a reinforcing socialized dimension of sin.

A significant feature of modern economic life which has an intimate connection with sin is advertising. In the elementary microeconomics of choice there is no scope for advertising as we live in a world of perfect information with known preferences. Broadening the model to allow costs of acquiring necessary information opens the door for advertising to serve a socially efficient function of letting consumers know about price cuts, product improvements and new products. The idea that advertising determines preferences is not particularly welcome within the confines of orthodox economics, but leads a healthy life amongst Marxist economists such as Cowling (1982), neo-liberal dissenters inspired by Galbraith (1958) and ecologically minded critics of economic growth. The precise nature of the role of advertising will be taken up fully in Chapters 4 and 5. For now, let us note that, if advertising does change tastes it may serve to break down the specific sin barrier causing resistance to consumption of certain goods. Generalized sin might be used as a way of adding value to goods by conferring status to them as special events in the chronology of consumption where the user 'gives in' to temptation. One does not need to embark on a full-scale semiotic decoding of the messages in television commercials for chocolate products to be aware of this phenomenon.

Having said all of the above, it needs to be emphasized that the specific word or concept 'sin' leads a somewhat fugitive existence in economics compared with its currency in the wider world. Even in largely secular Western societies, the language and culture abound in expressions involving sin, and works of art and entertainment in which it is a prominent leitmotif. Such is the pervasiveness of the idea of sin in popular song, movies, television, novels and so forth that it might be claimed that it has escaped from being a symbol of religious thought into becoming a significant independent element in how the individual decision-maker visualizes their position in the social world and its networks. Many works of art and entertainment, in modern times, have been centred on the 'seven deadly sins', such as the major Hollywood movie *Seven* in which detectives are tracking down a serial killer who is killing a victim for each of the sins. In their last collaboration together Kurt Weill and Bertold Brecht produced a sung ballet called *The Seven Deadly Sins* where the sinner Anna was played by two different people. The piece consisted of a prologue and an epilogue between which were sandwiched movements entitled: Sloth, Pride, Anger, Gluttony, Lust, Avarice and Envy. Despite the unlikely setting, this was devised as a stern attack on the impact of capitalism in degrading humanity, although this is not immediately apparent from the libretto.

A rare exception to the omission of sin in economics titles, albeit quite an old one, is a short paper by Rendig Fels (1971) entitled 'The Price of Sin', which turns out to be an account of how the US military became involved in the supply of prostitutes to soldiers due to the need to maintain efficiency in soldiering. A recent paper by Posner & Rasmussen (1999) skirts round the issue in an analysis of social norms which distinguishes between guilt, a self-inflicted anguish cost from failing to keep to a social norm, and shame, where the failure is known to others. A pioneering work on sin, in an economic context, was written in 1907 by the maverick American sociologist E.A. Ross. He argued that business culture, combined with the doubt cast by science on older notions of spirituality, thrived on what were once deemed to be sins and thus sought to promote them. He was the first social scientist to look at the issue of the formation of social groups from individual action; this led to the notion of 'social control' in sociology. Much of his thinking on the dynamics of social groups is extremely compatible with what we term the CORN model of right and wrong (in the latter part of Chapter 2). One major difference is his perception that the group-imposed control, or punishment, is an outgrowth of intuitively sought individual controls rather than a purely instrumental value which brings benefits due to the action of the social group. This contrasts with the guilt/shame costs enumerated by Posner & Rasmussen (1999), although there is no intrinsic reason why Ross-style self-control should not be incorporated in a formal economic model. Further, it has some resemblance to the meta-preferential discourses in economics dealt with in Chapter 2.

A good proxy for assessing the cutting edge or vogueish ideas in economics is to search the titles of one of the enormous economics working paper databases on the internet. In January 2001, I visited IDEAS (http://ideas.uqam.ca) which had 115,000+ paper titles logged and not one featured sin in the title. Searching on some cognate terms, particularly envy, did produce a flurry of titles. Perhaps not without significance is the fact that many of the papers that did turn up with envy in the title were heavyweight exercises in game theory. Titles of papers do not tell the whole story, but there is no speedy way to appraise large amounts of text content. Perusal of economics texts in a number of areas is unlikely to reveal the word sin in the index. Not surprisingly some of the perceived categories of sin do make frequent appearances in some specialized areas of economics. Lying and deception (see Chapter 6) are often analysed in models of negotiations and collusion as it is blatantly obvious that the rational strategist, in a situation of wage bargaining or price fixing, may attempt to increase their utility by sending a false message to those with whom they are dealing. One arena that affords scope for strategic misrepresentation is the search for a marital or relationship partner. Although economists have carried out a considerable volume of research on family formation and dissolution, it features surprisingly little emphasis on manipulative signalling to attract a partner [but see Cameron & Collins (2000a)].

As we shall see, economists do think and write about sin without naming the name. There are seemingly good reasons for the lack of explicit economic attention to sin. For one thing, the tradition of professional economics post-war world was to endorse a clean break in the code of how an economist should go about their work. The break, derived from the philosophical work of Karl Popper (1935) was reduced to digestible form by Milton Friedman (1953). From this came the simplistic opposition of positive economics which deals with things as they are, thus confining itself to the isolation of cause and effect with the intent of generating accurate predictions: the holy grail of properly scientific research and normative economics where the researcher now considers issues of right and wrong but may well feel inclined to delegate some of this responsibility to philosophers or the ultimate clients of ideas in the form of policy makers. A full analysis of the compartmentalization of these strategies can be found in Machlup (1969). It should, of course, be borne in mind that the above discussion relates to Western economics: as we shall consider in Chapter 3, the body of thought known as 'Islamic Economics' does place heavy emphasis on sin and its avoidance.

In this schema, the proper process for the professional economist is to work in a neutral vein with an analytical model which has had all values purged from it. Sin as a highly charged emotive term was quite wisely to be avoided. Indeed, Fels's rare usage of it in an economics title was inclined to the ironic and provocative, as his paper conveys no sense of disapproval of the military regulation of paid sex to its recruits. Since the decks have been cleared of positive/normative fusion, even highly morally charged economists are unlikely to say 'Mass unemployment (or huge income inequality or crime or whatever)' is a sin, but rather inclined to say 'the theoretical model allied with the simulations and or statistical analysis in my paper suggests that the externalities are such that policy measure X is needed'. The positive/normative distinction does not rule out analysing the choice behaviour of individuals with respect to their own normative preferences, which is indeed the way in which we begin addressing the subject of sin in the present work in the next chapter.

Before going on to the plan of this book (and finally getting down fully to the definition of sin) it might be instructive to ask whether economists have been symmetrical in their (non?) stance towards sin. That is, how has the opposite of sin fared? I will assume that we can call this virtue or goodness. Probably on balance this has acquired more attention in the abstract and almost certainly more attention in the concrete. Back in 1759, when economics and philosophy were freely intermingled, Adam Smith, in his *Theory of Moral Sentiments*, roamed widely over human actions, sentiments and the judgements passed on them. Although he contributed some incisive chapters (to which we return in Part II) probing the possible desirability of the sides of human nature more generally frowned upon, at least three-quarters of the book is exclusively devoted to debating virtue and goodness. General discussions of virtue take place in the minority field of social economics and might be considered by many mainstream economists to be not really economics at all. Notwithstanding my experience of this work is that, whilst focusing on advocacy, it has stuck very much to the issue of promoting virtue or good and paid little attention to downsizing the sin economy. Turning to the concrete manifestations of virtue, altruism might be seen as the mirror state of malice, jealousy or envy as particular facets of the sinful life. This received a full-length book treatment in terms of theory, policy and evidence over 20 years ago [Collard (1978)]. It continues to get attention in the leading mainstream economic journals, most usually in the case of analysing intra-familial altruism inspired by the air of paradox in Gary Becker's 'rotten kid theorem' [Becker, (1991a)] and more widely in research on charitable donations.

The opposite of altruism, via philanthropic income transfer, is theft which may be broadly construed to include fraud. There is a massive literature on this, again inspired by Becker, stemming from his 1968 article in the *Journal of Political Economy*. In true positivist vein, this literature neither condemns nor condones acts of theft. Theft (and other related categories like burglary) and crime in general become crimes because of the externalities they generate not because of any intrinsic immorality implicit in a forced income transfer. Indeed, the economic model of crime may predict that some thefts are beneficial through improving the distribution of income or otherwise being correctives to the problem of the 'second best', in which optimality conditions are not being met due to some barriers in certain sectors of the economy [see Boadway & Bruce (1984)]. The amorality of all this is seen at its most transparent in a general equilibrium model of crime due to Usher (1986), where individuals make a rational utility-maximizing choice over whether to be fully specialized as a criminal, producer or law enforcer.

As economists have not been partial to devoting explicit attention to sin as a subject in itself, we might, to a degree, be involved in the making of the definition of the word for economic purposes. In colloquial usage, sin seems to connote simply doing something one shouldn't do, but there is usually a sense of rank ordering of the amount of wrong involved in terms of what precisely constituted the sin performance. In the *Oxford Companion to Philosophy* edited by Ted Honderich (1995), the definition of sin (p. 827) is given as:

> moral wrongdoing, or in some cases the omission of what one ought to do. It is usually thought of as the violation of natural law or the commands of a deity . . . From medieval times the Church has distinguished mortal sins from venial or less serious sins. . . . Some religious traditions allow for the possibility of the forgiveness of sin.

The price of sin in religious symbolism will ultimately be a trip to hell, but things are not that simple mainly due to this possibility of forgiveness. In Milton's *Paradise Lost*, Sin is a (female) keeper of the gates of hell who sprang from the head of Satan. Sinners have been promised a stay in purgatory waiting until their sins are purged if they are not to go to hell. Purgatory was sanctioned by a decree from the Council of Florence, rejected by the Church of England in 1562. In some traditions, there has been the notion that special sites could be visited to do penitence and thus gain absolution during one's lifetime; for example, there is a legend that Christ revealed to St Patrick that a cave on Station Island in Lough Derg in County Clare in the Republic of Ireland was reserved for this purpose. Another method of avoiding purgatory, in Britain, was to have 'sin eaters' hired to eat beside the corpse at funerals, so that they would take on the sins of the deceased in some cases via bizarre rituals involving salt and bread. This has the neat mathematical property of ensuring that no one goes to purgatory so long as the balance of population is sufficient that it can always be passed on to someone who passes it on to someone else when they die. In popular usage, the word purgatory seems to have become detached from sin as it now seems to mean any form of unbearable suffering inflicted on one, regardless of it being a payback for sin, even applying to things like sitting through a very boring play, sports event or economics lecture.

In many cases, activities deemed to be sins might also be described as the breaking of a taboo, that is, something that by convention one 'simply does not do' and any violation of which brings anguish costs to the individual. To a degree, taboo is a term more favoured by anthropologists and not much by philosophers. A word is perhaps needed on the terminology employed in this book and the relationship of the economic approach to sin with that in the mainstream of philosophy. Generally, I have tried to use economic terms in the way in which they are normally used by economists, but have made no attempt to ensure that philosophical concepts are rigorously employed or introduced. This has been done to avoid cluttering the text with excessive numbers of detours or footnotes. Hence broadly philosophical terms that appear are to be read in the way which they would be taken in everyday discourse, unless some further elaboration is provided. Having said that, the economic approach to sin corresponds broadly to what is termed 'modernist' philosophy. The axioms of rational choice are taken as self-evident and largely not open to doubt. Ethical relativism is applied rather than any attempt to deduce notions of the good from tenets beyond individual welfare maximization. By its very nature, economics tends to come down quite heavily on the side of individuals having free will, albeit in the presence of strong forces determining their choices, without engaging in the voluminous debate on the conflict between the two things which has long gone on in philosophy [for example, Moore (1912), Smart (1961), Baier (1966)]. The relativism of modern economics is fairly reflective of the society which hosts it: for example in 1981 an opinion poll question asked in Great Britain, France, West Germany, Italy and Spain showed around 60 per cent in each saying that the proposition:

There can never be clear and absolute guidelines about what is good and evil. What is good and evil depends entirely upon the circumstances of the time

was closer to their own point of view than an absolutist statement given for reference [Webb & Whybrow (1982)].

A number of schemata suggest themselves for a book like this. One such is to divide the chapters as per the seven deadly sins or the ten commandments of the Bible. The widespread usage of the 'seven deadly sins' concept emerged from monastic philosophy early in the sixth century, and there were originally eight according to Sidgwick (1919, p. 129). Opinions differed on what was in the list: the sins featuring in all lists were Pride, Avarice, Anger, Gluttony and Unchastity, with the remainder coming from Envy, Vainglory and the somewhat unlikely Gloominess and Languid Indifference (presumably this became Sloth). They were termed deadly sins as their perpetrator required absolution from them if the soul was not to be doomed. This quality was reinforced in religious iconography such as the engravings in the work of the eighteenth century German priest Romedius Knoll, which portrays seven sinners, in chains, being led to their doom by seven devils holding up cards illustrative of the sin the victims had been guilty of [de Givry (1971), p. 39)].

The list does not include many things that would be universally considered to be so extremely sinful that no possibility exists for redemption of the soul before it departs the earth. Invariably all of the items in these lists are dealt with at some point in the text. There are disadvantages of following any well-established sin listings. For one thing it might be seen as endorsing or confronting a specific viewpoint of a particular religion. It would also produce an imbalance in the amount of meaningful discussion that could be allocated to each, from an economic point of view.

The plan of the book is as follows. Part I is essentially the background in terms of economic analysis, with particular reference to the economics of religion which is now a substantial sub-field within the discipline. Part II delves into some of the seven deadly sins grouped into three chapters. The final Part III descends into more concrete issues with reference to particular acts of consumption that have attracted universal concern, on account of their inherent sinfulness, at some points in history. Not unreasonably, the final chapter reviews the journey we have been on and speculates on the future of sin, particularly the cultural formation of post-modern sins, most notably the expanding role of the notion of addiction in social discourse. The approach taken is eclectic. I start by riding the neo-classical economics horse, but whenever the fences in front of it look too formidable I resort to excursions into other disciplines. Inevitably some of this branching out will succeed as an integrated synthesis, whilst other parts will languish before the reader like ill-disciplined oil and water.

2. Tools of the trade: Rational choice

I'ld be a dog, a monkey or a bear, or anything but the vain animal, who is so proud
of being rational.

John Wilmot, Earl of Rochester, *A Satire Against Mankind*

INTRODUCTION

Since this is an economic analysis of sin, this chapter begins with a review of
the relevant tools of the economist's trade primarily with reference to
demand/consumer choice. Having done so, we then scrutinize the assumptions
of rational choice commonly said to underpin the use of these tools. This leads
on to a consideration of attempts to push back the boundaries of economic
models of decision-making by increasing the complexity of the representation
of the utility function, and/or incorporating newer psychological ideas than
those which entered the foundations of neo-classical economics. The final
section of this chapter looks at the extension of individual choices into social
group processes in the form of CORN models (Collectively Ordained Rational
Norms). Having developed these, we propose an extension of the models via
'voice entrepreneurs' with a specific illustration of the case of some notable
'sin entrepreneurs'.

MODELS OF SIN BASED ON RATIONAL CHOICE BY ISOLATED INDIVIDUALS

The standard introductory economic approach to decision-making supposes a
fixed utility function which is maximized subject to constraints of price and
income. When factor markets are included, income will not be fixed but will
be determined by the amount of factor supplied and its rate of return. Factor
rates of return may be influenced by investments made in the past such as
those in the form of human capital. The utility function will contain arguments
generally in the form of goods plus any external effects imposed by the behaviour of other individuals. Maximizing utility subject to constraints is the core
of the economist's definition of rationality. Utility is derived directly by
consuming goods. The fixity of the utility function comes from the assumption

14

that tastes are inherited from somewhere outside the choice-making environment. Out of these ingredients we derive the expectation of market supply curves which are positively related to price and market demand curves which are negatively related to price. As in any scientifically styled field of knowledge, anomalies to this 'normal' state of affairs do crop up, but their impact is reduced precisely by them being granted anomaly or curiosum status.

As indicated in Chapter 1, sin may be modelled as a component of the matrix of the exogenous tastes assumed to be imposed on the decision-maker, and therefore it will not appear as an overtly displayed element in a formal theoretical model. Its impact will be felt in terms of the relative marginal utilities of each good with respect to the quantity consumed. That is there may be, in a sense, an implicit 'sin tax' on a commodity which will lower its consumption relative to other goods compared to a world in which the individual could view it as sinless. Conversely, in cases where the sinfulness of a good is attractive to the consumer there will be an implicit 'sin subsidy' which increases consumption of the sinful goods. If sin were an arbitrarily arising individual emotion, rather than a socially formed experience, then we would have, in a population with diverse tastes for sin, people who are high consumers of sin goods and people who are low consumers of sin goods in the way that we have people who consume many fatty foods and others who consume few fatty foods.

A frequent criticism of economics is its asocial nature. The model implied by the above brief outline leaves out the presence of external effects in the form of utility interdependence with other people's endowments and choices or, even, opinions. These were incorporated, strictly within the assumption set of core microeconomic theory, by Leibenstein (1950) in his analysis of bandwagon, snob and Veblen goods. Evidently, a few of the deadly sins are embedded within this rubric, notably envy and pride but also possibly gluttony. This analysis is 'social' in the sense that it acknowledges the dictum from John Donne's 'Devotions' that 'no man is an island', but it does not deal with social processes in terms of the interactions between individuals. This is taken up at the end of this chapter and further in Chapter 3.

In the case of bandwagon goods, the quantity of consumption of the good by others enters as an argument in the utility function with a positive partial differential. Leibenstein formulates this variable as the total demand in the market minus one's own demand, thereby avoiding the need for any kind of social group analysis such as would be needed if the bandwagon being followed had an exclusively referential element to it, as would be the case where selected 'leaders' exist in the market. The issue of market leaders in promoting or inhibiting sin is clearly an important one. Bandwagon effects cause few problems for positive economic analysis in terms of deriving the demand curve and analysing the properties of the market equilibrium. Under conventional assumptions, a long-run stable equilibrium should exist, although the slope of the demand curve is different from what it would be in the absence of bandwagon effects. At a point the price elasticity will be greater than it would have been without the bandwagon effect.

The snob effect is simply the reverse of this, where the partial differential is negative. The same comments about equilibrium and the slope of the demand curve (but this time it will be flatter) would be expected to apply notwithstanding the tendency of the pure snob effect to be positively related to prices. It would be somewhat inconsistent to have relatively large negative income effects for a snob good, hence there should not be any independent tendency towards an upward-sloping demand curve from that source.

In the case of the Veblen effect, the consumer values a good more the higher is its perceived or 'conspicuous' price. This good serves the function of creating ostentatious display and thus is a flag of the status or wealth of its purchaser. This is not to be confused with the use of price as a quality signal which may also be present. Take the case of what marketing researchers would term 'premium brands'. In the specific case of ice cream, high-price brands have only really penetrated the UK market in recent times. Price is a quality signal here as the consumer can readily accept that higher-cost ingredients are needed to make the luxury brands, but it may also enhance utility through its conspicuous consumption properties. This is a long-winded way of saying that some consumers will derive utility gains from knowing that other people will experience envy. In the Veblen case there may be an upward-sloping segment as the market demand curve could be non-monotonic. This could cause problems because the intersection of downward-sloping supply and demand curves will cause the equilibrium to be unstable, with the possible consequence that a market may not exist. However, it is a little paradoxical to suggest that a market would not exist for a good in which consumers are deriving utility from the high price. Problems of existence and stability of equilibrium would evaporate if the market were supplied by a pure monopolist rather than a large collection of competing firms, as the monopolist would simply set the price which satisfies its objectives. Markets in which heavy elements of conspicuous consumption figure are likely to become extremely non-competitive, in a stable way, as there are incentives to create consumer loyalty and the heavy promotional costs of so doing are likely to constitute substantial barriers to entry for potential rivals. There is no reason why the above, externality-derived, effects should apply exclusively to consumer goods. Employers of labour are just as likely to be snobs, bandwagonists or Veblenites.

There have been two main extensions to the depiction of the programming problem facing the, perfectly informed, choice-maker in modern economic theory, both of them appearing first in the mid 1960s although, as always, one can find precedents. These are the Becker allocation of time model and the Lancaster 'goods characteristics' model. After these have been briefly discussed we will, in future, lump them together as the Becker–Lancaster approach. I deal with this literature as it makes it possible to fit some aspects of sinful consumption into economic modelling with less awkward contrivance than in the basic 'goods are goods' model implied above.

In Lancaster's (1971) approach utility is derived indirectly from the 'characteristics' that inhere in goods. Goods are no longer 'just goods', but rather factors of production which households purchase in order to combine them to produce utility. For example utility from a television is a function of size, picture quality, sound quality and programme quality. There is assumed to be continuous substitutability between characteristics in the individual's utility function. For many goods the optimal solution involves combining different 'brands' of the same good. This implies that giving producers freedom to proliferate brands will be welfare-enhancing provided other conditions are favourable. As part of market entry, a producer may engage in research and development to add characteristics to a good which will compensate for the presence or absence of sinful elements perceived as archetypal attributes of the good. Although not exclusively concerned with sin, examples of this kind of thing abound in the cases of vegetarian meat alternatives and slimming foods. This presentation follows the simple 'goods are goods' model above in so far as the sin characteristic is regarded as 'normal' in the sense that it has a positive income effect and any negative effects from sinning are seen as overwhelmed by this. Lipsey & Rosenbluth (1971) developed an extension of this model where normal goods may have inferior characteristics which may give rise to some discontinuities in the demand function. This might work in various ways: for example the desire to be virtuous in eating and drinking might be an inferior characteristic in the sense that its utility declines with income.

In Becker's (1965) model utility is derived from commodities which are made up of combinations of time, market goods and home-produced goods. Take the example of painting a room. This could be done in different ways. All require the purchase of market goods in the form of paint and brushes. At one extreme the owner of the house could use all her/his own labour, thus making this a very time-intensive form of production. At the other extreme an outside contractor could be used, making this a very low time-intensive product because of the purchase of time inputs from the market. How would economic man choose which method to use to paint the room? The correct approach is to compare the cost of the two options. The value of an hour of the hired painter's time will be known, whilst the value of an hour of the owner's time will be set equal to his marginal productivity in the labour market as represented by his wage rate. There are implications for the effect of wages on production. Someone with a low wage, *ceteris paribus*, will tend to be more likely to paint their own room and vice versa. There is a straightforward substitution effect away from time-intensive goods in proportion to their time intensity. Thus rising wages throughout society would lead us to expect to see more airplane travel and more frozen foods. There is a qualification to this: we should not ignore income effects. Leaving them out of the picture might seem to imply that rising wages might eliminate long walks, pleasure cruising, bird-watching and other like time-intensive activities. Similarly we would expect the highly paid worker to live off fast food. The income effect will reduce the impact of time reallocation on time-intensive goods. Some products may even have inferior characteristics, such as frozen food, hence their consumption could fall when their price falls.

Painting a room is not normally likely to be viewed as a sin, assuming that the paint is not produced under some unethical conditions and 'slavery' is not a feature of the employment of the painter's assistant. Nevertheless, as with the schoolboy footballer in Chapter 1, there is scope for the commodity becoming sinful when it is produced using labour from a religiously tabooed time zone when it would not otherwise be so. The allocation of time model predicts that, other things being equal, wage rate changes and technology changes would alter the levels of sinful consumption and production unless there were very unlikely restrictions placed on the technologies of production and consumption and the utility function. A broad conclusion would be that rises in the wage rate would tend to lead to increases in sin activity if sin goods are less time-intensive than sin-free goods, unless there was a sufficiently large income elasticity for the avoidance of sin. Within the frameworks considered so far there is no scope for the proposition that the wage and technology changes themselves will alter intrinsic preferences for sinful versus non-sinful goods. Economists have not entirely ignored the issue of taste formation, but it is probably fair to say that, in the mainstream, they only meet the problem half-way. As so often in the widening of economics, we encounter the fertile suggestions of Chicago's Gary S. Becker. He pioneered the concept of human capital. Human capital is defined as any investment in the development of skills in order to gain higher returns in the future. Thus an individual will decide on schooling versus consumption. Becker & Stigler (1977) extend the human capital idea to consumption capital. Consumption capital encapsulates things like acquired tastes, where the individual may need to sacrifice current consumption where the good gives less utility per money unit than rivals, or even outright disutility, for a greater discounted flow of future utility.

Let us consider this in the field of sins. The positive utility from the inherent properties of some goods labelled as sinful may be 'acquired' tastes. We can acquire such tastes by investing in things which raise the ability to enjoy them, or more simplistically by varying the time pattern of their consumption as in Becker & Murphy's 'rational addiction' model. A different Becker, sociologist Howard Becker (1953), had earlier obtained fame for his work implying that becoming a drug addict involved learning and effort and is therefore different from say buying a pair of trousers, in ways other than its ambivalent social status and any potential health damage. In a sense some of this form of social learning is the type of behaviour discussed in Chapter 1 in that people can choose, at the margin, between investing in raising the direct enjoyment of the sin good or in lowering the negative feelings from sin. As we are still assuming a perfect-knowledge risk-free environment, the factors influencing this choice would be the profile of returns over time from these strategies and the individual's discount rate. It is difficult to generate any plausible clear-cut predictions about this as various scenarios are possible. Take an individual who is 'impatient' (high discount rate), with a large stock of negative sin capital, being tempted by a heavily addictive good (one with strong complementarity over time in consumption), then the likely outcome is extreme feelings of sinfulness as consumption will be rising more rapidly than guilt or shame feelings are falling. If indeed it is of net benefit to induce them to fall at all. This is as far as we will go at this point in contemplating endogenous tastes within a mainstream economic model.

So, let us turn to a feature of the economics of sin that I have thus far neglected, viz. its inherent tendency to involve stochastic elements which are resolved by some economists into separate categories of risk and uncertainty following the pioneering work of Frank Knight. For those who accept a distinction between risk and uncertainty, the usual distinction is that risk comes from a known probability distribution and therefore can be quantified and factored into decision-making algorithms whilst 'genuine' uncertainty is totally unpredictable and thus cannot be. Although frequently assailed by contradictory evidence and alternative models, the central model for risky choice in economics is still the Subjective Expected Utility (SEU) model, which interestingly has an origin in worries about sin. The acknowledged start of this type of decision-making model is 'Pascal's Wager', wherein seventeenth century French mathematician Blaise Pascal explored the wisdom of deciding on the existence of God by way of calling heads or tails on a coin toss, viz. a 50–50 bet. So should we bet on God existing or not? Bernstein (1996, p. 70) summarizes the situation as follows:

> If God is not, whether you live your life piously or sinfully is immaterial. But suppose that God is. Then if you bet against the existence of God by refusing to live a life of piety and sacraments you run the risk of eternal damnation; the winner of the bet that God exists has the possibility of salvation. As salvation is clearly preferable to eternal damnation, the correct decision is to act on the basis that God is.

This takes us close to the rudiments of the economic theory of suicide, another Gary Becker spin-off brought to fruition by Hammermesh & Soss (1974). The SEU model is represented in the Von Neumann–Morgenstern utility function [see Machina (1989)]:

$$\text{SEU} = pU(Y1) + (1 - p)U(Y2) \qquad\qquad (2.1)$$

in which p is the probability of outcome $Y1$ and $1 - p$ is the probability of outcome $Y2$ where $Y1$ and $Y2$ are different levels of wealth. Essentially this is a straightforward gamble if we simplify by allowing one act which turns out to be a major sin with probability p and not a sin with probability $1 - p$. Let $Y1$ be a level of wealth attained after sinning and $Y2$ be the level of wealth if the individual is found to have sinned. For example, think of the archetypal Roman Catholic confession where a young man finds himself compelled to an experience whose sinfulness is in doubt until he contacts the agent of the church in the form of a priest.

Use of this equation is premised on a list of axioms and assumptions:

i.   transitivity, i.e. if situation A is preferred to B and B to C then A is preferred to C;
ii.   the individual is able to perform the necessary mathematics to obtain the best outcome or at least can behave, like the snooker player, as if these calculations have been done;
iii. a monetary equivalent can be found for all sets of outcomes;
iv.   linearity in probabilities; which implies
v.   the independence axiom which says: if the lottery P^* is preferred (or indifferent) to the lottery P then the mixture $aP^* + (1 - a)P^{**}$ will be preferred or indifferent to the mixture $aP + (1 - a)P^{**}$ for all $a > 0$ and P^{**}.

Assumptions (i) and (ii) are simply carried over from the choice without risk situations analysed earlier in the paper.

An important feature of the model is that decisions are not based on the expected money value of the outcome, rather they are based on the utility at different levels of wealth. In this model there would be different types of risk-takers: risk-neutral, risk-averse and risk-preferring. Membership of these categories is determined by the marginal utility of wealth being constant, declining and increasing, respectively. Economists normally assume risk-aversion or risk-neutrality because a rising marginal utility is usually ruled out. However, Becker's 1968 paper did lead to a brief period in which risk-preference was invoked in order to explain why so many criminals appeared to persist in the face of negative returns. Risk-neutrality means that a fair gamble will be taken. Risk-preference means that an unfair gamble will be taken. Risk-aversion means that a fair gamble will be rejected.

A straightforward prediction from this is that, assuming all other things are equal, a risk-averse individual is less likely to put a sin activity in their portfolio than a risk-neutral one, who is less likely than a risk-preferring individual.

Accepting the frequently used assumption of diminishing marginal utility would then lead to the conclusion that rising levels of wealth/income will bring falling levels of sin. This is a different proposition from that of any negative time-intensity effects of rising wage rates made above. Pursuing the line taken in Becker's 1968 article would imply that only risk-takers would sin when it may have a negative *ex post* return, which is certainly a proposition in keeping with the thoughts of Blaise Pascal.

Consistent rational behaviour, in this set-up, implies that an individual will not simultaneously take risks and insure against them. In terms of sin, where the individual has a meaningful mental image of hell and/or purgatory, the inconsistent behaviour pattern would be simultaneously putting resources into devotion, for the purposes of possible salvation, and repentance whilst actively sinning. A utility function could be devised that incorporates all three types of behaviour and this is often used to explain the paradox of the 'insurance buying gambler'. This was proposed in the inflected schedule of Friedman & Savage (1948), which in a way is an *ad hoc* opening into the world of 'framing' models which have arisen to cope with anomalies in the SEU.

Before shifting to more 'behavioural' economic models, I now briefly consider the lives of the saints in terms of game theory. Saintliness is a most peculiar phenomenon; its strangeness is well demonstrated in the tale of the hermit Iakovos and the daughter of a rich man who:

> was possessed by a demon who made her call out the hermit's name. Her parents brought her to Iakovos to be healed. After expelling the demon, the hermit began to be attacked by desire. He was defeated and slept with the girl whom he subsequently killed. Such was his remorse that he buried himself in a grave and through repentance was so purified of his pollution that he was able to perform a miracle assuring his sanctity. Thus his sin was corrected, and his saintliness increased. [Laiou (1993, p. 217)]

The archetypal path to sainthood involves suffering in a state of social isolation in a hostile physical environment (graveyards, arid barnyards, etc.). Saints can become cults in their lifetimes but are most prone to this after death, when people visit the sites of their suffering in order to seek solace, miracle cures, and so on. Lecture 11–15 of James (1997) gives a detailed analysis of the psychology of saintliness in the context of the strains of religious belief. In the lexicon of sin, saints fulfil the role of showing the power for good that can come from having the willpower to overcome sin. At a less grandiose level the 'sin eaters', discussed below, also serve an agency function of drawing off the costs of sin from the rest of us and thereby helping us avoid hell or purgatory. Figure 2.1 is the game tree for the would-be saint. Assigning payoffs to outcomes would make this the extensive form: it is

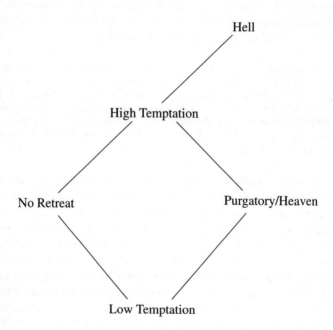

Figure 2.1   Game tree for a would-be saint

difficult to think of what the difference between heaven, hell, heaven via purgatory, and hell via purgatory might reasonably be in terms of utils, but there is an obvious rank ordering between them.

The would-be saint is playing a game against the 'state of nature' which determines their probability of salvation in the 'retreat' or 'no retreat' states. 'No retreat' involves pursuing the same life as other people whilst retreat involves hermit-style withdrawal into deserts, caves, farmyards, etc. If rational, sainthood is a game involving lifetime and post-existence utility calculations and all the relevant payoffs will be compared. To simplify the problem we need to assume a known lifetime with fixed imaginary time periods for purgatory and the afterlife, and a constant discount rate, fixed risk-preference and other tastes. The sainthood game is played against nature in the sense that nature determines the probabilities of high and low temptation and the probabilities of heaven, hell and purgatory following each node. Thus arises a rather paradoxical aspect of sainthood: the saint may become a cult with shrines and so forth when they have gone to hell rather than heaven. After all, assuming free agency for sin (i.e. one is not born evil), temptation can be lowered in the retreat but not reduced to zero as even the hermit can practise bodily sinning and entertain sinful thoughts. It is therefore necessary, if the sainthood game is to be an attractive lottery to enter, that the ascent to heaven is validated by a regulatory body in the shape of a church not perceived to be corrupt.

The existence of the sainthood game then serves as an incentive for the church to maintain its integrity as the licensor of the product. Further, the patronage of sites of sainthood serves a useful function to the individual who aspires to go to heaven. That is, uncertainty is reduced by clarifying the requirements and also the saint provides inspiration that the goal is attainable. In the game tree of Figure 2.1 the states of nature are assumed to be such that whatever temptation is present in the retreat is much lower than the 'low-temptation' outcome in the strategy of leading a normal life. As many saints lead supposedly normal lives in the period prior to retreat, economic modelling might suggest that they could operate a mixed strategy where they make a rational choice over all three alternatives: some retreat, low-temptation and high-temptation non-retreat. However, it seems more realistic in terms of the broad historical facts to take would-be saints as being at a node where the option is only of discrete strategies, that is go into retreat versus non-retreat where nature may deal a high- or low-temptation outcome for the rest of the game duration. It is then feasible in such a scenario that a person may undergo sufferings conducive to sainthood as a rational choice based on forward induction to solve their game-theoretic problem.

RATIONAL CHOICE OR NO CHOICE AT ALL?

Before going on to more behavioural models, I will revisit the rational choice assumption in greater detail. So far, in order to fit sin into the rational choice model as conventionally construed, we have treated sin as an unambiguous single-valued experience. Granted, the marginal value may change from positive to negative or vice versa with investments and the passage of time, and sin may be present as a characteristic with an opposite value to other characteristics inherent in a good. Nevertheless this is a presentation where experiences are unambiguous, in the sense that the individual does not have wavering or contradictory feelings about the elements in their choice. They may anticipate a 'pain' cost of being caught and punished for a sin and going to hell or purgatory, but that is an element of the 'hedonic' price of engaging in it along with the usual price elements.

Economics is founded on the bedrock notion that individuals engage in rational choice. There are a number of elements to the definition of rational choice, some of which are more fundamental to microeconomic modelling than others. Regardless of this, the goal of the enterprise is commonly agreed to be the positivist one, endorsed by Friedman (1953), of generating accurate predictions of human behaviour. In the extreme view expounded by Friedman there is no time for ethnomethodology: it does not matter whether the actors in the model would necessarily agree with the assumptions of the model or find them rational if asked to make an introspective or subjective judgement on them. This position was, to a degree, inspired by hostility to questionnaire studies of businessmen showing they did not follow textbook economic pricing strategies.

The opposite pole to this perspective is to see rational choice as a value judgement in itself, specifically one which accords the desires of the individual decision-makers autonomous status as the source of measures of well-being. In terms of sin, the economic argument, in rebuking a stern moralist, would be: 'you may say these people are sinning and would be better off if they desisted but as far as I am concerned they are entitled to determine their happiness so long as they do not impinge on the rights of others'. This embodies the essential small 'l' liberalism of the mainstream of the economics discipline, in which the infringements on others' well-being is dealt with via the concept of externalities, which reached its full flowering in the work of Cambridge economist A.C. Pigou early in the twentieth century. The simplistic concept of the externality has been battered somewhat by capital 'L' Liberals, as in the total rejection by Austrian economists and the revisionism of 'Law and Economics' emanating from Coase (1960).

As Ken Arrow (1986, p. 203) points out, 'Rationality hypotheses are partial and frequently, if not always, supplemented by assumptions of a different character.' He goes on to argue that rationality is often invoked ritualistically in applying models rather than being justified from within the essential logic of the problem being analysed. To a large extent this reflects the methodological individualism of economic thinking which [cp. Schutz (1943)] may run into problems when confronting social behaviour. Let us now unpack the elements of this thinking a little further. Rationality is generally discussed by philosophers in terms of whether or not individuals have free will. In economics there is the additional concern of underpinning models that are empirically testable within the confines of the many variants of multivariate classical statistics. Hence, the first component of rationality is consistency in that the same sort of choice will tend to be made in a given situation if it is repeated. Such stability says nothing about the desirability of the outcome which is generated. This is derived from the central proposition of microeconomics: utility maximization. It is portrayed as self-evident that only a fool would shun any opportunities which offer scope for making their personal feelings of well-being greater than they currently are. The objections that individual satisfaction cannot be measured and that individuals also care about other people have been readily disposed of as threats of any kind of breach in the armour of the rational choice model. Genuinely measurable utility in the sense of absolute cardinal measures, in the vein of height or weight, is rejected by almost all economists; it would be hard to find anyone who believes in the existence of the 'utils' which are brought into introductory quantitative economics books as illustrative material. This does not matter for the explanation of individual behaviour, and in the ideal world of elementary welfare economics it does not matter for social welfare either. As Clarence Ayres (1962, p. 76) so eloquently puts it:

> Price seems to have solved the immemorial enigma. To the question, 'What is Happiness? Who Shall Say?' the classical economists seemed to have found a final answer; no one can say but no one need say since the precise system provides a subtle instrument through the operation of which every man can have his say.

Economics of the recent modern era works in terms of preference orderings where we assume that an individual has a known rank ordering over all the possible combinations of goods that they might be offered. Thus, an individual offered the choice between two baskets of goods (a, b, c) and (a, b, d), where a, b and c are fixed quantities of three sin-free goods and d is a quantity of a sin-infected good which is otherwise of identical utility-giving capacity to c, would not take the second choice. Let us then take our first economic definition of a sin good as the case where the negative utility of sinning outweighs the gain implicit in the attractiveness of the sin good. Further, let us assume that individual perception of sin is not a function of being caught, that is the negative utility from d regardless of who knows about it. Being caught introduces an independent factor of costs if a punishment is imposed on the individual due to the decisions of other people in the group. This was briefly considered in the simple SEU-based model of sin as a portfolio choice in the last section. The issue is taken up again in this chapter on the general category of CORN models.

This definition leads us straight into a cul-de-sac as no one would ever sin. Some individuals will prefer the second bundle to the first and thus engage in an act that their reference group attaches the 'sin' label to, but this has to mean that they personally do not experience the negative utility in sufficient volume to be deterred. The only thing that can put them off is shame, guilt or explicit punishments, which are just price signals and not full-blown feelings of sin. Note that we have slipped into the practice of adding things on to rationality in the way that Arrow suggests. Or rather, conveniently not considering certain things. If preferences determine utility why should individuals not engage in large-scale attempts to change their own preferences? This is clearly the underlying rationale in the lives of various saints and the Calvinist protagonist of James Hogg's novel, set in seventeenth century Scotland, *The Private Memoirs and Confessions of a Justified Sinner* (1997). From one point of view it might be said that living in a cemetery, dependent on food thrown over the wall for subsistence, as did St Antony, the founder of monasticism, is a highly rational choice and from the other it might be argued that the complete opposite is more rational as tastes are being changed in completely the wrong direction. This view is taken up in the latter part of this chapter when we look at entrepreneurs of sin.

META-PREFERENCES AND SELF-CONTROL

The story so far is as follows. Sins can be fitted into economic models as externalities. The Becker–Lancaster model allows us to handle them in terms of being 'bad' characteristics of an otherwise pleasurable experience. If part of the price of sin is being caught and made to suffer, then we can handle that in terms of an SEU model or some variant of game theory. All of this is premised on a rational choice foundation. Is there something unsatisfactory about thinking in terms of rational choices over irrational emotions and passions aroused by the punitive dimensions of sin? If so, is it possible to open up the toolbox of economics to let a little air in without the equipment becoming rusted and useless? I should note in passing that there have been attempts [Collins (1993), Frank (1993)] to deal with emotions in terms of methodological individualism where they are regarded as socialized intentions which are acted on, instrumentally, in the vein of the traditional instrumental utility-maximization model.

Some apparently irrational behaviour can be treated in terms of responses to the risk of a loss of 'self-control'. As Oscar Wilde, not a neo-classical economist so far as we know, says in *Lady Windermere's Fan*, 'I can resist everything except temptation.' Some economists have attempted to take this dilemma on board in multiple utility models [Thaler & Shefrin (1988), Schelling (1984), Etzioni (1987)]. The traditional model of choice rules out any kind of judgemental ordering of the arguments of the utility function. If we relax this requirement then individuals have preferences about preferences. Models of self-control argue that individuals have 'higher' preferences which lead them to seek additional constraints to incomes and market prices which will reign in the drive to satisfy 'lower-order' preferences. We can see these added restrictions as 'utility enhancing consumption constraints' [Levy (1988)]. Firstly, you may seek to impose constraints, additional to price and income, on yourself (i.e. utility-enhancing constraints). Compulsive sinners might pay to have their sins reduced via religious consultations or the secular consolation of therapy, or, indeed, having themselves temporarily locked up in a religious or secular 'retreat' in order that the impulse may diminish due to lack of stimulus and a possible revision of preferences through a prolonged period of contemplation.

One strain of self-control thinking is the 'mental accounting' proposed by Thaler & Shefrin (1988). The solution proposed above, of external curbs or routines, is, they say, not available across all the areas where self-control may falter. So there should also be internal rules which need to be habitual in order to be effective. They must be simple to follow. Complex rules are likely to weaken the ability to exercise self-control. Habits also have the advantage of driving out forgetfulness, which can be as serious as passion in driving individuals off their optimal paths. In the case of sin, mental accounting could involve simple budgeting rules like not to drink at all or not to have an internet connection in one's house. Not all individuals will necessarily follow the same rules in the same situations. What looks rational to one individual will appear not so to another.

It has been argued, from an empirical viewpoint, that the introduction of control problems adds an irrelevant fifth wheel to the machine of microeconomic theory. Brennan (1989) claims that all the behavioural phenomena which intrigue control theorists can be accounted for using a 'mono' utility function model. But, do we now run the risk, as theorists, of going round and round perpetually trapped in an empty box of rational choice: viz. how do we answer the proposition that someone who has the foresight to erect these constraints or pay the costs surely must be able to deny themselves the behaviour which must be a net welfare loss in the first place?

Maybe we can escape from this conundrum with the distinction between long-run and short-run adjustment to optimal choices. Much of the treatment of sin in religious thought has been about the long-run payoff of short-run indiscretions, implying that a change in the discount rate might be enough to rescue a sinner. In broad economic terms the reason for foregoing the required willpower constraints, in the short run, is that these impose costs in the form of psychic effort [Thaler & Shefrin (1988)]. Emotional impulses, such as desires to sin, may bring exogenous (at least in the short run) doses of pain which need to be dealt with. The process of dealing with these may bring further pain. The pain of deciding to face problems may be of various sorts. There is the anguish of tergiversation, as examined by Akerlof (1991), if contemplating adopting a ready-made rule of action or devising a brand-new strategy custom-made for the occasion. In addition, there is the possible pain of 'regret' in the form of the utility loss from foregoing an opportunity due to adopting the wrong rule or a misguided custom-made strategy. One response to alleviating such pains is through careful choice of membership of a religious organization, which we address in the next chapter.

So much for actions or choices, but an individual does not derive utility merely from the outcomes of their preferences as revealed. Beliefs are also a component of individual welfare. Maintaining beliefs that conflict with the environment imposes further costs in the form of the strain of reconciliation. Here we seem to be encroaching on what many economists might consider the psychological boundary with economics. As has been pointed out by Sen (1976/7), economic theory has soldiered on for a very long time in isolation from psychological input other than that acquired when it first firmed up into a 'hard' neo-scientific social science. Inevitably as time passes and the research paradigm has been extended into hitherto untilled areas, particularly via Becker's corps of empire builders, the strains begin to show. Part of the rationale for the present work is that many of the 'social' areas into which economics has strayed can be brought into some kind of unity when viewed through the lens of sin. As will be apparent from the earlier part of this chapter, the standard microeconomic decision model is pushed into various twists and turns when we try to do this. And so, we find ourselves at this point reaching out for some more modern psychological input than the hedonic calculus of the nineteenth century to attempt a meaningful closure in the face of the self-control issue.

The main contender is the idea of cognitive dissonance, although noted heterodox economist Peter Earl (1983) favours Kelly's 'personality construct theory'. Cognitive dissonance was first propounded by psychologist Leon Festinger in 1957. A modified variant of it has been incorporated in economic models by some fairly mainstream economists [see Akerlof & Dickens (1982), Gilad, Kaish & Loeb (1987)]. Dissonance is the opposite of consonance, or harmony between the elements of one's life. For example, someone who believes that they live a decent and honourable life in the face of opposing evidence will experience dissonance. The historic legacy of the concept of sin is riven with the potential for dissonance. Such dissonance can cut both ways. That is, a person endowed with a large stock of guilt from their sin capital may experience strain in coming to terms with the inherent virtuousness, or at the very least sin-neutrality, of much of their conduct, or of course the perpetual sinner may operate in a state of denial of their persistent fall.

In their formal model, Gilad et al. (1987) assume individuals will try, as rational *hominis economici*, to reduce the level of dissonance because dissonance causes negative utility. Dissonance is reduced by selective exposure via the deliberate evasion of dissonant information. Individuals may play down the importance of potentially dissonant information or simply make sure that it is not received. Dissonance may be defined as arising from a 'surprise', defined as expected minus actual utility at time t. Decision-makers ignore surprises so long as they fall below a threshold level denoted as k; i.e. unless a surprise is a sufficiently big surprise individuals do not change their perceptions of the environment. Dissonance may trigger an information filter which selects in favour of information that confirms the wished-for belief that is otherwise contradicted by the world.

It must be stressed that k is a choice variable. Individuals choose a k value which balances the cost of blocking dissonant information against the gain in terms of avoiding mental strain by maintaining an inaccurate view of the choice environment. The literature [cp. Gilad et al. (1987, p. 67)] recognizes individual differences in tolerance towards cognitive dissonance. The level may depend on constraints in the decision-making environment. It must be stressed that the economists' version of cognitive dissonance makes quite a departure from the original work of Festinger [see Earl (1990)]. In particular the economic models of cognitive dissonance ignore the issue of prior choice of desired lifestyle. Dissonance reduction in Akerlof-inspired models is through avoidance of information which contradicts an exogenously given image. To put it in self-control terms, meta-preferences are treated as given whereas Festinger (1957) explores the origins of these. As Gilad et al. point out, the level at which k is set will depend on the environment in which the decision-maker operates. Variability of k can provide the linkage with the traditional approach. Hence, we can expand the model to allow for personality simply by allowing a new argument in the utility function (k) and seeking to measure it.

The idea of filtering has been extended in a paper by McCain (1990). In his model the notion of a two-tier preference system is replaced by the idea of an individual subject to a series of impulses. The choice decision then becomes one of deciding whether or not to obey impulses. The decision is made according to a series of filters. These filters may be motivational, attitudinal, expectational or the 'real' resource constraints which microeconomists are familiar with. On the latter point there is a price and income filter. This need not serve as a binding constraint. A poor individual with a sudden wish for a costly durable could first encounter filters for: (i) morality, whether or not it is all right to perpetrate crime to obtain the good; and (ii) debt attitudes, whether or not it is all right to take out a penurious loan to obtain the good.

CORN MODELS

Although it may be derived from some 'deep structure' in the human psyche about the rules of deities, which has been transmuted into notions of a natural order, the notion of sin clearly partakes of the quality of a social judgement. There is by now a fair amount of economic analysis on the degree to which individuals follow social conventions [for example: Akerlof (1984), Axelrod (1984), Bannerjee (1992), Bernheim (1994), Bikhchandani, Hirshleifer & Welch (1992), Coleman (1987), Gifford (1999), Granovetter (1979), Heiner (1983), Hirshleifer (1995), Jones (1984), Kandori (1992), Manski (2000), Young (1992)]. Social conventions, in a public good-like manner as mentioned in Chapter 1, are the most logical and consistent way of analysing the emergence of sins within the rational choice model.

One basis for institutions is the proposition that curtailment of individual drives to sin is needed to enhance group welfare. Take for example the issues of promiscuity, and even rape, counterbalanced against the opposing notion of marriage as virtuous, which was once so prevalent that cohabitation was widely known as 'living in sin'. Sociobiologists [Barash (1979), Wilson (1975), Buss (1994), Wright (1994)] posit that the pursuit of regular sexual intercourse is a basic human desire arising from the instinct to propagate one's genes. Even in a wild and unfettered 'state of nature' its frequency and timing in the lifecycle would be constrained by the additional desire to maximize the likelihood of success of each conception to which one has been party. There is no intrinsic conflict between the sociobiological premises and the economic analysis of customs, as the latter can be seen as modelling a collective compromise, which attempts to bring about an optimal regulation of these individual interests. Within the paradigm of economics, the core view of sexual intercourse is merely as an input into child production, where children are a local public good [Becker (1973, 1974, 1991a), Weiss & Willis (1985)], or more recently also as a pure consumption good [Grossbard-Shechtman (1982, 1984, 1995), Cameron & Collins (1997, 2000a)]. Abstaining from pre-marital sex would ensure that the abstinent can offer themselves to a partner as being virginal. Leaving aside the issue of proof, this would bring some expected benefits to the marital partner. The fundamental gain for a man is that the woman cannot possibly be bearing someone else's child and both partners would be free from the risk of sexually transmitted diseases. The woman also gains from knowing that the man is not beholden to some other woman through paternity. It follows therefore that under certain circumstances, virginity may be in the nature of a capital asset, although there have been instances in ancient societies such as Peru and Tibet [Ryley-Scott (1953, p. 37)] where it is looked down on. Indeed some societies supposedly instituted 'temporary marriages' purposefully for the loss of disadvantageous female virginity. Where virginity does have a positive value, this varies with the passage of time but once it is surrendered, like the traditional capital investment appraisal textbook example of a bottle of vintage wine, this value can be decimated unless it has been sold to the right buyer. Most societies characterized by high levels of religiosity and/or social taboos regarding contraception accord significant capital value to virginity in the unfolding of their social customs [Ryley-Scott (1953)].

Akerlof (1984) follows in the straightforward neo-classical tradition of prior work by Arrow & Becker in treating such customs, or social institutions, as consumer or investment goods with the public good dimensions elaborated above by Gifford. Choice of observance or disdain follows from the standard utility-maximization postulate that an individual is motivated by a cost–benefit calculation. Akerlof focuses on a possible prisoner's dilemma. There are two extreme sub-optimal scenarios, one where the custom is obeyed even though all agents are disadvantaged by so doing and the other where the custom is overthrown by all agents despite ubiquitous welfare losses.

A social custom or habit [cp. Heiner (1983), Coleman (1987), Twomey (1999)] can serve the same economic functions as the routines which become embedded in the conduct of a firm, the principle one being to reduce the various costs associated with risky decision-making. Thus the evolutionary analyses of firms stemming from Schumpeter (1934) [which reached full fruition in Nelson & Winter (1982)] are also of relevance. By supporting or dissenting from the prevailing customs, individuals resemble firms in the standard models of reputation games [Kreps & Wilson (1982), Rasmussen (2001); some extensions of this point can be found in Cameron & Collins (1999)].

In Akerlof's formal model utility has three arguments in addition to the usual ones, social reputation (R), belief in the customary code of behaviour (B) and conformity with its conventions (A). I now briefly outline his general model with several changes in notation. Reputation is a continuous variable with dummies being added for 'belief or disbelief in the code' (1) and obedience or disobedience of the code. There is not a one-for-one mapping of (dis)belief in a code into (dis)obedience of it. Obedience of a code one believes and disobedience of a code one disbelieves are obviously the most expected of the four contingencies between these two dummies, as costs of disobedience may prohibit indulgence in the disapproved taste. Reputation is

characterized as depending on the obedience dummy and the observed fraction
of other people who obey. This gives rise to the individual utility function:

$$U = U(G, R, A, B, e) \tag{2.2}$$

where

G = commodity consumption
R = reputation
A = obedience or disobedience of the code
B = belief or disbelief in the code
e = personal tastes

   The reputation function is:

$$R = R(A, B\%) \tag{2.3}$$

where $B\%$ is the percentage of the community believing in the code. The equation for aggregate changes in belief in customs is:

$$B\% = g(B, A\%) \tag{2.4}$$

where $A\%$ is the fraction obeying the code.
   The presence of reputation is necessary to ensure the possibility of an equilibrium with non-zero compliance in the absence of very strong beliefs.
Presumably there should be a corresponding function to Eq. (2.4) for $A\%$ such
as:

$$A\% = f(A, B\%) \tag{2.5}$$

but Akerlof does not write this down explicitly in the section where he gives
his general formulation. As his subsequent discussion makes clear there are
many possible combinations of equilibria for $A\%$ and $B\%$. Belief in a code can
be substantially backed by conduct or, equally plausibly, not and vice versa.
   Figures 2.2 and 2.3 further illustrate the model. The 45-degree line is a
benchmark as it shows positions where belief and obedience occur in equal
fractions. The other functions show the percentage observing the code given a
fixed level of belief and vice versa. The line of causation in both directions is
through reputation building or losing. As Akerlof rules out dissonance, within
individuals, in the model of social customs we would take this to imply that the
obeyers and believers are the same people. Assuming different tastes or returns
from compliance across the population implies that the observer function

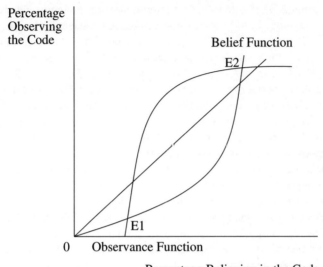

Figure 2.2   *Equilibria between observance and belief functions*

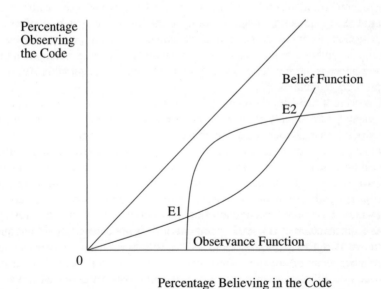

Figure 2.3   *Equilibria between observance and belief functions: permanent under-observance*

shows the cumulative likelihood of an individual succumbing to observance. If there are variations in the rate of impact of reputation/belief rates on obedience rates and vice versa, multiple equilibria are possible. The cases shown in Figures 2.2 and 2.3 have two equilibria and three different zones of divergence between optimal belief rates and observance rates. In Figure 2.2 the lower equilibrium shows belief rates falling below observance rates, whilst the upper equilibrium shows the reverse situation. In Figure 2.3 the observance rates fall below the belief rates at all times, even in both equilibria. These very simplified schemes may be a fair approximation of the historical lifecycle of some of the religions alluded to in the next chapter.

The relevance of the possibilities shown for any particular activity or commodity depends ultimately on the precise property of the utility function and the punishment cost function that Akerlof does not explicitly include. If we take something like an addictive commodity, that is deemed sinful in the religion of the consumer, then compared with a non-addictive commodity the observance function (i.e. the aggregate zero consumption percentage) may shift down and the belief function shift up, thus creating two opposing effects in terms of the likelihood of obtaining equilibria like those in Figure 2.3.

This type of model has links to Becker's celebrated restaurant pricing analysis (1991b). His example involved two fish restaurants which were similar in all respects, except for the one with the lower price having substantially excess demand and the other having excess supply. His answer to the question: why not change prices to enhance profits? is that there is an external effect on consumption, from the perception of consumers, that the persistent excess demand is symbolic of high status or fashionability. The price analogue in the present paper is the reputation capital the individual has acquired from other people's good opinions.

Lowering 'prices' for short-run gain runs the risk of destroying this reputation capital permanently if there is no corresponding ripple or cascade of behavioural change running down the chain of trend-setters. Cascading is examined in more depth by Bikhchandani et al. (1992) and Hirshleifer (1995). The essential feature is that each agent decides whether or not to enter a particular activity on the basis of the actions of prior entrants. The decisions of other people, who are assumed to have more information, is here a substitute for increased usage of objective information to inform one's own decision.

As Bikhchandani et al. (1992) point out, it does not necessarily follow that the move is a Pareto improvement as the followers' use of the leader(s)' compliance as an information signal may prove to be inefficient. This being the case we will have instability of code behaviour. Hirshleifer (1995) sees this as an advantage over the Akerlof model which he regards as inherently stable at the local equilibrium unless shifted by an exogenous change in sanctions for deviance/observance or technical change. This may be so for such things as trends in fashionability of pop music, restaurants, drugs or food fads (like the craze for baby vegetables), although it could be argued that a traditional 'product lifecycle' explanation based on the individual need for variety would suffice. All of the CORN-type models capture certain elements of a total picture of how institutions, norms or conventions are formulated, but seem to leave out others. Some focus exclusively on punishment as a means of maintaining the status quo, whilst the cascade model seems to imply that each social group consists of a tiered network of individuals who follow their relevant leader like firms in the traditional Stackelberg models of industrial organization theory. Granted, there is some rational choice justification for 'following' behaviour in the cascade model due to limited information, whilst there is none in the elementary Stackelberg model.

There is in either of these branches of the literature something of a lacuna as to the process by which the rules change. Akerlof's model identifies that change may be needed as voluntarily evolved norms may result in a standard prisoner's dilemma outcome where the current equilibrium is stable and Pareto inferior to others. The cascade models seem to imply the same possibilities of sub-optimality but a much greater degree of fluctuation in conformity to particular standards. This fluctuation is, of course, change in a truistic sense as collective behaviour is altering but it need not be purposefully towards a superior outcome. Group choice is simply trapped into bouncing around the optimal outcome because of severe limitations in attaining ideal world standards of information-gathering and processing. Inevitably, deriving group outcomes from the assumption of individual choice subject to constraints is going to rely on technological change as the driver moving us to different rules.

How do we fill this gap? Some link from the micro-organizational to macro-organizational is needed. A promising start in this direction can be found in returning to the perceptive work of Albert O. Hirschman (1970) on the exit–voice tradeoff. Much of Hirschman's book is a straightforward punishment cost model plus the additional feature of loyalty that predates the Akerlof model of social customs. The problem with loyalty is that it makes it harder to leave the worse the situation is. Individuals may become imprisoned by the existential asymmetry of institutions in that they subscribe to a belief or cause that they would not have chosen if they had known how things would turn out. Being 'inside' the institution there is a degree of 'locking in' due to emotional investments made over a period of time. Thus, there is an incentive to exercise the voice option. For religions, this would be quite difficult as individuals would need to become scholars and/or high in the administrative hierarchy to have much impact. The exit option will appeal where these costs are too high. However, entrepreneurs are needed to spot the opportunities for rebranding the product in such a way as to suit exiters. This is discussed further in Chapter 3. For some, the repression of sin will be so strong that they wish to exit the market and create a new market in which what is regarded as sin becomes acceptable. Such leaders we may term 'sin entrepreneurs'.

SIN ENTREPRENEURS

Sins are not firms as such but they are, in a loose sense, institutions. Let us adopt a stylized assumption that when capitalism emerged on a large scale many people found themselves in sub-optimal positions of observing codes that did not suit them. Feelings of sin, being part of this, are a form of negative capital and it is this dissonance which gives scope for entrepreneurs to exploit the opportunities for gain. There are three types of entrepreneurship involved: the promotion of ideas, selling of products, and finally setting up of communities to promote ideas. In the last case, various forms of communal living have been attempted to erode the negative effects of jealousy, sexual possessiveness, and so on. Product retailing is dealt with in various sections of Part III of the present work.

I will here deal purely with ideas, firstly in the work of Nietzsche. He derived from Schopenhauer the notion that the world was not a rational construction and that there was no evidence for the existence of God. This was extolled in specific works such as *Beyond Good and Evil*, in 1886, and most notably his final piece consisting of 62 observations, each of about a page long, called *The Anti-Christ*. In *The Anti-Christ* it is argued that sin cannot be naturalistically derived from the edicts of a supreme being. Sins are merely restrictive codes which weaken human nature and are therefore ultimately detrimental. Nietzsche gives the example of Blaise Pascal as a victim of serious welfare losses, due to his feelings of sin, when the blame should really have been laid on the shackles imposed on him by the organized lies and deceits of established religion. The essence of Nietzsche's position is shown in his remark in observation 25, where he claims that priests 'interpret all good fortune as a reward, all misfortune as a punishment for disobedience of God, for "sin" that most mendacious mode of interpretation of a supposed "moral world order" through which the natural concept "cause and effect" is once and for all stood on its head' [Nietzsche (1990, p. 148)].

Amidst his rhetorical flourishes and invective, the author seems to be taking an entirely rationalist perspective on the function and status of sin. In observation 49 he argues that priests are opposed to scientific thought because its pure logic will undermine the totally unnatural concept of sin which has been imposed on us. Elsewhere he argues that what is 'natural' is to pursue the 'will to power' which would come under attack in various sin catalogues as vainglory, etc. This is not an advocacy of total freedom of action, rather the end in view is that those who are superior should rise to the top and lead those who are of lower calibre in terms of their development potential as humans. Repressing such a process (which is seen as 'natural' in Darwinian terms) Nietzsche feels will be harmful to well-being. It is perhaps no coincidence that the writer came from a constricting Calvinist background. His philosophical writings could not make him a leader in the sense of creating an informational cascade as he would be unlikely to have high-end information-chain status.

Therefore, the mode of change must be that knowledge in the form of philosophy is a public good which may, in the end, alter preferences. Although Nietzsche rails relentlessly against the doctrines of sin, and some of his ideas point in directions that his opponents would consider sinful, he was a long way from advocating sin as a way of life. To find an illustrative specimen of this in action we turn briefly to the lives of the self-styled 'black' magician Aleister Crowley and the erotic novelist the Marquis de Sade. Crowley was brought up in the outstandingly repressive religion of the Plymouth Brethren which led him to remark of his schooldays: 'We were allowed to play Cricket, but not to score runs, lest it should excite the vice of emulation' [Booth (2000, p. 16)]. In terms of a rational choice model, the extremity of rules imposed by the agents of a single, vengeful deity formed such a drastic restriction of choice that the ensuing conflict would lead to rebellion against the preference set that is being invested in the author. As with Nietzsche the problem is laid at the door of the single deity wielding punishment for sin. The authority that agents (priests) claim for the deity derives from the prime mover proposition. That is 'he' made the world and is responsible for all events that take place in it. Undesirable events are the work of the devil and those who sin are fuelling his potency. Crowley did not go to the level of devil worship per se: this was not popularly exposited as a doctrine until the Church of Satan leader Anton LaVey began his publications[1] in the 1960s. Despite calling himself 'the Beast' and adorning himself with the number 666, Crowley produced writings on 'magick' which in many cases drew on religious traditions which had become marginalized by mainstream Christianity. He showed no reluctance to lie, cheat, engage in sexual promiscuity and so on, but the grand overarching emblem of his sin was the attempt to perform magical transformations by performing rituals, calling on spirits, and so forth. Essentially, this is the ultimate sin, from a doctrinal perspective, as it wrests from the single deity its unique selling point. Organized religion persecuted 'magical' rivals in the form of witches, cults and so on because they posed a threat to its monopoly on miracles which, to a degree, were franchised to agents ('priests') who might attempt miraculous changes by invoking the power of God. Certainly, enlightenment thinking such as David Hume's 'Essay on Miracles' had ridiculed this but it would, of course, be equally scornful of rival franchisers such as Crowley and de Sade.

Crowley, even in court in the absence of compelling evidence, set out on a crusade to show that he and others could do miraculous things and that this in no way needed to be predicated on a life free from sinning. In fact, the message in Crowley's exegesis is that specific acts of sin are likely to increase the power of the magician. He did embark on some entrepreneurial exploitations of his position in the strictly economic sense: such as selling tickets to ritual performances and, for a time, having a commune-type structure in which he attracted other people's money. He also wrote novels and books extolling his position, but these barely sold at all. In this regard he may have been ahead of his time as, in modern times, the veneer of 'black magic' helps turn over millions of dollars in various niches of popular entertainment such as 'goth' and 'death metal' rock music and Hollywood movies aimed at the younger market. These products are berated by Christian activists, such as Kraft (1997), although they may be mere cathartic outlets which enable disaffected individuals to abstain from more widespread practical sin.

De Sade's entrepreneurship, on behalf of liberating us from the fetters of sin, was more narrowly focused on sexual matters. Like Nietzsche, his writing is aphoristic and elusive and hence prone to varying interpretations as can be seen in the heroic attempt by David Martyn (1999) to compare his economic ideas, on exchange, with those aspects of Adam Smith which we look at in Chapter 6. Not surprisingly, de Sade's ideas are quite different from those of Smith. He criticizes virtuous behaviour in markets, and beyond, as hypocritical masquerades concealing motives that are intrinsically selfish. In this he is in good company with Mandeville and some of the more pessimistically inclined mainstream economists discussed in Part II of this work. De Sade goes so far as to claim that theft is a more honest form of exchange, in that the stealer makes no pretence of their intentions. In the specific matter of the sexual relationships between the characters in his novels it can be argued that he is positing equality of exchange between dominant and submissive individuals who would elsewhere be labelled as sado-masochistic perverts. It would be quite straightforward (although no one has done it) to set up conventional economic rational choice models where social welfare is maximized[2] by facilitating efficient interaction between sadists and masochists.

De Sade, much more than Nietzsche or Crowley, was trying to break the straitjacket of sin from a rational choice perspective. They all had in common that they were actively campaigning for their point of view, which makes them entrepreneurs of sin. Given the high money and stigma costs this brought to them one is entitled to wonder why they did not just get on quietly indulging themselves in their favourite sins without incurring the wrath of the established order. The rational choice answer would consist of some of the following: they hoped to capture an offsettingly large share of the spillover gains from promoting their views, other people's welfare loomed large in their utility functions making them deeply altruistic, or they were simply misguidedly irrational sociopaths. The last explanation would not be acceptable in the case of those who support the most extreme versions of the rational choice model.

SUMMARY AND PROSPECTS

In this chapter we have explored the relationship between rational choice economics and sinful activity. Initially sin was treated as a commodity attribute which might bring positive or negative utility. It was then considered in terms of risk-taking as the outcomes of sinful activity are often not exact. Certain strains arise in keeping sin within a narrow rational choice framework so some psychologized economics, mainly cognitive dissonance, was introduced. Finally we considered how sin is a social code which might be maintained and regulated as a type of public good. Social codes are not under any automatic pressure to bring social optima. Accordingly it is possible that the sin element, at any point in time, in choice-making is a serious barrier to the attainment of satisfaction. Explaining why this should be so necessitates consideration of the role of religion in the erection of codes around sin. The reaction against the dominant long-established religions was encountered and saintliness was briefly rendered into economic terms but it is now time to look, in Chapter 3, at religion in greater detail.

ENDNOTES

1. A good example of his work is *The Satanic Witch* [LaVey (1989)]. Contrary to the title this book does not seem to instruct women to devil worship. However, it is more or less a manual of how to deceive, torment and possess men which, as it is a debunking of conventional morality, must give it the status of being a sinful book.
2. Disregarding the negative externalities which their sin may impose on other people IF they know about it [cp. Sen's 1970 discussion of the *Lady Chatterley's Lover* case]. Even then the optimal welfare arrangement may be to make sure those who suffer from knowing about the activity are kept ignorant.

3. Religion

God will not suffer his people to be tempted above what they are able to bear.
I Corinthians 10:13 [as quoted in Scott (2001, p. 49)]

INTRODUCTION

The last chapter concluded with the issue of collective regulation of individual behaviour. The paramount element of this, with regard to sin, is organized religion. Granted, formal regulation is in the hands of the government, but even where state and church come to be formally separate there is still a powerful cultural influence of religious ideas through lobbying by religiously motivated groups and from the continuance of religious notions embedded, in subtle ways, in everyday language and discourse. This is particularly the case in life and death matters such as abortion, euthanasia, suicide and capital punishment.

There is a large literature on the economics of religion which proceeds without any real necessity of actually defining religion too precisely. As the present work concerns sin, we cannot really avoid giving a definition which, unsurprisingly, is not an easy thing to do. In his key work, of 1902, on religious experience, William James openly invited vagueness by defining it as:

> the feelings, acts and experiences of individual men in their solitude, so far as they apprehend themselves to stand in relation to whatever they may consider the divine. [James (1997, p. 53)]

In the *New Fontana Dictionary of Modern Thought* [Bullock & Trombley (1999, p. 745)], the definition of religion begins with:

> An attitude of awe towards God, or Gods, or the supernatural, or the mystery of life, accompanied by beliefs and affecting basic patterns of individual and group behaviour. In Latin, religare means 'to bind' . . .

Here the private experience, defined by James, is required to have a social component before it can be called religion.

It may be very difficult for a person ever to be non-religious under such comprehensive definitions. Clearly, modern revivals of Paganism and Wicca have no difficulty being counted in under such definitions since the presence of the deity, as in the market leaders of world religion in the last 100 years or so, is not essential to the concept. Going further back in history, the original Greeks, Romans, Norse, Celts, or anyone else in whose lives a body of myths and legends played a major part, would have to be considered religious. These bodies of thought certainly contain notions of sin as they consistently depict unpleasant consequences flowing from acts of hubris, greed, lust, etc. Going further afield, the last definition quoted implies that a person who is awed by the mystery of life and in some way changes their behaviour (even say keeping a horseshoe for good luck) is being religious. Once they know at least one other person who shares this belief 'binding' is taking place. So the only person who would not be religious is a secular humanist, shorn of any mystical experiences, who attributes the emergences of norms of right and wrong to purely instrumental considerations of their being utility-enhancing constraints as discussed in Chapter 2. In short, the sort of person who might be found in rational choice economic models including those devised to explain religious activity.

One reason for *homo economicus* not to be excessively inclined to mysticism is the absence of direct involvement with the fear of death. In most economic models, death is simply a known point at which the utility-maximizing machine, of the human entity, ceases to exist. Or, in extension, this is a stochastic event which the individual will take into account in planning their investments and consumption stream over time.

So, an organized religion tends to involve connection with one or more deities, or, failing that, a diffuse sense of wonder, and some form of social binding. Sin emerges in terms of private feelings of falling short of the requirements of the deity or deities and/or being punished by the social group to which one has bonded. This creates various economic roles for religious doctrine and religious organizations. In a deity-based religion, the individual may directly experience the anguish costs associated with sinning through being told that they have violated the divine precepts of correct conduct. Religious organizations function, as agents of the deity, to manage these precepts. Through cultural diffusion, certain codes of deity-based religions may acquire the veneer of being 'natural' as in such terms as 'natural law', 'natural justice' and 'natural order'. Or, being more up to date and down to earth, changes in the potential for altering human experience such as cloning, genetic manipulation of foodstuffs and births without procreation can encounter the objection of being 'not natural' in everyday arguments. This may also arise in objection to conduct such as transvestism, homosexuality, sado-masochism, and so on. The idea of all of the above contravening 'nature' derives from nature being implicitly defined as 'the way we are made', which more or less implies that some 'cosmic watchmaker' made us and hence regresses us back to feelings of sin that are consequent on defying the will of a deity.

The whole area of natural states is a very slippery one and there have been religions in which sin can be defined away by arguments about the inherent predestined logic of the natural order as one in which individuals fall short of perfection but will be redeemed in the afterlife. Going even further down this road, one might claim, with the sin entrepreneurs from the last chapter, that the human being's animal nature hardwires them to dominate and survive by whatever means possible. Hence, the natural order would be one with no religion as trying to discipline people into a sinless state is distinctly 'not natural'.

Religions based on a personal path to wisdom, such as Buddhism and T'aoism, have been characterized as non-naturalistic for example by James (1997). Essentially, these religions propose a model along the lines of the meta-preference route, but with the higher-order set of preferences being revealed through experiential learning. Every individual will go on a journey of some sort and hence pilgrimage is a daily way of life as opposed to the case of Christian religions where the pilgrim was a specific individual who literally made a journey, involving risks and suffering, to become some special kind of exemplar. Or, in the case of writers like John Bunyan, the pilgrimage was made through allegorical writing while imprisoned for his beliefs. The story of Jesus is of course the ultimate in such cultivation of exemplars. The personalized religion of permanent pilgrimage thus fits into the following quote from Jon Elster (1993, p. 179), who seems to be as close as makes no difference to advocating rational choice theory as the new religion:

> Rational choice theory is far more than a technical tool for explaining behavior. It is also, and very importantly, a way of coming to grips with ourselves – not only what we should do, but even what we should be.

One might be tempted to suggest that this takes us back, full circle, to the early nineteenth-century beliefs of Bentham and the other philosophical radicals (fundamentally the originators of the cosmology of neo-classical economists) who found 'all ecclesiastical establishments to be at best of dubious utility, and expected them to vanish away with the progress of enlightenment' [Dicey (1962, p. 321)].

For convenience I shall distinguish, in what follows, between 'deity-based religions' and 'person-based religions', although the distinction is not rigid. For example, the Jewish mystic Isaac Luria (1534–1572) put forward the doctrine that individuals could bring the godhead within themselves and achieve perfection. Having done so they could further improve the world. This is a person-based religion but he extended it with the traditional proposition of

Judaism that, whilst all people could do this, God had selected the people of Israel as the special agents for the task. The more person-based a religion is the less is the emphasis on sin as the significance of the Fall (discussed further below) will recede. The decreased emphasis on sin tends to be furthered by the inclination of person-based religions to accept doctrines of transmigration of souls (reincarnation), as did Luria, which afford scope for the belief that the soul will come back until reaching the form in which it will be perfected. Sinning or being the victim of sin is then susceptible to a karmic interpretation as part of the inevitable journey of the soul to perfection or the individual, in their current incarnation, to enlightenment.

In some person-based religions, the main reason to join a group is to make use of gurus as temporary inputs, along with all other relevant experience, to the pursuit of the correct personal path. Elevation of the gurus to become leaders up to the point where they take on entrepreneurial functions effectively leads to the degeneration of the non-naturalistic religion into a naturalistic one as the leader has taken on the role of divine agent or in extreme cases aspires to being the deity.

RELIGION IN THE MARKETPLACE

It is unclear what the first economic analysis of religion was, although some priority might be ascribed to Marx's dictum that 'religion is the opium of the masses'. Inspired by the work of Becker, economists have made many contributions to the study of religion [surveyed in Iannacone (1995, 1998)], some of which have led them into conflict with more traditional scholars in the field [see Bruce (1993)]. The most basic application of economics in this area is to subject the household to analysis in the form of a demand for religious products (services, holy books, icons, TV shows, etc.) and a supply of time to religious activities (going to church, arranging flowers, helping in fund-raising activities, etc.). More broadly, there is the application of the traditional analysis of firms and industries to interdenominational competition [e.g. Hamberg & Peterson (1994), Stark & Iannacone (1994), Hall & Bold (1998)], with this also being applied to the determination of financial contributions [Zaleski & Zech (1995)].

The seminal paper by Azzi & Ehrenberg (1975) focused solely on attendance at services. Azzi & Ehrenberg, and economists who follow them, are engaged in 'empire building' for the Becker–Lancaster model by moving it into religion as just one more area of application in which predictions can be derived and applied to data that have already been produced by researchers with no cognizance of the economics of religion [see for example Long & Settle (1977), Ehrenberg (1977), Sullivan (1985), Neuman (1986), Smith (1993),

Sawkins et al. (1997)]. Thus the analysis is totally founded on the microeconomics considered in the early sections of Chapter 2. It is convenient to
divide the following discussion into two parts. Firstly, I shall consider the
determination of frequency of service attendance for a given level of religious
conviction, or strength of faith, which I shall denote as GAC (God
Appreciation Capital) and then go on to consider the simultaneous dynamic
linkage of GAC and service attendance. Tastes are assumed to be given and
utility is derived through combining goods, purchased from the market, and
time to produce commodities. The relevant commodity here would be the
overall 'religious experience' which might derive from service attendance,
scholarship, pilgrimage, watching religious television or giving to the church.
The ultimate constraints are therefore prices of goods, rates of return on
human and non-human capital, the fixity of time and the state of technology.
From such a model, there emerges a derived supply of time to service attendance with some fairly clear predictions for the impact of the key variables.
Increased costs of attendance in the form of travel time required, or fixed pre-
commitment time requirements to other activities, plus monetary expenditures
should decrease the level of attendance as there is substitution at the margin.
Income should be positively correlated with attendance, *ceteris paribus*, so
long as religious services are a normal good. Services are, of course, only one
element of the religious experience and, as such, may exhibit a declining
income elasticity if there is substitution to other elements such as donations or
consumption of religious products like television shows or music, which have
a much lower time intensity. On the other hand, religious services may confer
certain network externalities that are not available for less time-intensive
forms of religious consumption. For example, one's business prospects may be
enhanced through regular meetings with key individuals in the church. On a
more personal level, the worship site has been a historically important mode
of searching for a marital partner. These factors impart a 'club good'
[Buchanan (1965)] dimension to attendance at a service. For historical and
sociocultural reasons such benefits will vary across denominations; for example in a faith where 'out-marriage' faces relatively high stigma costs there is a
greater incentive to attend services frequently in the implicit search for a partner. In extreme cases, with inclusive religions, marriage out of the faith will be
a sin and lead to dismissal.

Religion conveniently fits into the Chicagoan model of rational 'addiction'
or 'habits' [Iannacone (1984), Becker & Murphy (1988)], discussed further in
Chapter 8, which is, after all, only the Becker–Lancaster model with intertemporal dependency between marginal utilities of an 'addictive' good. In this
framework, addiction is only a strong habit and religion is widely known to be
habitual. Now, GAC becomes endogenous with the frequency of service attendance. A high level of attendance helps form religious capital which in turn

increases the level of attendance because the marginal utility of an extra minute of service will be rising over some ranges of increasing belief capital.

Obviously, some individuals have neutral, or even negative, tastes for religion and will never develop GAC regardless of sustained levels of exposure. At the other extreme, some individuals may have sufficiently strong intrinsic beliefs that there will be no diminution in response to changes in exogenous variables. However, even these individuals will exhibit some responsiveness of frequency of service attendance to economic factors such as the shadow price of time. Our expectation is that they will have little consequential loss of GAC. The GAC factor will differ across individuals due to exposure at an early age to parents' views on religion, that is formation of religious capital within the home, as well as exposure to services. The level of adolescent exposure will also derive from varying 'denominational strictness' [Iannacone (1992)].

If the demand for religion is derived from such a framework then, if we are to be consistent, organized religions must be treated as firms supplying the product of worship. So far we have treated the product as religious experience which simply appears in the utility function of the individual. Given the discussion in the Introduction, this might just be a relatively sin-free 'sense of wonder' as retailed in 'New Age' religions, or in the traditional Christian religions the product sought may be 'salvation' of the soul as in the discussion in Chapter 2 on the lives of the saints. As ultimate salvation is intrinsically unknown to the individual, the strictly correct representation within the SEU framework is to include the discounted costs of the afterlife torment and the probability of receiving this torment. If we do stay within that framework, then the more risk-averse an individual is the more likely they are to pursue religious consumption. This is discussed in detail in the model developed, to deal with the provision of religious indulgences, by Cassone & Marchese (1999). If we switch to a cognitive dissonance type of model then the individual will not make marginal adjustments to the probability of damnation. Rather, they will maintain a self-image from which dissonant elements have been filtered out until a large enough shock, such as suddenly finding they are dying of cancer, comes along. This might lead to a sudden increase in perception of the sinful components of the life one has led to date and a consequent investment in atonement capital. The expectation then is that individuals will settle into polarized states. One would be that they are sinners and must do all they can to overcome a gaping gate of hell at the end of their lives. The opposite is one of being convinced that hell does not exist or even if it does exist then none of their current range of sins is likely to cross the threshold to cast them into it. The current range of sins might be minor acts of theft, lust, envy and so on, which a sudden death sentence at the hands of cancer might throw into a relief which opens the filter so that religious consumption–investment becomes necessary.

Whilst there are notable declines in church attendance within many Christian religions leading to closure of worship sites and recruitment problems within the labour market for service-administering personnel (priests, vicars, etc.), it would be a mistake to jump to the conclusion that the rising wage rates of developed economies have led to an overall decline in religious activity due to a large time-substitution effect or pervasive dissonance with respect to eternal damnation. Work by Finke & Stark (1992) on the history of religion in America claims to show that 'religiously active' individuals have grown from one-sixth of the population in 1776 to over three-fifths in 1980.

Organized religions may have their origins as club goods arising from small collective provision of a local public good. This is the sort of idyll to which modern 'New Age' religions hark back, where the community would come together to perform rituals intended to banish evil and ensure bounteous harvests and so forth. With sufficient growth, they become firms albeit not usually in the 'classical' sense of there being a residual claimant who pockets profits as a return on being the principal risk-taker. The near-firm status was recognized in the Ecclesiastical Commissioners' Acts of 1836 and 1840, which reformed the Church of England 'as a sort of quasi-corporation' [Dicey (1962, p. 338)] to be regulated by the 'perpetual corporation' of the Ecclesiastical Commission, which held the residual claims of the Church as a trustee. In some cases, religions are huge multinational conglomerates. In a not unduly restricted sense the product they are selling is sin, or rather sin removal, as sin is the determinant of the probability of damnation of the soul [Schmidtchen & Mayer (1999) analyse thirteenth century friars along these lines]. Having attained large size they inevitably have to evolve governance structures which creates scope for all the problems of rent-seeking, opportunism and optimal contracting that arise in the modern theory of the firm. Indeed the modern theory of the firm is to a great extent the economic analysis of bureaucracy, and there were large religious bureaucracies in the world centuries before any large corporations emerged in the business world.

Many economic analyses of the supply of religion focus on the monopolistic firm analogy. Finke & Stark (1992) argue that large dominant religions are rent-seeking monopolists which are therefore bad for the religious economy. The rents appear in terms of esoteric philosophizing by church hierarchy who are indulging in consumption of high doctrine which detracts from the service offered to consumers. This is a straight transfer of the model developed in Newhouse's (1970) model of the non-profit hospital in which the managers exhibit a 'quality bias' in determining the treatment mixture, thereby depriving the customers of less exciting or vogueish measures which would lead to a higher level of welfare. In the case of church doctrine, sub-optimality may, in some cases, be due to not providing enough punitive vim, on the matter of the consequences of sin, to the rank and file member. Declines in quality or quantity perceived by consumers may lead to 'exit', via quitting, or to 'voice', via lobbying for alterations in the product supplied. Either the monopoly churches will change their product to bring increased consumption or the consumers will switch to new churches. Finke & Stark show that the mainline churches in the USA (Catholic, Jewish, Baptist, Protestant) have lost their market share to the 'new churches', some of which are transplantations of older doctrines from other cultures.

The extent of slippage between the utility function of the 'religion manager' who supplies doctrine and the rank and file member will depend on the type of doctrine we start with. It is worth bearing in mind that many religions are examples of what we might term 'existential asymmetry' which has been discussed in the rational choice literature on institutions. That is, they may exist at a point in time despite the fact that there is no logical justification for them emerging, all other things being equal, if they were not already here. Given the assumption that the religion manager's utility functions will be like any other manager's, dependent on income, size of the body, prestige and 'on the job' consumption, then it follows that having been granted existence in a sub-optimal world they will seek to maintain it. A religion then might be expected to grow as a means of ensuring survival and enhancing the utility of its top-line managers. This is less likely to conflict with members' interests when there is a high degree of inclusive orientation. In the extreme case of inclusivity the individual member will perceive the optimum as being when the whole world is in the religion due to the gains to be had from the externality gain of reduced sin by others. This is, of course, just the standard argument for the optimal provision of a pure public good. If the religion provides other goods which are necessary to the members and these do experience congestion, then the member will benefit from some degree of exclusivity even if the doctrinal stance is inclusive.

Paradoxically, the very extreme case of exclusivity would involve the whole world being in the religion also, as outsiders branded as 'infidels' who are condemned as sinful beyond redemption purely by dint of birth would be eliminated via wars and thus removed from the world.

Let us return to the inclusive and bureaucratically expansive religion. Expansion brings a gain to the rank and file member in terms of the 'warm-glow' externality of a perceived fall in others' sinfulness. The mere fact of joining should produce this, even prior to behavioural change by the incomers, as a member will anticipate the probability of a decrease in sin by incomers. Assuming individual contributions do not decline as membership rises, and that pure rent-seeking deadweight loss does not absorb the growing income, then the organization must become more powerful in terms of lobbying for its standards to be applied in the world. So expansion seems to be good for all concerned, but how is it to be done? A number of strategies exist, being mainly: straightforward promotional advertising, association with 'good-cause' events, provision of charitable goods and services which may help catch the especially fallen, and the traditional door-to-door 'cold calling' of the old-fashioned salesman. The last two strategies are a commercialized version of traditional missionary work and are primarily associated with modern-day American religions like the Christian Scientists and the Church of the Latter-Day Saints (Mormons). Such missionary work may be seen as voluntary labour and is thus a tithe of time rather than income to the church of one's faith. If such labour had high productivity in terms of conversion rates then it may be a more efficient method of resource extraction, from believers, than simple income transfers. Against this must be set the obstacle of the opportunity cost of wages foregone by missionaries: in particular as missionaries may well have to work in economies run by those outside the faith there is a potential decline in the return to human capital due to interrupted work patterns.

All of this sounds like a strong disincentive to running any kind of mandatory missionary service (*à la* military conscription) in which, for example, all are liable but only those selected in a lottery are sent to serve. However, there is one big promotional idea which missionaries are a good way of pushing and that is, of course, sin. The Christian missionaries of Victorian England were propagated on a quest premised on the idea that the less developed world contained savages steeped in sinful depravity such as naked rituals, cannibalism and devil worship. The idea that one is saving the world is an attractive positive externality to many people. The promotion of the idea of sin may also be useful as a means of attracting missionary work, and other forms of labour transfer, as the individual can be sold the notion that this is one way of increasing their personal probability of salvation. In the extreme case, where religions adopting such a view dominate the state, this may be inhibitive to economic growth and development. This proposition is turned on its head by Weber's thesis of the Protestant Work Ethic, which is discussed later in this chapter, where economic activity itself becomes the mission of the religious individual.

To put it in a cynical nutshell, religious leaders need sin like doctors need illness. Neither would, *en masse*, overtly go out to encourage the existence of the causes of their existence. Yet, given the existential asymmetry noted above, they have a self-evident interest in managing the perceptions of their potential clients in order to sustain and nourish their existence. Sin attracts members and can also attract voluntary member labour inputs. Thus 'sin innovation' is needed to replenish the latent demand for religion, or as they say in marketing literature to 'refresh the message'. Older sin 'sites', in the sense of activities designated as sinful, may be eliminated from the agenda of scorn/punishment or become stale with tolerance. New areas need to be colonized as focal points for membership welfare. The primary means of doing this is to start, or whip up an already growing, moral panic. In 1930s England the prime site of moral panic was the cinema. Pearson (1983, p. 32) quotes the following from a work, by Hugh Redwood, describing the work of the UK organization 'The Salvation Army': 'The boys of the slums are wonderful training material for good or evil. They are children in their love of pictures and music. Hollywood's worst in the movie line has recruited thousands of them for the gangs of race-course roughs, motor bandits, and smash-and-grab thieves.' This litany has been rolled out for each new consumption good or technical innovation that threatens the established order: the campaigns against sex and violence by The National Viewers and Listeners Association in the UK have lost their edge but periodically new demons emerge in the form of video nasties, Japanese cartoons and currently internet pornography.

The opposite strategy to colonizing features of modern life as sin sources, to rouse moral panic, is simply to accommodate to social change. This involves watering down the doctrine of the religion. By itself this would not attract many people away from secular activities and so an increase in joint products is likely to be needed, such as social activities for young people and more modern services with greater levels of member participation. Under this strategy the quality of product will fall for some insiders, but this could just lower intra-marginal rents they were receiving from the prior product mix. The individual will not quit unless such rents are dissipated to a sufficient degree. Quitting is further circumscribed by holes in the product space of religion characterized as in the Lancastrian demand model. Such holes create a discontinuity where the move to another religion is a sudden jump in the product characteristics mix rather than a gradual transition. Uncertainty reinforces such exit barriers, for example if one contemplates exit on grounds of substitution in the product mix away from a hard line on long-established sins (e.g. more liberal attitudes in sexual matters etc.) there is a potential 'better the devil you know' factor in terms of worry about risks of the group one now joins turning out to be even worse (viz. more 'soft') than the one just left. In the case of religions, quitting, in the face of a perceived decline in the 'quality' of product received, is further inhibited by loyalty. Loyalty is fostered by the capital formation of compulsory adolescent consumption, discussed at the start of this section. It may also be fostered by the public-good dimensions of the faith in terms of a specific doctrine of the Fall and the 'chosen ones' element that tends to prevent all-out inclusiveness in many religions.

The dilution of doctrine and the accommodative expansion of joint provision of other goods and services may worsen the sparsity of the product space to the point where there may not often be many feasibly 'different' rival products anywhere in the characteristics space. Harold Hotelling (1929), in his pioneering analysis of competition argues in the final paragraph, of a discussion that producers fill up market segments with too many similar products, that the Methodist and Presbyterian churches are too much alike. Douglas

(1973) notes the increasing tendency for Jewish and Christian denominations to become more alike, in the USA, via emphasizing social betterment and downplaying the core doctrine. As we have just argued, loyalty prevents mergers, which might benefit those who are happy with the product mix, in such situations. Some potential quitters will refrain from shifting to a person-based religion on the grounds that it does not adequately provide for the sin element. Loyalty and side benefits (or more often costs), such as the regulation of the marriage market, may make it difficult to leave a religion which is providing a product mix that is less than optimal for many of its clients. Holes in the characteristics space for the product create opportunities for entry by the classic entrepreneur as defined in such Austrian texts as Kirzner (1973). At the end of the last chapter we encountered some pro-sin entrepreneurs who sought to undermine the whole basis of religion. None of them attracted movements of any note as that was generally not their intention.

Recent acts of anti-sin entrepreneurship have been highly successful. It is worth mentioning two characteristically American cases as illustrations of how a basic religious product which has languished has been relaunched through energetic promotion and judicious alterations to the product characteristics mix. Firstly, there is the case of Billy Graham who was ordained as a Southern Baptist minister and took the human capital of the 'fire and brimstone' preaching tradition, which is predicated on the potency of the legends of the Fall, into his Billy Graham Evangelistic Association. The fact that his promotional activities were called crusades is indicative of the usage of moral panic fears to create a notion of a war on the sinfulness that the modern world is prey to. He combined this with usage of modern media, and a shifting doctrine which was highly inclusive of other religions, even up to the point of alliances with the ancient established religions of many parts of the world. One sign of the potency of Graham's mission is the estimate from a church attendance regression equation for Scotland [Smith (1993)] that he created an average rise of 16 per cent in church-going against a backdrop of steadily falling attendance. Ironically, perhaps, one of his broadcast speeches containing the Fall-derived remark 'there must be something wrong with human nature' became the basis of a successful dance record by Gary Clail (UK Top Ten hit in 1991) which must have boomed through the heads of thousands of drug-saturated dancers. So we find the very media which have served time as the scapegoats of moral panic entrepreneurs being used to keep the driving wheel of religion, man's intrinsic failings, to the fore of public consciousness.

Secondly, the Church of Jesus Christ of Latter-Day Saints (Mormons) which I shall refer to as LDS, gives a most interesting case of both product differentiation and marketing strategy. It is one of the largest and most successful religious groups ever started in North America, having about 10.8 million members world-wide spread across 150 countries. Post-war growth has been extremely rapid. The product differentiation follows the classic formula of reviving an older doctrine (the original Church of the Apostles) in a strict form at a time when other religions are losing their edge. The LDS put forward their ideas as corrections to lapses in the interpretation of the King James' Bible which are supplemented by numerous revelations which have been passed to their own special agents of God. They reject the Fall doctrine of original sin but retain the idea that mankind is inherently sinful. The organization is extremely hierarchial and excludes women from all managerial levels, thus resisting the modernization that has recently characterized old-established religions.

Their centralization in the State of Utah and Salt Lake City in particular gives them further scale and scope economies in promulgating their faith. It might be thought that having the advantage of such an economic enclave they would strictly enforce their doctrines. This does not seem to be quite the case. As far as one can tell pornography is not openly available in Salt Lake City but the vices of cigarettes, tea and coffee do not seem to be curbed and alcohol is more tightly regulated than in other comparable American cities. It also seems to have the usual city difficulties with harder drugs. Nevertheless, as suggested in the later parts of Chapter 2 a strict doctrine can bring utility gains to a member who does not fully adhere to it because the mere attempt to comply is a form of assistance to self-control. In this respect, someone shopping for a religion to improve their physical health may see LDS as an enticing product which takes us to the next topic.

There is one benefit which may be supplied as an 'atmosphere' or positive externality rather than a specific output: good health. This has sometimes formed part of the campaign for religious expansion: gross outcome statistics on comparative well-being are cited in some LDS campaign material. In a sense this is moving the boundary of sales from the afterlife into the here and now as the client seeks not only salvation of the soul but elevation of the body. In terms of the analysis of Smith (1999) this will shift the tradeoff function between the afterlife and the present outwards at all points. I will now consider the evidence on health benefits which is, of necessity, specific to deity-based religions as there is little material on person-based religions.

In his wide-ranging survey on the economics of religion, Laurence Iannacone (1998) draws attention to the presence of a health–religion correlation. It is obvious that any such correlation may be due to beneficial effects that arise from behavioural differences between the religious and non-religious, rather than being due to religion per se. Generally, more religious individuals are less inclined to engage in health-harming investments such as the consumption of legal and illegal addictive drugs and would therefore be expected to show a better performance on health outcome measures. This is a straightforward gain from reductions in sins of the flesh. As unsurprising as this is, it is a surprisingly neglected feature in a lot of economic work on health-harming consumption: for example the recent NBER volume on substance abuse [Chaloupka et al. (1999)] has no mention of religion in its fairly comprehensive index and, as far as I can see, none of the studies therein uses any religion variables. Many papers have looked at the religion–health correlation although quite a lot of them failed to do much to separate the direct effect of changed consumption/time allocation patterns from the indirect atmospheric influence of religion over and above this [see e.g. Levin & Vanderpool (1987), Ellison (1991), Levin (1994)]. The statistical work reviewed in the above papers covers a wide range of possible measures of health. Health status measures have included scales for 'life satisfaction' and 'general happiness', death rates, suicides, physical illness, diagnosed mental illness and blood pressure. Many of the studies have appeared in the world's leading medical journals. There does seem to be a raw statistical relationship between measures of health status and religious observance. As suggested, some of this seems to be due to health-harming consumption being lower amongst more religious persons, thereby improving their relative health. There are several other reasons that might account for a raw positive correlation between health and religious activity.

It is possible that the more religious segment of the population may be investing, at a higher level, in preventive measures that protect the health stock. Religious belief may be a proxy index for risk-preference (and/or the discount rate) in that the more religious may be more risk-averse. This has been brought out at various points above. A little elaboration is needed with respect to the current point. If those who are sufficiently weakly religiously motivated not to join a religion with any vigour are merely less risk-averse, then any poorer health they suffer might all be attributed to risk-taking and *not* to the direct absence of religion in their lives. It is also possible that more religious individuals may make better (i.e. more efficient) choices in areas of life where complex matching problems arise, such as the choice of job or marital partner, through associated search and transactions cost-reducing network externalities. This may result in lower levels of stress which may feed through to a higher level of the health stock. If all of the above could be accounted for and there is still some residual difference left between the health of the religious and the non-religious we could then go on to claim that the difference is due to religion and not its by-products.

There are epistemological problems in any claim that such a positive pure atmosphere effect is a priori to be expected. Firstly, it seems far from axiomatic that sustaining a high level of religious belief and/or observance is conducive to well-being. To take one crude simple case: a person who belongs to a strict faith might come under health-threatening stress from constant feelings of failure at being unable to live up to the spiritual requirements they have thereby had imposed on them. This argument about 'sick' religiousness is made by William James in *The Varieties of Religious Experience* and was encountered in the last chapter in the rather more florid and unfocused musings of Nietzsche. In a world of perfect rational choice, an individual who is thus-wise sick should of course quit, but there are obviously limitations to this approach as discussed in Chapter 2. The individual may have inherited a legacy of negative sin capital which is costly to move. The more risk-averse they are the greater is the disincentive to try to move it, particularly if the probability of transition to a happier state is perceived to be low. Further, cognitive dissonance models of choice suggest that individuals may, under such circumstances, be in a state of 'denial' over the causes of their diminished health.

There is a further problem that adherence to a religious belief may generate a bias in subjective health measures due to a 'mood differential' for the religiously inclined. Health is difficult to measure objectively. So, we inevitably must resort to objective measures of lack of health or subjective measures of perceived utility from some health-related state. The five-point 'Likert' scales normally used as subjective measures in this kind of situation are purely ordinal; nevertheless the type of analysis required imposes comparability of scaling across individuals if the results are to have any validity or meaning [cp. Alchian (1953)]. Even if we assumed identical parameters on the variables in all the relevant functions for the religiously inclined and those who were not so, there is still a problem of a shift in baseline utility even if the function maps onto the subjective health rating index in a non-problematic way. In the light of the above, Cameron (2000a) sought to test the claim of a pure health agio for the non-sinner using a large representative national survey. Little support for an independent effect of religion was found except in the case where a rather arbitrary five-point scale is used to measure the self-rated stock of health. Even then, the effect of maximum religious commitment is so small that it is hard not to dismiss it as a manifestation of subjective bias in a crude measure of ordinal utility. One study does not finish off any argument and it may be that a substantial effect can be uncovered. Even then, it is possible that the person-based religions may have a greater health effect. Whatever may be the case the prior studies have overlooked the question of how big the effect is in favour of the rather meaningless activity of treating statistical significance as numerically meaningful.

THE RISE AND FALL OF THE ECONOMIC INFLUENCE OF THE FALL

The discussion above took for granted that religions may exist to satisfy a latent demand for their products and went on to look at some influences on the ebb and flow of membership in particular religions. It did not make deeper forays into the sources of this demand or the consequent question of why it might need to be supplied in a group or 'club' mode of production. Club production does exist in person-based religions as well as deity-based religions, but both do not contain the same mix of factors that might justify this form of provision. Both types may experience economies of scale, scope and marketing which would suggest expansion beyond purely personal worship. On top of this, the external supply may serve a 'public good' function or if you prefer it might be regarded as an 'intermediate public good' function, like pollution-abatement or crime-prevention expenditures which do not themselves bring utility but reduce the disutility from a public bad.

The public good here is the body of doctrine. If tensions within the body of doctrine are resolved satisfactorily by its guardians then this is a pure public good as, once it has the seal of approval, all subscribers to the belief receive the benefit [cp. Smith (1999)]. A good example of such revisionism is the decision of the Church of England, in 1562, to reject purgatory as being not only without foundation in the Bible but repugnant to the word of God, being a mere invention of Roman Catholicism. There will thus be no problems of congestion costs from crowding in the consumption of this product innovation. They will only be excluded if they exhibit dissent. Obviously, any arbitrary set of doctrines cannot attain public good status as it might conflict with the needs of the client base as examined in the last section when we looked at product differentiation and entry and exit. So a core, that appeals to a wide range of people, has to be found in the doctrine. It is possible to find an underlying thematic unity in the most seemingly diverse bodies of religious thought, which is the notion of a Fall. In a sense the public goods role of organized religions is to regulate the legends of the Fall. In traditional Christian doctrine (i.e. a single-deity model) this is given in the tale of Adam and Eve who are pure beings until they fall prey to sins of the flesh. In other thought systems, including classical mythology and Hinduism, which use a multiple-deity model of the world, the gods 'fall' and are, in the process, agents of creation. Such systems include myths of not only how the world, in toto, came to be but also specific features such as plants, animals and geological features. These are sometimes reflective of virtue but more often are linked to sin as in the story of the origin of the Narcissus flower (cultivated as the Daffodil) which follows from sin of excessive self-regard (or vainglory).

A differentiated product from the biblical version of the Fall comes in the visionary doctrines of Sun Myung Moon, founder of the Unification Church, the so-called 'Moonie church' sometimes represented as a dangerous cult. According to Moon, events in the Garden of Eden were prefaced by a spiritual sexual relationship between Lucifer and Eve which contaminated the children of the Adam–Eve union, thereby imbuing them with 'fallen natures'. God's plan is then to send key individuals to help rectify this malaise and Jesus failed because he did not get the chance to breed and thus proliferate the unfallen. As with the medieval Roman Catholic Church, the Unification Church offers a side order of marital regulation at which purification rites are performed in order to remove the sin of the Fall from the children of married couples.

This takes the kind of paranoia that was rife in medieval Christianity over witchcraft but with the novel twist that the fear of sexual vampirism from the Devil is taken back to a pre-history of the Garden of Eden rather than being an epidemic which spread after the wrath of God following mankind's continued sinfulness [see Stanford (1996)]. Historically the central concept of the Fall has become diffused into other cultural areas such as the idea of demons/devils as fallen angels. Some medieval illustrators (as quoted in Chapter 1) portrayed the seven deadly sins as being under the stewardship of specific individual demons. The legacy of this kind of thinking is still thriving in everyday language. Such phrases as 'coming to terms with personal demons in the form of drink and drugs' serve to keep afloat the idea of the sinfulness of these consumption areas, which we deal with in Part III of the present work, in our overtly secularized mass culture.

The notion that demons could infest otherwise pure individuals thereby leading them into temptation was a useful notion for the established Christian churches. Demonic possession could take place in three ways: involuntary possession 'by accident' as it were, voluntary possession by invoking the demons through sorcery or involuntary possession through some invocation of sorcery by an enemy. Cases where people were said to be so possessed would now often be treated as mental illnesses of various types and delegated to appropriate professionals. In medieval times, the competing suppliers of demon-removal services were the established churches and folk practitioners of medicine. A monopoly of the demon-removal trade was highly useful for any established church [see Thomas (1997)] and hence the 'witch hunt' of mass slaughter, in many parts of Europe of suspected witches, can be seen as a particularly unpleasant piece of rent-seeking.[1] The long-run rate of return on witch persecution was raised by the promulgation of the claim that those suspected were, in fact, part of an organized body sending demons abroad to undo the Fall-remedial work of the church. Even where there was no overt persecution of witches, as in Russia, the established church used the notion of sin as a means of controlling rival belief systems. In the mid seventeenth century, individuals engaging in the supernatural practice of divination were punished by being beaten with rods [Ryan (1999, p. 31)]. An eighteenth century manuscript shows the Russian Orthodox Church describing a huge range of seemingly innocuous practices as 'accursed' (ibid.). These include: playing musical instruments, playing chess, listening to animal noises as a means of foretelling the future, rolling in the snow (a means of forecasting marital prospects) and believing

that itching palms means one will receive money. There are minority religions, in the UK, which have shown this obsessive level of anti-sin mentality. The logic of all this is Fall-derived, as the notion is that any display of
human weakness that passes unchecked will lead to total moral disorder as
mankind is inherently unable to resist temptation.

The Fall fables are an answer to the question: 'why are we not happy?' The
person who could answer this question would have created a most wonderful
pure public good assuming, as an idea, that it could have a near-zero distribution cost, particularly if the solution follows from the explanation. A convenient solution for economic growth and development (for what else can we
call the rise of capitalism?) according to Weber was the Protestant Work Ethic
(PWE). In terms of basic microeconomics, the discussion revolves around
changes in tastes rather than price and income variables. Weber's basic story
is that capitalistic development was hindered by the religions which treated
making the maximum amount of money as evil and not the correct way to
serve God. In such a regime consumption will, along with the supply of labour,
be modest. There will also be a problem of raising the levels of investment. In
the UK usury laws were not repealed until 1834. There were isolated sparks of
capitalism before the PWE took hold, but in no way was there a capitalist
system.

Weber's approach is pretty much the opposite of Marx, who would argue
on the basis of economic determinism that the pattern of religious observance
was a by-product of the mode of production. Weber's story is that a taste
change, the spread of PWE, brought about the systematic transformation of the
economy. He analysed the shift in the economy of Renaissance splendour to
economic calculation in the sixteenth and seventeenth centuries. He contrasted
this with an earlier Catholic mode that deprecated accumulation. Only in the
Protestant mode was saving seen as virtuous. In Protestantism, reward was to
be had on earth as all forms of earning a living were treated as a calling. In
Weber's schema the taste change is ascribed to an independent variable 'the
spirit of the age'. This is criticized by anthropologists [Douglas & Isherwood
(1979)], who maintain that the 'spirit of the age'/PWE should be treated as
endogenous, i.e. the analyst should explain where the spirit of the age comes
from rather than treating it as a predetermined fact.

Weber's secularization thesis proposes then that the market institutions
usurp the religious institutions. Some modern economists contend that the
process is one of absorption rather than usurpation. Goodwin (1988) and
McCloskey (1985) point out that religious metaphors are absorbed into the
market mentality. Goodwin even goes so far as to suggest that economists are
new secular priests, advising on the economic equivalents to the ten
commandments. We will take up this issue further in Chapter 11 when we
conclude by speculating on the future of the current array of leading sins.

RELIGIOUS–ECONOMIC FUSION

Given the claims at the end of the last section, we might expect some doctrinal response to modern capitalism that tries to 'capture' or at least integrate economic ideas to ensure the survival of the major religions. Since the emergence of modern capitalism, mainstream economic theories have met with religious opposition as Weber's thesis would predict. In nineteenth century England, a strong moral tone was to be found in the opposition voiced by critics such as Ruskin, Carlyle and Dickens. The sin aspect of this was felt in their horror that capitalism seemed to be spawning apologists for greed in the form of the 'political economists' of the day, particularly the Ricardian school. Later writers such as Nassau Senior and the French economist Bastiat were singled out for vitriolic attack by Karl Marx for being apologists without any redeeming merits of insightful theory to exonerate them.

Neither he, nor the literary critics, did anything much to construct an alternative moralized version of how the economy might work. Indeed, Marx's work, like Nietzsche's, is one in which nature will have its way and traditional Christian morality is thereby an irrelevance, albeit he does hold forth with a certain amount of moral invective. In fairness, one could construct a thesis that the predicted inevitable explosion of capitalism into socialism is the ultimate nirvana/utopia fantasy in which we finally return to the 'garden' where Adam and Eve first made their mistake.

By the late nineteenth century, some more coherent attacks on economists were forthcoming: in the UK from Roman Catholic economists and economic historians and in Germany from the 'German Historical School' which was to influence the emergence of 'Institutional Economics' in the USA. These critiques emerged at the time when marginal analysis and subjective value were transforming microeconomic analysis into what it has become today. The overwhelming focus of such critiques, as far as anything sinful might go, was on the topics of unfair income distribution in the form of great extremes of wealth and poverty and the destruction of the environment. There were also occasionally arguments that the pressure of the capitalist system was forcing the working man into lust or sloth depending on his fate, and thereby undermining the sanctity of the family which is an institution most organized religions have sought to regulate. Two things emerged from this. Firstly, as indicated in Chapter 1, possible accommodations within economics itself in the form of Pigouvian Welfare Economics which sought to derive rules for the optimal intervention of the state to cushion the blow of unfortunate side-effects of a free market system. Secondly, Christian and neo-Christian policy proposals which invariably tended to be some sort of vague social democracy with protection for the underprivileged, measures of worker co-operation, and so on.

Some religions evolved a distinct body of teachings in economics, covering both macro- and microeconomics. By far the largest amount of such writing comes from Roman Catholics. Several popes have written encyclicals which convey papal thinking on economic and social matters [see Charles & MacLaren (1982) for an analysis of the papal encyclicals]. The Catholic Economic Association launched an academic journal in 1942 to explore this kind of thinking. This journal, *Review of Social Economy*, still exists although it publishes a wide range of other types of thinking in 'social economics'. The organization is now called the Association for Social Economics and its membership contains many non-Catholic economists. Indeed, a good deal of Judaically based economics has appeared in the *Review of Social Economy*.

ROMAN CATHOLIC ECONOMICS

Roman Catholic economics centres on the dignity of labour, the sanctity of the family, ethical responsibility by business leaders, the need for justice in income distribution and the over-riding goal of social harmony to which these contribute. As must be the case, a lot of this is simply traditional doctrine imported into the economic field. Roman Catholic economists have not accommodated greatly to free market economics, although even recent papal encyclicals have shown some drift towards the inherent relativism of economics. Ultimately there is a suggestion that maximizing economic growth is not necessarily the proper goal of government policy. Excessive growth will jeopardize the institutions of the family and workplace relations on which the stability of society relies. Catholic economics may have its problems with growth but it has been fairly flexible with respect to issues of money, banking and interest. Scholastic philosophers approved of borrowing with interest so long as it was not in excess of a 'just' return. This concern with justice is also shown in acceptance of the fact that there may be circumstances where labour disputes are permissible, most notably if they are required to redress infringements of justice in wage payment or the dignity of labour. Such a focus on justice is capable of being incorporated within neo-classical theories of distribution once the required adjustment is made for externalities. The overall thrust of these ideas then is not innately hostile to capitalism but rather tends towards 'responsible capitalism' akin to that found in secularly advocated social democratic politics.

ISLAM

At present there is a very active literature on 'Islamic economics' [including the publication of a journal of *Islamic Economics*; see for example Abizadeh,

McCormick & Yousefi (1995), Presley & Sessions (1994), Kuran (1995)].
Islamic economics emerged in India in the 1940s and blossomed in the 1970s.

The subject holds a fascination for Western economists because of the
question as to whether an economy can survive and grow when placed under
the restrictions of the Islamic system. With respect to the Weber thesis, it is
interesting to note that the world's Muslim countries have tended to be under-
developed economically [Kuran (1999)] yet countries which are beginning to
expand their world trade, notably in Africa, are converting to Islam
[Ensminger (1999)]. Islamic economics was originally developed as a counter-
balance to Western economic ideas which showed signs of undermining
Islamic society. It has three key elements, the best known being usury. The
others are zakat, which is a redistribution system, and a set of moral precepts
which economic decisions must pass through. Usury is rejected altogether and
this has been introduced into the banking systems of Iran and Iraq since the
mid-1980s. The ban on interest does not prevent banking from emerging as
profit and loss sharing; Islamic economists disapprove of interest being made
when the lender has taken no risk. In practice the banks have operated in a
different manner from that envisaged in Islamic economics. It is not clear
whether a zero rate of interest is meant to be real or nominal, although the
balance of doctrine is on nominal interest rates. In an inflationary economy
this will mean a negative rate of interest. This has happened in Iran and
Pakistan because of an over-large expansion in the money supply [see Yousefi
et al. (1995)]. The Islamic banks operate on profit and loss sharing which turns
out as depositors' profit shares closely following the interest rate, especially in
mixed systems where Islamic banks compete with secular banks [for example
Turkey, see Table 1 of Kuran (1995)]. The system of murabatha functions as
essentially an interest-type mechanism. Under it the bank buys an item and
marks up the price, gives it to the customer and receives payment in one year.
This is clearly a roundabout method of absorbing a traditionally sinful practice, which is necessary for economic expansion into the established doctrine.
In Western religions where usury was rejected, the ease with which it could be
enacted without punishment meant that there was no parallel contortion. Ease
of avoidance seems to characterize the zakat system which may then facilitate
expansion through sinning. It is, of course, possible that, at some stages of
economic development, stricter enforcement of zakat may prove Pareto optimal due to the need to cushion some of the blows of rapid change on the social
order.

The ethos of Islamic economics promotes waste avoidance, elimination of
negative externalities, generosity, hard work, fair prices and fair wages [Kuran
(1995)]. These are similar to the ideas to be found in Roman Catholic economics above, the person-based religions of Buddhism and Wicca below and the
more mixed doctrines of Rudolf Steiner's anthroposophy [see Seddon (1993,

section 7)]. These issues, in general, will be taken up in the next section of this work.

Person-based religions are somewhat difficult to pin down in terms of their economics. I will briefly consider the position in Buddhism and then the increasingly popular 'New Age' variants of Paganism/Wicca.

BUDDHISM

The first overt attempt by Schumacher, in 1968, to claim that there was such a thing as 'Buddhist economics' began with a startling claim: 'Right Livelihood is one of the requirements of the Buddhist's Noble Eightfold Path. It is clear therefore, that there must be such a thing as Buddhist Economics' [Daly (1973, p. 241)]. Indeed there must be if one were to go along with the position of Elster quoted earlier in this chapter. Many would not go that way and might stake the claim that simply stating the propositions of Buddhism as they apply to the economic sphere of life does not a body of economic thought make. Notwithstanding, practising Buddhists, who are also economists, have attempted in recent times to advance the Schumacher position: the key statement of this is in Zadek (1993). Explicating the Roman Catholic approach to economics is relatively easy because of the papal encyclicals and the numerous commentaries on them by economists. In the case of Buddhism, experts have studied the practice of Buddhism in use [Pryor (1990, 1991), Zadek (1993)] rather than the canonical texts which are not enlightening.

Schumacher's vision of a Buddhist economics has come to imply a set of organizing principles for practical alternatives to dominant modes of arranging capitalist economies. Work is seen as a vehicle for further development of the self, not just as a means to an end (not that conventional economics rules out someone doing this, but it is not regarded as a core right of all persons). Economic organization is to be in small local units. Consumption is intended to be purposive in terms of the individual who is rising to a higher level of consciousness and thus frivolous consumption is to be shunned. It is unlikely that Buddhists would adopt the neo-Christian proposal of sumptuary taxes to curb any such tendency. Rather, the public good of providing information about the Buddhist way of life would be used to enlighten the victim of consumption folly.

Buddhist practice indirectly curbs frivolous consumption by the levying of substantial taxes on the laity to support the Sanghas (monks): reportedly as high as 55 per cent of the total income of some communities in Thailand. Frederic Pryor, in two articles published in the early 1990s, took the Weberian view that the more that the laity gave to the Sanghas, the less will the economy grow [Pryor (1990, 1991)]. This was based on a textbook static macroeconomic model. The more that the laity give to monks, he argues, the less will the economy grow. Furthermore, if reaching nirvana depends on being freed from the conditions of production and reproduction (i.e. requires one to be a monk), then the best strategic approach to pursue in maximizing the number of people in a society that can reach nirvana is to maximize the rate of economic growth. There will be an intertemporal tradeoff of enlightenment, that is supporting a high proportion of monks now may reduce the total access to Sangha status, and hence enlightenment, in the long run. Here is the Weber growth retardation argument again with the added twist that the religious practice defeats even the welfare objectives it has assigned itself.

Buddhist economist Simon Zadek (1993) contests the rigid implications of Pryor's proposition by giving a number of reasons for long-run economic growth being high under Buddhist economic regimes. One argument is that the transfers ultimately equate to social expenditures that maintain the coherence of the community and thus aid productivity. For example, some resources passing through the 'monk sector' in Cambodian peasant society are used to provide social services, such as health care and education. Further, there is the positive externality of 'radiation' offered by Pryor himself. Pryor offers an interesting, although ambiguous, mixture of interpretations of the meaning or root of radiation. First, he quotes Reynolds and Clifford's argument that, 'as a result of the monk's pure and selfless actions, the laity flourish' [Reynolds and Clifford (1980, p. 62)], but does not attempt to explain exactly what is meant by this. The general implication seems to be that productivity may rise due to this atmosphere effect. There seems to be a contradiction in attempting to argue that Buddhism will be a highly useful instrument in long-run growth rates to the point where it might replace Protestantism as the Work Ethic that drives us to higher levels of collective well-being. The ideas contained in the eightfold path suggest that pursuit of high rates of growth is not good for individual well-being and therefore the *bona fide* individual Buddhist ought not to exhibit a preference for institutional forms which support such a goal. They should then oppose any dilution of the doctrine which emanates from the pressures of the market for beliefs in a developed economy. Dilution however, cannot be ruled out, particularly once religious pluralism enters the community structure and the faith is subject to the ill winds of competition from rival faiths which may appropriate some of its more marketable characteristics and jettison its less palatable ones. One area where diluted Buddhism rears its head is in the final faith we wish to consider in this chapter: Wicca.

WICCA

Unlike the previous cases, there has yet to be any attempt by a professional economist to present a synthesis for this belief system. So, in this section I will briefly attempt to elucidate what its economic principles might be as judged from some representative contemporary texts. As with more conventional churches, Wiccans do have orders of status within community organizations, such as a coven, and beyond this do form larger federations from these bodies. Again, they have variations of doctrine within their ranks such as feminist strands, gay and lesbian bodies and such supposed breakaways as 'Chaos Magicians' [see e.g. Hine (1995)]. Evidence of the popularity and visibility of Wiccan doctrines is found in the large number of books being published on the subject and the attention given to campaigns for recognition as a *bona fide* religion, for example in the US military. The underlying features of Wiccan beliefs are as follows.

i.   Rejection of the single deity belief system of Christian religion as just another mythopoetic system amongst many with a tendency to favour classical or Celtic mythology as an underpinning of the faith. This will tend to be portrayed as Paganism.

ii.   Negative forces leading to evil are characterized as demons. Individuals may be the victim of demons that others have sent or that they have inadvertently conjured up themselves. It should be noted that this approach can still be found in mainstream Christian works which confront the problem of evil [cp. Kraft (1992)].

iii.   In some cases there is an attempt to forge a tradition of Wicca as having been a fully fledged original religion of the common European people (despite the discrediting of this in historical research), which was brutally crushed by the established church.

iv.   As part of (iii) the 'Pagan' element is emphasized in the form of worshipping nature and the earth with the consequent duty of the individual not to defile it by pollution and excessive usage of natural resources leading to their depletion.

v.   Personal growth is emphasized through various exercises which may include borrowings from other religious traditions such as yoga, in the physical domain, and elements of Jewish mysticism in the mental domain.

vi.   There is a tendency towards vegetarianism but more broadly organic dietary lifestyles where processed food and 'non-natural' growth methods are frowned upon.

vii.   Ritual and symbolism is encouraged in terms of clothing and group worship ceremonies which are linked to the seasons.

viii.   There is a belief in the efficacy of 'spells': that is, that a person can will certain things to happen if they follow rules which have been devised by wise precursors in the tradition.

There are some implications of these for economics in general and the economics of sin in particular. Doubtless the strong portrayal of Wicca as 'white' magic (i.e. a force for good) in promoting the faith is a response to its being labelled as sinful or even Satanic by oligopolists of established deity-based religions. Hence, this is a deft piece of product positioning. The whole-hearted exponents of the darkness of nature were discussed at the end of Chapter 2. More specific economic doctrines are sporadically scattered in Wiccan texts. For the most part, these would be fairly congruous with Buddhist doctrine. There is a pro-environmental stance and a hostility to modern industrialism and rapid economic growth which is manifested in antipathy to cities as denying access to communion with nature. The main microeconomic sin issue derives from spells, which takes us into the question of money. Many of the more specialist texts in the field [e.g. Farrar & Farrar (1996), Fitch (1999), Hine (1995)] shy away from giving very specific instructions on how to conduct spells for love or money, but it is not hard to find them. For example, chapter 6 of Cunningham (1999) is titled: 'Simple Folk Magic Rituals' and gives a procedure involving flower petals to bring love to the caster; it goes on to a week-long 'silver spell' to bring prosperity which is not really much different from the ideas on 'creative visualization' one might find in purely secular works on 'the power of positive thinking'. Cunningham remarks in the run-up to this that 'money is a state of mind'. At first glance this might seem like mere hippy philosophizing, but the context of the remark shows that it is the standard subjective value theory of Austrian economics.

We have reached the point at which monotheistic established religions would accuse this of being a sinful endeavour. If spells work then individuals can surely will themselves huge amounts of money and power to do what they wish without any moral responsibility whatsoever. The fear of trips to purgatory and/or hell will exercise no deterrent effect on members of a faith who do not believe in these contingencies. Even if spells, *per se*, are ineffective there is still the risk that attempting them is a route to developing the kind of powers of telekinesis that Chinese researchers claim exist in their country, whereby gifted individuals can move money and objects from other people to themselves simply via concentrated willpower [see Dong & Raffill (1997)].

It should of course be pointed out that praying itself, and many of the rituals of established Christianity, are a form of invocation to achieve results. In addition, the tales of Jesus and other major figures in the Bible basically portray them as magicians in the strict sense that they bent the conventionally understood rules of nature: making a few scraps of food go round multitudes, water spring from rocks, mighty seas part, and so on. However, Jesus and other biblical magicians are the agents of God and in an economic sense have been franchised with his 'prime mover' agency of being the author of nature/fate. The Christian who prays is praying directly to the principal rather than soliciting a miracle from his agents on earth. So, in economic terms, the threat of Wiccan religions is that they usurp this monopoly power of the old established churches and their rebranded variants. Wiccan/New Age religions essentially seek to make the individual capable of performing their own miracles. This might seem to open the door to unlimited sin but Wicca, as now defined, rapidly slams it shut. The whole exercise of becoming a witch, magician or whatever in the huge battery of 'New Age' publications is seen as one in which the empowered individual is a virtuous craftsperson working 'with nature' and not against it. They are hemmed in from abusing their power by various 'natural laws' in which the Wiccan analogues of Christian sin ideas are enshrined in picturesque phrases and numerical formulae. Chiefly, we have the 'boomerang' effect whereby any misuse of power rebounds on the manipulator, often reinforced by the obscure notion of the 'threefold law' that not only does the individual get paid back for crossing the line into evil but the repayment is three times as bad as the ill-will directed outwards. From this position, a survey of the history of occultism is able to afford cautionary tales serving a parallel function to that of the Fall in Christian doctrine. One of the earliest concerns the fall of Solomon into black magic, but we encounter a steady stream of tales of disastrous demise such as the Dr Faust story and perhaps the ultimately unhappy ending of Crowley.

So it seems that, after all, Wicca is not advocating the possibility of a bizarre Hobbesian psychic world where wealth accrues in proportion to the marginal productivity of one's psychic potency. Adherents will not try to enter such a realm, as it contravenes the doctrine, and even if they did there is a powerful set of deterrent ideas. Indeed, Wiccan ideas are a long way from any kind of anarchism or even extreme liberalism. Detailed data on adherents' beliefs are hard to obtain because of suspicion arising from discrimination. Still, a useful survey of occultists in the UK in 1989 [*Occult Census* (1989)] gives a clear picture of the sort of views likely to be found on running the economy: the political parties supported are in rank order, for the top five: Greens, Liberals, Democrats, Labour, SDP. A menu likely to produce recommendations not dissimilar from the ideas of Buddhists and Muslims.

On personal matters concerning money, individual Wiccans seem to have a philosophy of moderate consumption, 'just wages' and 'just prices'. For example, it is generally advocated that those who may have extraordinary healing powers should not seek to profit from this by charging up to the limits of what the market will bear. A good example of this distinctly unsinful perspective is to be found in a biographical exegesis of the faith [Cabot & Cowan (1992)] by

Laurie Cabot, who recounts the tale of how a note of around the amount needed to pay a restaurant bill, when she and her daughter had forgotten to bring their financial resources, mysteriously floated out of the air. At no point does she go on to claim that she or anybody else can become rich by psychic theft via teleportation of liquid assets or alteration of electronic accounts or otherwise distorting the mind of someone who might be able to effect a transfer to the individual Wiccan.

Ultimately then the conduct orientation of Wicca is not unlike the traditional Christian religions and is buttressed by notions of payback for sinning which are also not dissimilar.

CONCLUSION

This chapter has considered the role of religion in managing and developing the notions of sin which would enter into the individual's decision-making processes as detailed in Chapter 2. Religious doctrines and the bodies which promote them fit quite well into the standard analysis of firms and industries from the industrial economics literature. Religions can be seen as supplying differentiated versions of the same underlying product. New religions enter and old religions rebrand their products in response to economic growth and development. There may be two-way causation, in that religions influence the economy; however, as economic development takes off it is unlikely that an individual religion can retain a strong direct influence. The indirect influence of religions through language and culture remains and is something that the opportunistic individual religious firm can manipulate. The legacy of such indirect influences is found in two main spheres. One is judgements about individual motivation and conduct, which we go on to in the next part of the book, and the other is concrete policy issues around matters of sex, drugs, life and death, which are the subject of the final section of the present work.

ENDNOTE

1. Witch hunts were partly justified by the claim that the Bible insisted that all witches should be put to death. However, this may have been a matter of linguistic confusion from the word for witch essentially meaning 'poisoner' [see Scott (2001)].

PART II

4. Greed, lust, sloth and waste

INTRODUCTION

Let us begin this chapter with a quote from the best-known poem (an allegory from the life of bees) in the history of economics:

> Vast Numbers thronged the fruitful Hive;
> Yet those vast numbers made 'em thrive;
> Millions endeavouring to supply
> Each other's Lust and Vanity;
> Whilst other Millions were employ'd
> To See their Handy-works destroy'd;
> [Harth (1970, p. 64)]

Admittedly Bernard Mandeville's 'Fable of the Bees', published first as a sixpenny pamphlet, *The Grumbling Hive* in 1705, is probably the only well-known poem in the history of the literature of economics. Further, by the final edition in 1724 the thrust of the book was also buttressed by numerous prose remarks which Mandeville had appended to the poem in response to his critics. The prose text had effectively overtaken the poem as an exposition of his ideas. Although he was attacked by noted critics using puns on his name as 'man devil', Mandeville was not actually advocating sin but was rather engaged in a polemic to highlight the hypocritical state to which society had sunk. Mandeville was essentially modernist. Commentators perceive his economic thinking as being mercantilist and thus devoid of the insights of marginal utility and general equilibrium models, even in the nascent form of Adam Smith's invisible hand. Yet his pithy comments on the subjects of this and the next two chapters are quite in line with remarks made from the mainstream of economics in those areas.

Mandeville identified the simultaneous presence of greed, lust, sloth and waste as essential to maintaining balanced high-level economic growth. He had no hesitation in proposing that these sins could be, as economists would say now, social-welfare-maximizing. This chapter and the next two explore the economic aspects of the sins Mandeville sought to legitimate. In so doing, we will encounter economists serving the function of being the new secular priesthood, particularly through the important service of providing a vocabulary in which the original deadly sins are modified in their tenor.

I now briefly contextualize the four sins dealt with in this chapter. Sloth is a habit or state of being, greed and jealousy are emotions, and waste is a blanket term of condemnation of actions and/or their consequences. Sloth is an intrinsically 'bad' habit which has come to connote mere laziness but originates in the idea of some kind of spiritual malaise within the individual. Waste in economic terms is inefficiency, as in the failure to produce the level of welfare that could be reached with given resources, but more widely there is the intertemporal problem of the destruction of non-renewable assets. The common usage of waste carries an implied condemnation of irresponsibility or, less seriously, frivolity of action. Greed and lust are emotions which are related to each other. It is common in the study of the emotions to distinguish between 'basic' and 'complex' emotions. Some work filtering into economic literature on addictions considers them to be due to basic emotions described as 'visceral', which means relating to inward feelings. This does not mean the brain is not involved (that is, the response is not 'from the gut') as the brain is categorized amongst the visceral organs. Rather, the distinction is that cognitive processing prior to responding is not a large feature of a basic emotion, hence the response will tend to be spontaneous and more difficult to control. Anger is therefore a good example of basic/visceral emotions whilst envy/jealousy, to be dealt with in Chapter 5, are more complex. Greed and lust veer towards the basic end of the spectrum but it must be admitted that, approaching the overall topic of this work from an economic viewpoint, it is hard to maintain the pure notion of entirely visceral responses that are not subject to delay and filtration of social perceptions. Economic problems may arise in group contexts: if envy, lust, greed, etc. are visceral, an individual would then generate involuntary bodily reactions such as displeased facial expressions and hostile posture [Carter (1998, ch. 1)]. If the subject responds in like manner then there will be a feedback loop setting up an environment of low levels of trust which may undermine group productivity. There is thus some incentive to encourage control of these emotions, by deflection of them into less problematic outlets or outright concealment of them at times when they cause greatest risk.

GREED

Biblical condemnation of greed is to be found in Timothy, where we find the well-known remark that love of money is the root of all evil and also the phrase 'greed of filthy lucre' in which we find the conjunction of dirt and craving for money or possessions. One of the signature episodes in the Bible as a teaching of 'right' conduct is the tale of Judas Iscariot's betrayal of Jesus in response to the temptation of earthly wealth. Part of the religious disdain for greed is the elevation of transcendence and demotion of the material aspects of life. The most important economic implication of the sustained perception of greed as a sin has been the ability of religions to sustain prohibitions on usury. Greed became a deadly sin due to the monastic devisers of the list of the deadly sins seeing it as an intrinsic part of man's fallen nature. This began with Adam's inability to resist temptation in the Garden of Eden. In a broad sense, any succumbing to temptation involves greed as it denotes mankind assuming 'too much' agency for its own fate.

Playground terms of abuse such as 'greedy guts' and 'greedy pig' are still with us and are both revealing of the basic Christian point of view. The cultural maintenance of greed as a sin has been through morality plays and tales. The children's bedtime story is a powerful instrument for the socialization of economic agents as it determines the given tastes which they are assumed to have in most rational choice models. Let us consider one of the best-known cautionary tales against greed, which comes from a collection of Aesop's fables. These are of pre-biblical origin and have filtered into everyday speech and thought. The high point of anti-greed sermonizing in this collection is the story of 'The Dog and the Shadow' in which a dog, who is carrying a piece of meat on his way home, sees his own reflection in a pool of water. Not realizing this is an illusion, he snaps at his reflection and because of having to open his mouth 'the piece of meat fell out, dropped into the water and was never seen more' [Jacobs (1966, p. 7)]. This fable could be recast in terms of the SEU model. That is, the dog takes a bet on the reflection being a real dog with meat and thus gambles on losing his existing 'wealth holding', i.e. the piece of steak in his mouth. This might be a perfectly rational choice if the dog is sufficiently risk-loving as he maximizes his *ex ante* utility. So far, this does not include any notion of greed *per se*. It is notable that the standard tellings of the tale are extremely bald in that the dog does not experience regret at his apparent misjudgement. The judgement of the observer would be, in terms of the SEU model, that the dog has made a catastrophic error in subjective probability assignment, that is assuming the other dog is real and, further, being real would be easily relieved of his wealth.

This is a straightforward control failure sparked by the cue of a vivid image of easy gain making the dog lapse into these prediction errors. Elster (1998) suggests modelling such visceral waywardness as 'temporary preferences' which quickly die out and then the agent returns to 'normal'. In this set-up, greed is really a form of impatience where the temporary preferences might be collapsed into a sudden rise in the discount rate which is a reversion to child-like (that is, before complex emotions have fully developed) behaviour. Research on savings, summarized in Webley (1999), suggests that economic socialization, in terms of virtue and vice, may be quite important. Around the age of six, children save reluctantly and, if at all, because they think they ought to in terms of its being good in a moral sense. By age 12 they conceptualize it as an economic strategy which may raise their welfare aside from issues of virtue.

From Mandeville onwards, through Smith, Austrian subjectivism and revealed preference, economists have striven to impart a gospel of efficiency to ensure that we do not become Aesopian, Pavlovian, or any other kind of dogs. Contradiction might seem to be looming over us, in so far as generally we would be inclined to think that a successful entrepreneur has something of the characteristic of the Aesopian dog but manages to get it right. Entrepreneurs may be driven into excess by speculation on ever-improving circumstances, and the same can happen to households with the same ultimate risk of crippling debt and, in the worst case, bankruptcy. These problems are inherent in a dynamic growing economy. In a dynamic environment, individuals are constantly bombarded with new information. This could be analysed with behaviourism, where the individual is treated in terms of stimulus–response. The stimulus comes from either the income or expenditure side. In the case of lottery winners the will to spend is over-stimulated by the receipt of income. Or, in the case of credit cards, the card itself is a stimulus. The lure of new, exciting and attractive goods may be a stimulus which elicits a response of procuring (legally or illegally) credit cards. Control is lost due to the overwhelming power of the continual stream of new stimuli. In terms of a satisficing model of uncertainty [cp. Earl (1990, pp. 47–51)] the level of constraint previously perceived as realistic is destroyed. Sudden changes produce psychic reactions that cannot be analysed with the marginal calculus. This makes the notion of a long-run static equilibrium irrelevant as the conditions under which it can be worked out are not known.

As one of the seven deadly sins, greed has its origins in the monastic life but why did it take root in the wider society to the point where it is still quite prevalently frowned upon in terms of behaviour and attitudes? Let us now consider the basic motivations which create the costs and benefits in those scenarios. There are a number of possible sources of disapproval of greed, which we might conveniently divide into micro and macro.

MICRO-GREED

As in Aesop's fable of the dog and the shadow, greed leads to an ex post short-fall in individual welfare over what could have been achieved with less distorted perceptions, that is perceptions not inflated by the visceral emotions. Greed may lead to health damage for the greedy individual whether this is due to eating too much food, excess stress from pursuit of goods or too much risk-taking in hedonic goods. They may also fail to provide adequately for their dependents, thereby imposing a burden on society. Thus for an individual who lacks self-control, welfare may be increased by the supplement from the stigma of social disapproval as is suggested by the analysis of social customs in Chapter 2. So, a rational individual may join in with condemning greed as a means of maintaining its status as a 'public bad' in order to use social stigma to help supplement their own insufficient self-control. In other words, we might join in the condemnation of other people's greed, with respect to certain acts, as a way of building up 'action-specific greed capital' so that it exerts a collective force pulling us away from performance of the act. This is just a mild form of the typical Hobbesian argument for social controls such as direct punishments on criminals. Being greedy may lead to crime but clearly in many cases, such as over-eating, it does not necessarily do so.

As with all the themes in this section of the book there is the prospect that the emotion of anger at someone else's greed may be more than just an investment in social capital to aid self-control. That is, it may be a projective justification for feelings of envy (rather than the control maintenance just mentioned) at someone else's superior allocation. Greed can be used as a *post hoc* justification to protect self-image or the super-ego from excess dissonance. This could amount to 'taste envy' as well as goods envy, as an inhibited individual may be jealous of a less inhibited individual's gaining welfare through indulging in the greed that the moral critics had held in check. This is a visceral aversion to other people's greed which poses problems for overall welfare as it is a negative externality in the utility function of the individual which may reduce the gains of economic growth if the envy outpaces the gains from one's own direct resource gains (see Chapter 5).

Going back to the role of religions, in Chapter 3, greed may be intrinsically displeasing regardless of the above factors as it is symptomatic of a fall from grace. It is a sin of the flesh which evidences the basic animal nature which religion/spirituality/mysticism strive to rise above. One of the clearest biblical depictions of greed is in Genesis 38 regarding the actions of Onan who is better remembered as the first conspicuous sinner, via masturbation, as discussed in the next section. Onan was faced with a classic problem in terms of rational choice. Exhorted to do the duty of impregnating his brother's widow he was confronted with the dilemma that, under the laws of inheritance, this would mean that wealth otherwise due to him would pass to the child in which he would not be allocated any property rights in the Levirate marriage, which passed the child on as being considered to be his brother's despite the biological parentage. As biblical scholar Jonathan Kirsch (1997, p. 139) says in his treatise on the pre-bowdlerized biblical texts, 'we realize that Onan is acting out of pure greed . . . [when] . . . he refuses to bring the sexual encounter to a climax that might actually produce a child'. Ironically Onan steps into the sin of greed by denying himself the pleasures of the flesh.

MACRO-GREED

In the previous chapter we encountered the conundrums surrounding the relationship between Islam, which maintains a nominal prohibition of usury, and the state of economic development. One direction of explanation is that, at low levels of development, such curbs may be efficient. In a society with low levels of economic development, greed threatens the community. Stocks of food, etc. may be a buffer against risk of natural disasters, attack by enemies, seasonal failures and so on. The greedy person may exhaust their buffer stocks and thus be pushed towards expending resources contesting transfers from the stocks of other individuals. The deadweight loss of these efforts further reduces output. Where there is an expansion of the frontier of technological knowledge and the opening up of new trade opportunities, greed may be a useful feature if it drives entrepreneurs into taking the necessary risks in these inherently uncertain ventures. Some kind of balancing act is required as the risk-taking entrepreneurs may need to raise capital from the savings of other individuals. This may be difficult as greediness amongst the potential savers would require high rates of interest in order to induce them to trade off present for future indulgence at a sufficient rate. Granted, the possible high rate of return from the expanding economy may offer them high interests on loans, but these may be too risky.

Notions of greed might then become mutated depending on the sphere in which they operate. Economists, and other secular priests such as psychologists, play a role in providing language to justify and control actions. Thus greed moves from being naked, which is unpalatable, into the clothing of business 'success'/'ambition'/'achievement' which are positive virtues in a secular society. Whilst not exactly things which would be heavily encouraged in traditional religions they are a long way from being regarded as sinful in the deadly sense. Individuals who have made a lot of money are seldom to be found saying 'basically I'm greedy and that is why I did it'. If they did there would be no basis for humour, or radicalism, in such attempted subversion as the attack on the Beatles' faux-Eastern spirituality by Frank Zappa and the Mothers of Invention in the 1968 record 'We're Only In It for the Money' or the Sex Pistols' 1970s film *The Great Rock and Roll Swindle*. So, we get the post-capitalist version of the 'dignity of labour' as achievement and, if it is wealthy achievement, additional justifications, from economics, such as the virtue of creating jobs for many other people are put forward. The true limit of financial greed, in the form of theft, is not ostensibly approved of, although we will have more to say on this at the start of Chapter 6. Success orientation derives psychological sustenance from ideas such as the 'Type A' personality of the high achiever.

In the macroeconomic arena, serious crises repeatedly occur [see

Kindleberger (1978, p. 216–17) for a historical catalogue] which are commonly attributed to waves of irrational speculation on the seeming perpetuity of rapid share and/or commodity price rises. Modern economics was supposed to put paid to the 'Mercantilist fallacy' that 'buying cheap and selling dear' was the road to national wealth. Yet these maniacal 'bubbles' show its endurance. The Aesopian dog seems to be always within us, ever waiting to materialize on the dealing floor. To mainstream economists, such events are disregarded as mere blips in a well-regulated world. To the mavericks who do pay them serious heed, the greed of the 'bubble' is linguistically altered to the notion of 'euphoria' which seems to originate with Hyman Minsky and, in the eighteenth century, Adam Smith gave it the neutral-sounding name of 'overtrading'. What is financial euphoria but a case of excessive focus on a favourable outcome that cannot be sustained? In Elster's terms a temporary switch in preferences, which is how we have been claiming greed fits into microeconomic analysis.

Thus we find greed rebranded by the secular priests going about their innocent business of striving for scientific value-neutral analysis of human behaviour. What would be the final proof that it has lost its full sting as a deadly sin? Undoubtedly the presence of rituals that were essentially more ceremonial rather than directly useful. Briefly, let us consider one example from casual empiricism and one from an arch cynic of rational choice economics. Firstly, there is the social etiquette of group eating whereby food may remain uneaten (or alternatively be covertly procured), especially of the more frivolous variety such as cakes, because no one wants to be seen as the person who has the remainder at a point when everyone has already eaten sufficient to meet survival and comfort needs. Granted this may be a problem of *ad hoc* risks of inequity, but even so a repressed feeling of having too much fun lurks in the problem. Finally, in such circumstances a justification of capitulating to desire may be given in terms of avoiding the waste (a different sin) of throwing the food away. Ethically it might be preferred to transport the excess to a region of great poverty, but transactions costs prevent spontaneous redistribution of a cream cake in a fourth floor office in downtown New York to a Third World famine site.

Transactions costs also enter into Tullock's (1966) pessimistic take on more widespread organized attempts to be charitable. The existence of many large charities might seem to suggest that fears of accusations of greed still rankle heavily in the emotional complex of the modern individual. Alternative models of charities exist, but the approach which is in harmony with standard rational choice economics is to include the income distribution as an externality in the individual utility function. Those who do badly may experience negative externalities of envy whilst those who do well may experience negative sympathy externalities on the grounds that some individuals are very badly off. This could create feelings of being 'greedy' even if one's visceral emotions are staunchly regulated. Transfers from the better off to the worse off could solve this problem, particularly if non-profit firms designated as charities resolved the transactions costs problem. Here we enter the problem of the hypothetical microeconomics universe, in which there are no saints to save the sinners but rather all men (and women) are pretty much the same underneath the veneer of constraints and opportunities. Tullock attributes charitable donations to a 'warm-glow' effect which would expiate guilt from any accusations of greed. Charities spend on promotional expenditures, as firms do with advertising, to increase their revenues. However, if the warm-glow is largely a rhetorical gesture then the individual giver falls into a strategy of 'rational ignorance' as they stand to lose utility if they probe too deeply and discover that very little of their donation is going to the intended recipients. Under such circumstances, the bureaucratic charity may enter substantially into the region of its revenue function, where the marginal return from promotion is negative even to the point where the transfer to recipients falls to near zero. Studies of philanthropy [see Andreoni (2001)] in action are always fraught with difficulties of obtaining credible data. Nevertheless it seems that the giving of the very rich has dramatic patterns that might best be explained in terms of ostentatious motives such as greed/lust for recognition, praise and so on. Andreoni shows that the giving of the extremely rich, in the USA, seems to be disproportionately low. It seems unlikely that the degree of disparity could be explained by under-reporting of the forms of transfer. Further, there is dramatic variability in the charitable transfers of the ultra-rich which seems to be down to lumpiness from ostentatious donations which will exalt their name on the brass plaques of buildings or new facilities within existing institutions.

Thus, charity may become a ritual to purge the individual of greed-induced guilt. Charity was once mainly a church function, so the large bureaucratic secular charity usurps this role of absolving the individual from sin. The possibility that the individual is buying absolution to increase the risk of ascent to heaven might draw some support from the estimated rising propensity to give with age which ties in with a similar finding that attendance at religious services seems to rise in later years.

LUST

Traditionally the distinction between greed and lust is that the former emotion is cued by money or goods and the latter by sexual stimuli. The distinction is not rigid as we have commonplaces of 'lust for life', 'lust for power' and even 'wanderlust'. There is also the phenomenon of 'blood lust' in early Christianity which is not, of course, seen as a sin.

Fitting lust into the rational choice economics model requires a little contemplation. As with greed it is some kind of externality in the utility function both in terms of one's own subjective lust and any externalities of discomfort from being the object, or more indirect victim, of other people's lust. The difference between greed and lust, from the rational choice viewpoint, seems to be most sensibly viewed as one of degree rather than kind. Greed is an emotion of strong desire to possess an object which may overwhelm an individual's normal process of planning to acquire it through allocation of part of their legitimate income to its purchase. Lust is a higher order of pyschic disequilibrium where an opposing negative feeling of suffering at being denied the item is a bigger element. This may consist of multiple components such as guilt at experiencing the desire and pain costs of repressing the wish to enact the desire even if one does not feel any guilt. It is repression that leads us into the more interesting issues concerning the relationship between lust and economics. Ultimately following the thread of repression takes us to a Marcusian critique of the self-control/meta-preference models of Chapter 2.

Being a basic emotion, we would predict that disincentivizing lust through price signal measures like taxes, fines and punishment is not very effective unless backed up with some prior social investment in guilt capital via religious and cultural shaming. Some economists seem to endorse this view, naturally with social norms as virtues. For example, Sawhill, writing in the area of economic analysis of teenage pregnancy rates lays most stress on upholding the idea that out-of-wedlock child-bearing is wrong, over and above policy measures designed to pull the cost and benefit strings of the problematic teens. Historian of the breast, Marian Yalom (1997, p. 52) reports that in the fifteenth and sixteenth centuries, in most of Europe, many sumptuary laws were passed to discourage sexually provocative dress such as the wearing of codpieces and the display of naked breasts, but proved ineffective. Is there any economic basis for such regulatory attempts? As implied at the end of Chapter 2 we may settle into an equilibrium where social codes are more honoured in the breach than the observance.

The 'economics of institutions' predicts that attempted crackdowns on the breach of a code will only take off if there are potentially significant costs of non-observance of the code. Dismay at the breach could stay at the level of personal anguish as the individual expends psychic energy that is wasted if they engage in heavy condemnation with no prospect of enforcing their preferences. So, waves of anti-lust activity are hard to explain away as simply the work of religious cranks who fail to see the writing on the wall. For one thing, the simple religious basis for disapproval of such things as masturbation persisted for centuries without severe attempts at curbing it through formal controls or widespread myth-making moral panic. Yet, from the mid eighteenth century there was an explosion of condemnation which rippled forth in the form of numerous myths about the effects of the vice on the individual's well-being (thus adding some early fuel to the religion–health link discussed in Chapter 3). Gathorne-Hardy (1993, pp. 267–9) discusses Victorian puritan writer, William Acton. In his view (a common one of the ruling/middle classes in England) women do not experience lust but it is a male bestial urge. Here are some highly evocative selections from his litany of the externalities of habitual male masturbation:

> the frame is sunken and weak, the muscles undeveloped, the eye is sunken and heavy. . . . His intellect has become sluggish and enfeebled and if his evil habits are persisted in he may end in becoming a drivelling idiot or a peevish valetudinarian. . . . self-indulgence, long pursued, tends ultimately, if carried far enough, to early death or self-destruction. [Gathorne-Hardy (1993, p. 267)]

Upon the discovery of female engagement in the 'solitary vice' women were locked up on the grounds that it was a sign of insanity. Men also received therapy and medical treatment in the early twentieth century campaign against this vice. This kind of thinking, which was devoid of any research basis, ultimately leads to outright physical measures to curb the act. Gathorne-Hardy (ibid.) reports the case of restrainers fastened on to male children, by English nannies, in order to prevent exploration of their genital regions. There were also the earlier isolated views of Jewish thinker Moses Maimonides (1135–1204), that circumcision was vital to curb onanistic and more broadly lustful tendencies apart from its ceremonial and (later) medical justification.

Maimonides aside, religious condemnation was purely moral. It came from the interpretation of the biblical evidence that God condemned Onan's deliberate 'spilling of seed' to avoid the enactment of his duty, under Levirate law, to impregnate his widowed sister-in-law. The big drive to stamp on this facet of lust sprang from an anonymous book called *Onania, or the Heinous Sin of Self Pollution* (pollution meant masturbation at this time and has only acquired the connotation of environmental waste in the twentieth century) published in 1710. According to health and perversion historians [see Youngson & Schott (1996, pp. 69–71), Rosario (1997, ch. 1)] this book swept the American–European world. By 1750 it had reached its nineteenth edition and almost single-handedly put its subject in the forefront of moral panic over sin. It is accredited with being the source of all the frightening beliefs catalogued in the quote from William Acton above.

So what economic factors are at work here? One has to rule out the scarcity argument as the typical male produces large amounts of reproductive fluid. Any discharge is quickly replaced in a healthy man. So this rules out any consequent fear of economic stagnation on account of under-population. Rather the particular explosion of the 'self-pollution' fear in roughly 1750 to the early/mid twentieth century surely links to Weber's Protestant Work Ethic. Although the condemnation escaped any confinement within specific religious doctrines it was highly congenial to the religions to whom enterprise and thrift have been attributed. The moral panic symbolized a fear that lust is an unstable cue with explosive potential to decimate the self-control faculty. This line of argument was fully taken up by Marcuse (1955) who, in *Eros and Civilisation*, blended Sartre, Freud and Marx.

The economic threats posed by lust are as follows.

i.   Pleasure-seeking may reduce the adherence to any work ethic. Ultimately this is reined in by zoning attenuated pleasure-seeking temporally and geographically and using its marketization as a further incentive to work. That is, fleeting and restrained indulgences of lust, at the weekend for example, may form a reward to the individual who has worked hard, during the week, to receive them. This kind of work–delay–reward system is particularly likely to be efficacious with someone subject to such a discipline in childhood.

ii.   Lust may influence the young to reckless behaviour which exposes the old to risks of not being financially supported.

iii. Lust may lead to unplanned population growth which could throw the country into a state of poverty. Hostility to pre-marital sex is a code which sought to serve this role. Where this collapses, risks of over-population can be reined in by marketization of contraceptive methods which help to reinforce the solution to (i).

iv.   Recourse to prostitution, which may add to the problems in (i) and (ii) by undermining family life which, as we saw in Chapter 3, is the core of the religious–economic fusion doctrine. There is further the potential for lost output through death and disease.

v.   Individuals driven to extremes may commit large numbers of rapes which deliver to society children with poor incentivization for efficient parental investments.

vi.   The amount of savings available for investment may fall if individuals have a high pleasure orientation.

vii. Resources may be used up competing for the objects of lust either through direct physical combat or via rent-seeking expenditures (which might be classified as 'waste' by some) used up in tournaments to win lust prizes.

viii. All of the above problems may lead to heavy expenditures to control lust which are themselves a deadweight loss to the economy.

It should be noted that we could construe 'self-pollution' as a substitute good for intercourse, rather than the dangerous complementary good envisaged by Moses Maimonides. In the context of a Becker–Lancaster time allocation model it reduces the search and transactions costs required relative to attaining a sexual outlet via copulation and related acts with a partner. This might be a less preferred commodity *in vacuo*, but the cost differentials could be such that welfare is higher.

One could couch the moral panic over Onanism in terms of tastes, *per se*, as its being a gross complement to other sexual activities, rather than a substitute, as envisaged in the previous paragraph. Alternatively, it might be seen as a form of capital formation which alters the tastes for ever more dangerous and socially costly sexual activities. This still assumes that tastes are constant and self-control is perfect. In a world of perfect self-control (with harmoniously reconciled beliefs) no one would stand to accrue rents from rolling out a moral panic. So the basis of the above grounds for the moral panic is fundamentally that of the deterioration of what Marcuse (1955) called the 'psychic thermidor', which is an inbuilt tendency for the individual to defeat their own basic emotional desires via succumbing to repression. Any escape from repression into untrammelled hedonism might alter the mode of behaviour in all other spheres of activity. The main one being the corrosion of the ability to defer gratification, leading to the individual's discount rate being too high.

Large-scale moral panics enhance the use of explicit means of control through child-rearing practices, the banning or muting of stimuli and, in the extreme case, mutilation of the sex organs sanctioned by religious doctrine. Muting is of course most explicitly seen in the case of pornography laws which are discussed further in Chapter 8. This has an earlier echo [see Yalom (1997)] in the history of religious art in which breasts moved from being prominent/celebrated to being absent, i.e. painted down. Muting is also found in the boundary case of total privatization of the marital partner, as a commodity, through the covering up of most of the face and the body so that temptation stimuli are not issued to other men. These are specific means of regulation but general 'repression capital' may also be formed by discipline in all areas of an individual's socialization. A good example is the strict regime of 'potty training' [see Gathorne-Hardy (1993)] imposed on Victorian and Edwardian English children by their nannies. This will build a habit of being reluctant to let go which can serve economic functions of altering the discount rate and resisting all-round cues for temptation.

Marcuse seems to suggest that there is a 'natural' tendency towards inhibition built into people, independently of induced repression, in the form of the 'psychic thermidor'. This constitutes a potential critique of the self-control model in Chapter 2. There is a tendency in such a model to slip into the habit of seeing the 'higher' preferences which should dominate the welfare function as ones of modesty, virtue, abstinence and low rates of discounting. One finds this throughout the Elster edited conference volume on addictions [Elster (1999)] which is preoccupied with the notion that addicts 'truly' want to give up. In the extreme case, this kind of normative thinking [e.g. in George (1993)] generates the argument that the lower-order preferences are being rewarded by the market which thus tends to 'over-create' them. This argument can be reversed in the Marcusian scenario. There, the market is creating repressed preferences and the individual who is exercising self-control is merely playing out a Freudian drama of id and ego. Marcuse's view is essentially the opposite: that the market is tilted excessively to rewarding repressed preferences which the individual is doomed to be unable to escape from. For example, in such a view so-called 'perversions' may be positive signs of variety and/or attempts to break through harmfully imposed preferences.

In this section we have stayed mainly on sexual themes as this is the commonly viewed locus of lust; nevertheless a Marcusian view of repression of lust as economically ordained control suggests that repression will lead to disequilibrium in the thermidor which may spill over into excessive behaviour in other areas, such as drug consumption (see Chapter 8) as an outlet. Of course the thermidor may falter in some individuals who experience heavy dissonance in conforming to the current menu of codes. In the extreme case they may be classed as having personality disorders by the judgement of the constrained society in which they exist. Within this boundary, they may respond to the fetters of repression by more erratic risk-taking, thus behaving in a way opposite to that intended by the codes. Thus, repressed lust may also spill over into general risk-taking activity. Lyotard (1993), in an attempt to marry economics and psychoanalysis, argues that the crises which were attributed to 'euphoria' by various writers in our last section can be regarded as libidinal, where erotic energy gets transferred into stock market speculation. The works of Marcuse and Lyotard are radical attacks on the 'dematerialized' nature of the neo-classical economic paradigm in which the existence of the human body is relegated to being a passive engine under the control of the rationalizing mind. In some sense, they show the neo-classical model to be both transcendent of traditional religious sin-orientation and yet covertly endorsing it, at the same time, by shunning the true nature of the body as a force bringing disruption to the celestial mechanics of the general equilibrium model.

SLOTH

Sloth is harder to get a clear picture on than the other sins in this chapter. In the King James' Bible, the censure of sloth seems to be of people who are 'sluggards', with this being concentrated in Proverbs. Proverbs depicts a number of bad consequences that may follow from 'idleness' as the state seems to have been translated, including death. As with lust, death is the extreme price signal to be used to deter a sin (but must not be confused with the reason for them being 'deadly sins'). Thessalonians sheds some light on the attitude to sloth in terms of the converse virtue of the 'dignity of labour'. Here we find notions which have endured, such as 'good' and 'honest' labour. The person who 'gets by' doing just enough work to survive is seen as falling down in their duty. It is not entirely clear what the motive behind the promulgation of such doctrines was. In economic terms there are a number of possibilities which revolve around the uses of a surplus over subsistence requirements. A surplus serves the dual function of providing resources for conspicuous religious spending on churches, art, clergy, etc. but also a reserve for war efforts against rival faiths and races. The stigma of sloth may also be beneficial to war efforts in that, if it works, energetic individuals will make better soldiers than those who lead a life of lassitude.

Any surplus could fuel economic growth, which takes us back into the Protestant Work Ethic argument. This would claim that Calvin and Luther's focus on centralizing the notion of the dignity of labour was a powerful force in expansion.

It seems that the monastic sin of sloth did not mean mere idleness or laziness, but some kind of overall spiritual malaise. In modern parlance it has tended to become equated with sheer laziness as personified by the animal called a sloth which leads a singularly unenterprising life. The stigma of being slothful is now muted as insults involving it tend to be light-hearted, except perhaps in the case of those refusing to do paid work who are variously termed 'spongers' and 'scroungers' in the UK. Experience of large-scale structural unemployment has possibly removed the weight of sloth that was once gathered behind criticism of idle or lazy workers. The term 'unemployment' is of comparatively recent incorporation to everyday language. At the turn of the twentieth century, those we would now term unemployed were still called the 'idle poor'. The emergence of unemployment as a neutral description of the state of worklessness probably stems from the introduction of legislation in the inter-war period that required the state to shoulder some of the burden for the condition.

The modernized version of sloth's essential meaning seems to be as the opposite of greed, that is procrastinating beyond what is considered a reasonable length before taking action. The end product of this may be the same as that of its opposite, in that the individual either misses out on an opportunity or inflicts loss on themselves. The addict, as portrayed in some writings, manages to combine greed/lust with sloth if constantly plagued by a failing intent to quit their addiction. Procrastination per se is not likely to be seen as a traditional sin.

On the whole, sloth is not a word in very common use and it is a little ironic to see how it has now appeared in economics contexts. Reporting on the award of a MacArthur Foundation 'Genius Award' to Berkeley professor Matthew

Rabin, for his work on 'psychological economics', Gerencher (1998) titles the piece 'the economics of sloth' and goes on to extol Rabin's putting 'some of the deadly sins to work mathematically where others have downplayed the role of human nature in their equations'. Yet red-blooded sin is a long way from any of the discussion in the interview with Rabin that follows. The main thrust of the conversation is how people, by procrastinating, forego opportunities to amass wealth. We find more of this astonishing secularization of sin into economic terms on the 'Motley Fool' website, in a piece by Barbara Elster Bayer [Bayer (2000)] which goes through the whole seven sins as a guide to investors and again extols Rabin as the anti-sloth guru. As his work is interpreted here, sloth is not importantly different from greed and lust as the words of caution are not to jeopardize your retirement by putting off savings due to an excessive present orientation which must be, as we have explained, the core economics definition of greed and lust. The hitching of Rabin's work to the notion of sloth is once more simply tying a particular sin to efficiency issues, as we shall shortly see in the case of waste. Moving on to consider waste cannot detain us long as the efficiency propositions on procrastination, as sloth, are really about waste.

Let us briefly consider social sloth as distinct from personal sloth. Sloth extends from being a purely personal issue when the person is responsible as an agent for the well-being of others. Neglect of this duty might be considered a sin: for example an airline crash which kills people because the executives of the airline have not enacted adequate safety procedures might still be laid at the door of the executives as a sin. Still, the methodology of mainstream economics would suggest that this does not materially matter as far as making the world a better place goes. All that matters is that means exist of enacting behaviour change in a politically acceptable way. Utility-maximizing agents might not be perfect but their sins are perhaps randomly distributed errors. Incentive mechanisms such as price/cost alterations via taxes, subsidies and punishment might be expected to be capable of efficient internalization of the externalities of sloth. Unlike lust, sloth is not a basic emotion and thus its elasticity with respect to incentives might well be larger and less variable in effect. Of course, the elasticity is again dependent on the social capital formation which most notably, in this context, comes from the Work Ethic discussed earlier. Remaining commentary on sloth fits more conveniently into the waste section to which we now turn.

WASTE

Like greed, waste may have lost its sting as a deadly sin but it is still something few are likely to say they approve of. Mandeville, and later Keynes

(1936), gave it a polemical elevation to virtue status on grounds of its macro-economic stabilization potential, but their insights have now been incorporated into a less disturbing body of thought.

Waste, in general, is a two-sided phenomenon meaning either the needless destruction of what exists, as in resource depletion or war, or a failure to create all that might potentially be brought into existence. Within the latter category one can make a further distinction between failure to do a physical act like fix a hole in the roof before the rain comes in and damages some property, and failure to take advantage of a latent opportunity such as not buying some shares before the price goes up. This is a personalized ethically neutral 'waste' which involves notions of regret being brought into the model of individual behaviour. The needless destruction of what exists might be viewed as leading to a socialized version of regret through widespread externalities. For example, I might intend never to go and see a site of natural beauty in a far-flung country but still condemn its destruction by ecological devastation from the by-products of a large multinational company.

Very early in the introductory microeconomics course, the 'missed potential' notion of waste is brought home to the student in the production possibility frontier diagram showing society's choice between amounts of two goods. If society is inside the frontier then more of both goods can be produced and this is deemed 'inefficient' as economists avoid the value-loaded term 'waste' in favour of other terms defined relative to the benchmark of efficiency. For the economy as a whole, efficiency is defined with respect to perfect competition which, some might say, is a value judgement being smuggled back into the analysis. Industrial economists in the 1960s computed many estimates of the loss to the economy from monopoly power with the repeated conclusion that it was not a very large figure. Against this backdrop, Harvey Leibenstein wrote his first paper (1966) on 'X-inefficiency', sparking a controversy which has raged on, leading him to various reformulations (e.g. 1978) of his be-leaguered concept. X-inefficiency now features little in the main intermediate micro textbooks which focus on allocative efficiency, and it is also little seen in specialist textbooks on welfare economics; that by Ng (1983) briefly considers it under 'advanced topics' only to dismiss it as irrelevant.

Still X-inefficiency lives on in the fringes of economics and has some currency in policy debate in developing countries. It also seems to be the motivating factor in frontier cost function analysis, which is sometimes used as an alternative to multiple regression models. Getting down to a definition of X-inefficiency is not easy as it often gets conflated with other things. It might help if we recall the impetus for Leibenstein's coinage, which came from the study of military aircraft where X signifies the residual or unexplained factor as in 'X the unknown', called up to account for substantial differences in the performance of two otherwise identical units of production.

This invokes the idea of waste as one is naturally led to regard the output of the more productive entity as being within the grasp of the less productive, which must then be wasting resources in some way either through their destruction or inefficient usage. It does not seem to make sense to talk of excess or over-efficiency, and thus the lesser output establishment is wasting resources unless there is some benefit gained from its actions.

Given the furore surrounding X-inefficiency one might expect it to be some marvellous alchemical elixir of economics leading to campaigns to better the world by eliminating X-inefficiency. Facetious as the last remark may be it has some of the air of discussions in developing economies sparked by Leibenstein's further marketing of his ideas as 'the economic theory of back-wardness'. In an attempt to clarify whether this concept does bring sinful waste into economics I will go through the various components of X-inefficiency which are in the original statement of the idea, the reformulations and glosses put on by other writers.

(i) Motivational shortcomings. Leibenstein (1966) was adamant that work-ers and firms often do not work as hard as they could nor do they search for cost savings as efficiently as they might. This seems to be more a case of waste attributed to economic sloth.

(ii) In order to fall short in this way opportunities must exist for such self-indulgence. One of these is incompleteness of contracts within the firm due to uncertainty. However, that is a constraint which if unmovable means we are only inside a notional frontier that could not exist in the given state of knowl-edge. In other words, contracts may be incomplete of necessity due to the dynamic of the situation. Comparing this with an ideal set of contracts in a perfect world is to lapse back into a version of the 'nirvana fallacy' of bench-marking the world against perfect competition.

(iii) Non-cooperation due to lack of trust in team production where free-riding is a problem. This is more a case of greed and envy which we address, in detail, in Chapter 5.

(iv) Personality. Individual tastes and aptitudes may differ. This is another 'team production' problem of putting together the wrong team. This can easily be solved by divisionalizing the workforce better and/or recourse to the outside market so long as other barriers do not exist.

(v) Lack of market pressure underlies all of the above. When X-inefficiency was first proposed this was seen mainly in terms of withholding quantity to force up the price. However, the degree of monopoly power will also cause waste by enhancing the scope for the factors in (i)–(iv) to persist through in-ertia. Nevertheless, countervailing factors can squeeze such opportunism out. The managerial theories of the firm prevalent in the 1960s argued that shareholders could not achieve this due to transactions costs arising from the diffusion of ownership. Thus, they are unable to excise waste from the corporation.

Contestable markets theory revived the 'workable markets' logic of J.M. Clark in the 1930s to suggest that so long as costs were mainly fixed rather than sunk, then the threat of competition would drive out waste without any need for it to be enacted.

(vi) Institutional inertia. The lag of custom and practice as explored at the end of Chapter 2 might form a drag on production and consumption efficiency. Thus, taboos could be seen to lead to waste. For example a cultural legacy of antipathy to eating particular foods may be causing deadweight loss. This is not just a feature of developing economies and one should not fall into the pitfall of judging their waste as a loss equal to the welfare they would have if they were given our preferences. An obvious counterfactual is that it is very unlikely that the UK would suddenly move heavily into squirrel farming even if it were the case that in pure cost terms it was more efficient than other meats.

(vii) Personal belief inertia. Outside of taboos and codes, an individual may be a victim of supposedly non-rational 'magical' belief. They might misattribute the sources of their own productivity to a 'totem' rather than their own efforts. An obvious example of this is the sports player who attributes high scoring to lucky charms and consequently panics when these are not present. Overcoming this inertia would require sending them on a management training course where they develop the skill to focus their concentration efficiently in the abstract without the need for the fetish object. A particular important fetish object (although not always detectible by overt image representation) is the job title and status of individuals within organizations, e.g. a priest is needed to do an exorcism or a computer specialist is needed to do a routine technical task. Such structural rigidities create waste, but the degree to which they can be removed depends on the management of envy over positional goods (see the next chapter).

The deadly sin of personal waste was expounded at times when the individual was simultaneously being exhorted to contribute to church buildings, ceremonies, etc. which came to be critiqued under the post-enlightenment thinking of Philosophic Radicals/Utilitarian economists as wasteful on the grounds that it served no useful purpose. This would be a case of 'agency waste' where an organization wastes resources held in trust for individuals who may be members or owners. We have already encountered the externality defence that some of this may not be waste at all in the course of the discussion on Buddhist economics in Chapter 3, where positive externalities on productivity where brought into the picture. After the separation of state and church the state becomes the focus of agency waste criticism. In the UK, John Wade's *Black Book* in 1820 attacked the squandering of taxpayers' money by state and church. During the 'marginal utility revolution' in economics (about 1890–1920) heterodox economists such as J.A. Hobson attacked the neglect of social waste by professional economists. In the inter-war period, American writer Stuart Chase (1930) included the 'frivolous consumption of unnecessary goods and services' in his extensive catalogue of welfare lost due to wastes on advertising, war-related expenditures and so on.

The full flower of this kind of thinking was to be found in the works of Marxists schooled in conventional economics. There is a certain ineluctability about Marxian condemnation of waste due to the dialectical materialist foundations of the doctrine. The gospel of capitalism was accumulation of capital which was seen to be self-defeating, as maintaining a balance between savings and capital was not possible in an unregulated world, therefore booms and slumps would occur with attendant waste. The waste is of both types. Idle resources in a slump which Marx was at pains to point out were not indicative of personal sloth but rather system failure. Then, in the antithetical boom phase, speculation (the euphoria discussed in the greed and lust sections above) leads to inflation of asset values which ultimately collapse leading to a 'slaughter' in the accumulated capital stock value. Contrary to Marx's expectations this cycle did not amplify to the point of system breakdown, but the agents of the system sought renewed stabilizers in the form of state–corporate control of spending and investing to smooth out the cycles. These lead to costs which can be bracketed as socially necessary costs of reproduction. The landmark contribution of this type was produced by Baran and Sweezy (1966).

Here we progress beyond the notion that waste is due to the mere innate and inevitable greed of business persons (fallen sinners like the rest of us) deliberately setting out to cheat us. This progress, beyond quasi-theological disdain of the literary humanist type, is in the interests of being scientific in the service of scientific socialism. The locus of waste is in the needs of the military–industrial complex where big business and big government seek to control the economy. Demand has to grow at a high rate but also be stable in the sense of generating balanced growth. High growth requires the addition of social costs of reproduction such as advertising to maintain consumer and worker enthusiasm which might, shorn of economic parlance, be construed as greed.

As quoted from Arrow (1986) in Chapter 1, we are inclined to emphasize the large element of unsubstantiated ritual in the way individuals are treated in the rational choice models of economics. That is, a leap of faith is made beyond mere application of principles to data. More specifically, it seems that conventional economists could never accept the notion that a large proportion of GDP in an advanced economy could be waste. The belief is that, the proliferation of prisoner's dilemma models notwithstanding, we could never tolerate a huge volume of X-inefficiency. Either we are rational enough to engineer change, up front, or intuitively our survival instincts push us on to a path of learning behaviour in which codes and institutions adapt. This is well illustrated in a short paper by McCloskey and Klamer (1995) which adopts the

ploy of pseudo-radical conservatism of hitting us straight off with a frightening fact and then explaining it away in a reassuring manner. They kick off with
the alarming title 'One Quarter of GDP is Persuasion' and seem quite willing
to believe that it is fairly socially efficient persuasion. This is instanced in their
remark that 'Persuasion is a rank-order tournament, similar to queuing (though
in most cases not a waste like queuing)' (ibid., p. 193). Along the way they
give us the handy euphemism of 'sweet talk' for the effort involved in encouraging someone to part with their funds in a world of imperfect information.
The implication is that we, as principals, are happy to employ persuaders as
agents to assist us in making choices. So back we go into the rational choice
ritual.

Apart from military expenditure and advertising the other main waste accusations are from vegetarians and environmentalists. Vegetarians might fairly
be said to regard taking animals' lives as a sin per se, but it has little history of
being so regarded as most religions have allowed meat eating and have even
encouraged sometimes gory blood sacrifices. Neither the ten commandments
nor the seven deadly sins had the slightest hint of support for animals. Thus,
critiquing meat eating as waste is a rhetorical strategy one would expect from
vegetarians as speaking the language of market economics is now the best way
to be heard. The logic then of the waste argument is that it would be more efficient to use the materials which animals are being forced to process as human
food. On its own this argument falls immediately as an economic proposition
as the willingness of individuals to purchase the animal products outputted
rather than their inputs must signify that sufficient value is being added to
support the meat-oriented economy.

To sum up, economics tends to subsume the word waste within discussions
of efficiency. Efficiency has tended to be benchmarked with respect to markets
at the broad grain level and perfect competition at the fine grain. Markets are
seen as less wasteful than other allocative mechanisms. Granted there is now
a large economic literature on how internal markets and other 'non-market'
devices might work efficiently, but these are premised on the notion of them
being situated within a global complex which runs on open market lines with
a market mentality firmly in place. This will be efficient for consumers with
well-defined and rationally controlled sovereign preferences. Terms of criticism of inefficiencies take the place of damning the source perpetrators as
sinners. Terms like managerial slack, bureaucratic incompetency and even
market failure are used. Incompetent managers are seen as a sign of market
failure as the efficient market will lead to their replacement or the absorption
of the company into a more efficient company. In a nutshell, the tale remains
the same, efficient markets guarantee elimination of waste and so sin is neither
here nor there; what matters is the achievement of perfect markets or at least
perfect solutions subject to the inevitable fetters of an imperfect world.

CONCLUSION

In this chapter we have reviewed four of the sins common in the original lists of deadly sins. Inadvertently or otherwise modern economic theory has served to legitimate or secularize these via the provision of a less charged vocabulary and a mode of reasoning which always reflects back to the individual's autonomous needs. Mainstream economics would not deny that these four sins cause problems for society, but ultimately the problems they cause would be addressed in terms of negative externalities. The solution to negative externalities is some policy change which will alter the incentives for individuals to engage in the sins. Not that we really any longer can call them sins, as the economic world sees them as both bad and good depending on the situation and is thus highly relativistic.

5. Envy and jealousy

> Jealous: adj. Unduly concerned about the preservation of that which can be lost only if not worth keeping.
>
> Ambrose Bierce, *Devil's Dictionary* (1911)

INTRODUCTION

I will defer for a short while discussion of the difference between envy and jealousy, as far as their uses in economic contexts go. First, I review the discussion of these in the Bible and some key texts from later rationalist thinkers. Envy and jealousy are part of the monastic 'seven deadly sins' discussed earlier. They have been condemned for much longer: in the King James' Bible we are told in Ecclesiastes 30:24 that 'Envy and wrath shorten the life', thereby depriving us of the atmosphere benefits attributed to religion which we discussed in Chapter 2. In the Bible, jealousy is cited in reference to the wrath of God, which may lead to vengeance if believers lapse into idolatry and false faiths in general. Jealousy elsewhere in the Bible is interpersonal, generally between brothers or between sisters, but is not particularly based on wealth or position. In the *Concise Oxford Dictionary* jealousy is unhelpfully defined as 'envy', although it is also given as 'resentment' and there is some discussion that jealousy is more used for situations involving sexual desire than envy is.

Envy has a slightly different biblical grid of reference than jealousy. It is brought forth as a factor in the misfortunes of Jesus and the prophets. Indeed, one could interpret the life of Jesus, in purely secular terms, as a broadly mythical morality tale showing how the power of envy (or jealousy) deprives the world of the full benefits of special individuals (healers, magicians). The Bible is also clear on the consequences of envy in terms of leading to fighting, to contest envied resources, at either the interpersonal or national level. The sinfulness of envy is clearly stated by the claim, in James, that it is a product of the devil, who is also blamed for the lies we encounter in the next chapter. Yet we have the contradictory proposition (at least so long as we think achievement is good) in Ecclesiastes that 'All achievement springs from envy.' This is a key notion in the economics of this particular sin as it implies that envy is part and parcel of economic growth and cannot therefore be excised, from a rapidly growing economy, like some unfortunate disease that has temporarily blighted otherwise perfectible humanity. This issue is what underlies most of the remaining sections of this chapter.

Envy and jealousy have also attracted the attention of pithy phrase makers. For example, the desirability of the state of being envied, as an achievement marker, is shown in the Greek proverb 'better be envied than be pitied'. The unavoidability of jealousy is recalled in the seventeenth century English proverb 'love is never without jealousy', which is what lies at the heart of the novel components of Robert Frank's 1999 book *Luxury Fever*, in which he allies sociobiology to conventional economics in the pursuit of policies which will optimally control envy and jealousy to the benefit of all.

Eventually, when rationalist thought started to undermine the power of religion, thinkers began to probe the functionality of the deadly sins in more detail and envy was one of those attracting the greatest attention. It was a favourite topic in the 'Fable of the Bees'; Mandeville appended a lengthy remark on it [Remark N, Harth (1970, pp. 158–69)]. He claims that envy is a universal passion which is found in all people but attracts disapproval due to the hypocrisy of our being unwilling to admit to the extent of self-love in all our actions. He says we are driven to anger by the pain of wanting what other people have (this is much closer to the definition I give later of jealousy). The universality of envy is depicted with reference to its being the factor essential to horse races (horses run faster because they are envious of each other), a characteristic of beautiful women (who are always envious of other beautiful women), and men of letters who respond to their envy of others' writing by nitpicking criticism of minor faults in their works. He then gives a definition of malice which is really just *schadenfreude* (viz. envy in the mirror of others' misfortune). His definition of jealousy is: 'Love, Hope, Fear and a great deal of Envy'. Hope is what we might more precisely call 'wishful thinking', that is imagining ourselves with the other person's allocation. Love and fear are elements in the functionality of envy, that is the sociobiological explanation, which we discuss below, of envy being related to the need of resources for survival.

Even before Mandeville's polemical poem, Francis Bacon (1625) argued for the benefits of envy. He distinguishes private envy which is purely 'one on one' as an evil (related he thinks to the 'evil eye' of witchcraft) from public envy which may serve as a good through 'ostracism, that eclipseth men when they grow too great' (p. 27). He further claims that private envy, like love, is continual rather than intermittent and thus most dangerous. It is not clear why a man growing very great is harmful. On a purely religious note it could be seen as sinful pride which is here regulated by the lesser evil of the jealousy of others reducing its volume. On an economic level, the hubris of the very powerful might be seen as a source of X-inefficient waste as they lapse back into a hubristic 'magical' attribution of high productivity to their own presence as an input. Thus the downsizing effect of group envy on leadership ego is a case of beneficial chagrin.

In his *Theory of Moral Sentiments*, Smith (1759, p. 395) adds to the normal condemnation of envy the notion that it has a functional use in preventing the poorly motivated individual from lapsing into self-pitying sloth. He says:

> Even that principle, in the excess and improper direction of which consists the odious and detestable passion of envy, may be defective. Envy is that passion which views with malignant dislike the superiority of those who are really entitled to all the superiority they possess. The man, however, who in matters of consequence, tamely suffers other people, who are entitled no such superiority, to rise above him or get before him, is justly condemned as mean-spirited.

As we moved towards 'scientific economics' inspired by Smith's better-known work, *The Wealth of Nations*, the focus of analysis was on economic growth. Growth was seen as arising largely from liberating markets from excess government intervention in order to improve the efficiency of factor utilization. When attention shifted to consumer choice at the end of the 1890s, economists strove for a unified approach in which all motives could be reduced to the abstract concept of utility with there being no need to inquire into any of the emotions or their consequences. The distribution of income was a by-product of consumer choice theory to the extent that they were lumped together as the 'theory of value and distribution'. One searches in vain for any discussion of envy or jealousy in the major or minor works of mainstream economics in the period from 1890 until the post-World War II era. Mostly indirectly, there have been scattered contributions since then, particularly in recent years. Some of these were considered in Chapter 2 and others are addressed in the remainder of this chapter.

CONTEMPORARY ECONOMICS AND ENVY

Whilst there certainly is some writing in economics relating to envy, a lot of the time it is below the surface of discussions about 'justice' and 'fairness' in welfare economics and public finance. In such work, just or fair outcomes are usually derived from an appeal to the judgements of idealized persons who are not contaminated by feelings of envy or jealousy, or indeed surges of passion in general. Envy is also invoked in some of the experimental economics liter-ature on 'ultimatum games' where being envied is absorbed, in the decisions of the offer makers, as a cost leading them to settle for 'fairer' distributions than might be predicted [see critical discussion in Elster (1998)].

Given the fringe status of the emotions in modern economics, some of what follows is inevitably my interpretation of what an archetypal mainstream economist would say, if put on the spot, rather than being derived directly from particular sources. Within the literature of economics, envy and jealousy might seem to have a paradoxical status as there are three distinct strands which are not transparently congruent. Firstly, there is the full-blown rational choice enlightenment perspective that such negative utility losses are pointless, as once one understands why the envied individual has their allocation, one will be better off if such feelings are discarded. Next, there is the use of emulative comparisons as motors for entrepreneurship, artistic achievement and so on which takes us from the 'neutral' position just described to one where envy may be a useful, as well as inevitable, feature of the capitalist economy. Finally, we encounter the notion that envy and jealousy are destructive to economic efficiency and individual well-being and thus it might be worthwhile to reinstate them as prominent sins. In fairness, this last position is a fairly minority one which has to be winkled out of the text of those inclined to a more 'social economics' such as the late Fred Hirsch.

Therapists prefer the word jealousy to envy, as it is deemed to be connotative of a problem state which in the extreme, of morbid jealousy, becomes an obsession. They also distinguish between healthy and unhealthy jealousy largely on the basis of the rationality of the individual in terms of the level of foundation there is for their beliefs [Dryden (1998)]. Economists nowadays seem to prefer the word envy to jealousy. This may reflect their tendency to avoid the 'passions' if one accepts the distinction I am about to make, which is that envy and jealousy differ in a similar way to greed and lust. That is, the difference between envy and jealousy is one of degree rather than one of kind. In economic terms we might create the distinction in terms of envy being a preference for the allocation held by someone else, and jealousy as a stronger version in which an additional externality occurs in the form of a lustful craving to possess the allocation held by someone else.

It should, of course, be borne in mind that envy of an allocation may take account of the effort and risk which the envied agent experiences, thereby ruling out the 'unreasonable' property of the accounts of Bacon and Smith in the last section. These now, more properly, belong in the category of jealousy where craving over-rides reason. It should be apparent that envy is a function of the knowledge possessed by the envier. Indeed, it depends not just on basic facts but also on what kind of personal mental construct they use to attribute causes to the observed outcomes of allocation mechanisms. Take the case of risk and uncertainty for example. It is inevitable that X may randomly be receiving above the norm for their inputs whilst Y may be receiving less. Is Y then warranted, given as we discuss below that they may have no choice in being open to such feelings, in processing their initial cues of the situation into a state of envy? Clearly regular deviations either way are more likely to be perceived enviously as they grow in magnitude, although it is possible that there are diminishing returns to being envious which create a plateau region where an individual goes beyond accruing further envy from others. This may be deduced from informational limits of the mind (i.e. the life of the envied may pass so far from one's own experience that the imagination hits a ceiling in terms of how much pain it can add to the envy) or to the costs of being envious. Envy of others, whilst it may be visceral in origin, can escalate into disapproval of the envied either in the form of critiquing their motives as greed, etc. or attempting to impose sanctions on them which curb their further acquisition of envied items. As Elster (1998) says:

> Expressing disapproval is always costly, whatever the target behavior. At the very least it requires energy and attention that might have been used for other purposes. One may alienate or provoke the target individual, at some cost or risk to oneself.

So, the mental model of the individual is a factor in envy and we come to the conclusion that knowledge of economics might be claimed to alter unreasonable jealousy into more tolerable envy as it provides a progression on 'lay' attribution of causes. Shortly, we will encounter 'lay' writers on economics making this very claim. There is no more obvious source of jealousy than craving someone else's take home pay. Maybe there is just cause for such feelings. Table 5.1 is a list of the most recent salaries of Hollywood's biggest box office draws in the year 2000.

Table 5.1   Last picture salary of the 12 most bankable movie stars in 2000

1	Mel Gibson	$25 m
2	Jim Carrey	$20 m
3	Tom Cruise	$20 m
4	Tom Hanks	$20 m
5	Bruce Willis	$20 m
6	Julia Roberts	$20 m
7	Eddie Murphy	$20 m
8	Robert DeNiro	$15 m
9	Harrison Ford	$20 m
10	Nicolas Cage	$20 m
11	Martin Lawrence	$12 m
12	Denzel Washington	$12 m

Notes: Rankings are made on the basis of the box office during the year from all of the stars' films. The salary shown is from their last film.

Source: http://www.boxofficemojo.com

This is vastly in excess, just for one film, of what workers, on average salaries, would earn in an entire lifetime. Economics provides a language which seems to say that envious wage comparisons are perhaps not odious but pointless. Textbooks in economics do not attempt to tell us that huge income disparities are just or fair as that is not the job of positive economics. Nor do microeconomics textbooks go out of their way to endorse the pursuit of high income per se as, after all, the utility-maximizing individual may trade off money income for other 'quality of life' aspects. Nevertheless, these textbooks, and a large body of work in labour economics, serve to (unwittingly or otherwise) legitimate some disparities in income as explicable by economic factors and not therefore entirely rational objects of jealousy. A standard textbook ploy has been to explain high returns to sports, musical and film superstars as indicative of economic rents accruing to unique characteristics that are not capable of being duplicated by other individuals. In such a scenario, jealousy is merely a pointless self-inflicted loss of utility as there is no feasible means of altering the situation. The simple economic rent story of very high earnings for superstars has been augmented, in recent decades, by additional sophistications originating in the work of Sherwin Rosen (1981). He argued that technological progress, in broadcasting, created a huge audience beyond that capable of live consumption of a cultural event and thus the rents to unique sellers will expand enormously.

In the case of movie stars, economists have been prone to argue that the high salaries are enhanced by returns derived from the use of a star name to reduce the risk of a flop in a high investment cost industry. Granted, the stars do not take the financial risks themselves or even accept a basic salary plus returns in the event of success. This could be attributed to efficiency in principal–agent contracts but it could regress back to the scarcity argument that only so many stars can exist at one time as stardom is a positional good, a concept generally beyond the pale of mainstream neo-classical economics, but which we discuss later in this chapter.

Star envy and jealousy do not seem to conspicuously plague the modern individual and may in fact be replaced by fantasizing about the stars' lives or indeed wishful thinking about emulation or outright attempts to enter this particular lottery. This may be due to the market, and its metaphors, becoming part of the mindset of everyday people who have never studied formal economics. Occasional outbreaks of envy/jealousy do occur. A good example of this is the case of salaries in the sporting labour market. Writing in the *Detroit News*, 15 December, 2000 under a heading of 'Fans who bash athletes' salaries don't understand basic economics', Rob Parker says, 'In case you are forgetting, this is a free market society. Salaries, both big and small, are based solely on what the market can bear.' He goes on to claim that fans who critique their star players' high earnings as ludicrous are being hypocritical and jealous as they would, in the same circumstances, be willing to accept these salaries themselves.

The mere fact that you would not refuse something if it were offered to you is hardly a sound basis for branding envy or jealousy as irrational or unwarranted. One surely needs to go on to defend the outcomes and/or the process that generated them as fair. Being explicable as a market process does not, in itself, make something fair but it helps grease the wheels of any subsequent argument about irrational passion being best dissipated. There is a certain ineluctable logic to the economic way of thinking. Just as the analyst of a great poet feels compelled to find profound meaning in every line, however banal, the economist feels there must be an explanation for all apparent discrepancies in market outcomes. Thus in the field of income there is a constant search for factors which account for differentials. In the beginning it was relative demand, skill, then successively trade unions, human capital investment, race and gender discrimination, religion per se, religious upbringing and now we have marital status and consumption habits like smoking and drinking [see Cameron & Ward (2000)] brought in to account for differentials. The net may have widened but the story always comes back to productivity in all these explanations, with the exception of some elements of the discrimination models.

Hammermesh & Biddle (1994) try to establish a new factor to economists albeit one we have long suspected, that physical appearance may be an influence in some people's larger salaries. They use a number of surveys to assess the statistical significance of height, weight and assessed attractiveness on earnings. As they admit, the results are not overwhelmingly strong: in particular, the 'above average' looks for females (the case we would most expect to count) dummy has fairly low 't' ratios in a number of their results. Further exploration of their data leads them to conclude that most of the differentials for 'looks' come from employers (and/or employees) discriminating in favour of the more attractive worker as a means of enhancing their own consumption benefits via interacting with and viewing the worker. Hammermesh & Biddle do not exactly say outright 'don't be jealous of the luck of looks', but they do go on to treat it as a highly rational choice economics issue by commenting on the incentives the labour market 'provides to expend resources on beauty' (p. 1193). They then slip in a telling use of the concept of 'natural' states when they say: 'The results also lead naturally to further examination of the sources of wage differentials and possible discrimination along various other dimensions, such as mental and physical handicaps' (ibid.).

In general, one would not expect to find explicit 'beauty' discrimination at the point of hire; that is a pool of candidates would not be interviewed and the more attractive one appointed on higher pay for the same work as the rest. One can see that such a mechanism, if pervasive, may give rise to substantial envy/jealousy externalities because of the notion that pay should reflect contributions to productivity not rent-seeking by the hirers. The premium for looks will thus occur largely through a 'behind the scenes' process of sorting people into jobs and generally will depend heavily on the rents available, to those with more product market monopoly power, to indulge the consumption whims of those most heavily involved in the hiring decisions. This segregates the discriminated against from the favoured and thus reduces the scope for reference group envy. Pay differentials will further arise if there are discriminatory elements in internal promotion. Envy arising from such situations may be a highly detrimental externality, especially where the winner of the promotion 'tournament' is now acting in a supervisory capacity to the losers. It follows then that promotion tournaments need to be designed in terms of fairness of process.

In the above discussion, the main material result of envy would be lost productivity through unproductive conflict between workers and also a possible X-inefficiency due to demotivated workers reducing their inputs as opposed to the 'desirable' (from the viewpoint of free market economics) consequence of emulatory rises in inputs such as in pursuit of winning the promotional 'prize' in a labour market tournament.

The problems entailed in envy are magnified in the case of group envy where a comparison is made with someone else's entitlement on the basis of them belonging to a social group which has been culturally delineated, such as a race, class, religion, gender group or elite (freemasons, graduates of particular educational institutions) which may be a source of attribution to any differentials. I am not claiming that individuals who are experiencing such differentials are not entitled to feel that these disparities are unjust. Rather, I am drawing the distinction between 'process envy' and 'outcome envy'. That is, an individual may be the victim of a purely random 25 per cent differential between themselves and a member of their own culturally delineated group and yet not feel envy because wishful thinking ensures that this return to themselves seems capable of being imagined. The out-group differential will be more envy-inducing, potentially tipping into jealousy, if the mental model used attributes a large proportion of the other random and systematic components in the differential to the group membership factor. The ultimate danger with group envy is the potential for group conflict such as wars between countries or civil and political conflicts within countries. One factor limiting this would be an (unrepressed) adherence to the notion of envy as a sin. This would also contain the lesser social strife of crime which is motivated by inter-group envy.

It is very difficult to apportion the envy component in crimes and conflicts. The kinds of measures which could be used in studies of crime are seriously prone to contamination by other influences on criminal activity. In econometric work, carried out for the World Bank, Collier (2000) reports econometric work on 161 countries since 1960 looking at the incidence of civil conflict and finds that income and asset inequality is not a predictor, nor is lack of democratic rights, nor is ethnic and religious diversity. Whilst this may be encouraging news, in certain lights, as it suggests the social and political processes within countries contain the potential for conflict, it is silent on the magnitude of welfare loss from envy or jealousy from inter-group comparisons.

An important tangible economic consequence of envy, on an everyday level, is on consumption behaviour. There may be effects on the distribution of spending across types of commodity, savings rates and in the extreme on the number of people who find themselves with debts that they are unable to repay. The logical way to tie these factors into a rational choice model is via the concept of a 'reference group' who may exist only in the mind of an individual rather than being an organized 'group' in any concrete sense. That is, the reference group do not have to be capable of issuing sanctions for nonconformity as in the Akerlof-type models discussed in Chapter 2.

The individual will, in effect, issue the cost to themselves via the reflected feelings of envy. In a pioneering contribution to mainstream microeconomics, Duesenberry (1949) argued that the acquisition of increasingly high-quality consumption goods has become a social goal which is 'in psychoanalytic terms incorporated into the ego-ideal. When this occurs a certain degree of success in reaching the goal becomes essential to the maintenance of self-esteem. The maintenance of self-esteem is a basic drive in every individual' (p. 28) [cp. Maital (1988)]. The message to be drawn from this is that a failure to obtain high incomes and/or corresponding high-status possessions will generate feelings of inadequacy in 'failed' individuals. For such a failed person, the utility loss will be exacerbated by increases in the visibility of successful individuals. It will thus be difficult psychologically for an individual to sustain a low-income equilibrium even if it is feasible in resource terms. If rising individual aspirations are to result in rapid economic growth they must induce extra efforts at labour and entrepreneurship to fund consumption. High aspirations could have the socially unintended by-product of diverting individuals into other activities of a predatory nature (crime), or excessive borrowing. Aspiration levels are set by social comparison [Vernon (1969)], an idea which can be extended to consumer behaviour [Earl (1983, pp. 176–7), Frank (1989)]; they are raised if one's reference group appears to be doing better, especially if they are perceived as being of lower status. In contemporary society an important pressure on aspirations is the social competition of children over status goods such as 'trainers' (running shoes), designer clothing and videogames. A case study by Lea, Walker and Webley (1992) finds that a group of delinquent Welsh Water Board customers see spending on such items, especially at Christmas, as a major cause of their payment failure.

Where do the high aspiration social goals come from? There are long-standing problems in conceptualizing the goals of a system as distinct from the goals of those who make it up. Walter Weiskopff wrote, in 1965, that 'A Gross National Product growing, if possible, at an increasing rate, has become a dogma of economic reasoning and an object of economic worship. There is an obsessive preoccupation with the growth and rate of growth of the GNP which one could call GNP fetishism' [Daly (1973, p. 241)]. Is GNP fetishism a collectively expressed outgrowth of individual cravings or is it a 'top-down' phenomenon? In the latter case individual impulses/responses are a product of the economic system rather than the architects of its design. One way of deriving systemic goals is to locate an organized group which stands to gain from growth. Political parties are the obvious candidates. In an economically static society, policies to improve the lot of any group in society require redistribution. In a growing economy the hope is that public spending or redistribution can take place against a backdrop of everyone becoming better off. The best way to guarantee growth is to engender growth-oriented behaviour in all individuals. A free market system does not allow pre-selection of the best potential agents of growth. The best hope for a high rate of aggregate growth is thus to cast the net of sustained effort as widely as possible. With such a 'scattergun' technique, many will fall by the wayside but this can be perfectly efficient from the aggregate viewpoint. Consider for example the recent governmental zest for small business growth combined with a total lack of concern for the extremely high failure rate and the devastating consequences of it.

Aspirations could drive a credit explosion. It is hard to check whether one's reference group's growing consumption level is based on current income or on borrowing. Duesenberry (1949, p. 50) presents interesting evidence that blacks in urban areas had much higher savings rates than whites, which he attributes to 'the making of invidious comparisons between consumption standards'. Indebtedness is private, in most cases, as regards one's reference group, whereas the goods purchased are often objects of ostentatious display. Individuals cannot collect objective information about reference group achievements; to a large extent they rely on media images. Developments in technology mean that one's reference group may be someone who you have never met, even a fictitious character in a soap opera. O'Guinn & Shrum (1990) find systematic over-estimation of other people's levels of high-status consumer goods, which rises with the amount of television watched. There are also frequent findings in the social psychological literature [Weinstein (1980)] of unrealistic optimism, whereby people view themselves as more likely to experience favourable events than the population average. This suggests a widespread likelihood of failure to achieve one's set aspiration level, which promotes dissatisfaction. The more insecure a person is the more unrealistic their aspiration levels are.

It could be argued that some societies such as certain less developed nations, Australia, Canada and New Zealand, have reached a level where national aspiration levels lead to spiralling comparisons between states; keeping up with the Schmidts as well as the Joneses. Individuals may have the relative GDP ranking of their own country relative to other nations as arguments in their utility functions. Thus governments may be elected with an implicit remit to copy the lifestyle of reference groups with whom they cannot compete in income. It is hard to see how this could be justified in Durkheimian terms as socially useful, unless we invoked a Darwinian argument that a debt hangover promotes fiscal temperance that equips the nation for a higher future ranking in world GDP tables. Failing this we would appear to have a classic contradiction of capitalism in that a factor in growth (emulatory behaviour) becomes a factor in retardation.

Economists concerned with issues of fairness and/or possible detrimental effects of rapid economic growth look for reference group effects in quantitative studies of happiness such as those surveyed in Easterlin (1995). Waiving, for a moment, the highly problematic nature of measuring happiness at all in the first place, we may note a number of consistent patterns in these studies:

i.   Within a country, happiness is positively associated with one's position in the relative distribution of income.
ii.   Over time there is not much relationship between average levels of satisfaction in a country and income growth.
iii.   Across space, there is not much evidence that higher-income countries have greater levels of happiness. Indeed, one finds figures showing that the three happiest countries are (flood-adjusted) Bangladesh, Azerbaijan and Nigeria [see Brittan (2000)].

One way of reconciling all the puzzling contradictions in this is to argue that envy is a big factor in happiness, as the relative position in the income distribution seems to be so crucial compared with the impact of the absolute level of income. Envy may be showing up in a number of ways. Those at lower ranking points in the income distribution may be unhappy even with growing incomes across the board due to an inability to catch their reference groups who are, in a sense, further away as technology-inspired growth also involves more conspicuous consumption. Those at higher points of the distribution may be happier than expected from income growth alone due to a positive external benefit of being envied. In addition, there may be an all-round atmosphere effect of envy and jealousy being both causes and consequences of higher growth in the form of a 'materialist' cultural attitude.

Given that Bertrand Russell spent thousands of words without being able to adequately define happiness, and hordes of academic philosophers have gamely and vainly followed, one is entitled to be suspicious of the validity of these studies based on a questionnaire demanding to know if one is 'very happy', 'fairly happy' or 'not happy'. In statistics however, the proof of the pudding is in the eating and economists are, in the use of such measures, simply hoping for a good proxy for the utility function and/or the capacity to experience levels of lifetime utility. So, the proxy might be validated by establishing its correlation with something else that we might think is convincingly related to measures of well-being. Frank (1985, ch. 2) surveys a number of medical studies which show that people who report unhappiness are more likely to have problems with headaches, accelerated heartbeat, digestive disorders and psychosomatic ailments. Those who report as 'very happy' are more likely to show well on measures of social adjustment and less likely to report attempted suicide. Whilst this is interesting, one must at least pause to point out that reverse causation may be at work here, i.e. those who are unhappy may be so because of exogenous factors causing these conditions. Whatever, we are back to the health factors discussed in connection with religion in Chapter 3. Someone inclined to dissent from contemporary growthmania might see a case from this evidence that envy ought to be reduced by a curb on GDP fixation.

Specific operation of the role of reference groups in stimulating activity has been shown in a number of different sources. For example, it is documented that in the early days of selling air-conditioning in the USA, salesmen were able to induce purchases of systems by telling households that other households in the same street were buying. This worked without the household bothering to check the assertion. More recent econometric evidence, on the impact of proximate referents, is provided in an ingenious micro study by Neumark & Postlewaite (1998) of sisters. Their specific focus is on the decision to work outside the home. In a strictly orthodox microeconomic model, a woman should make this decision purely on the basis of her own family variables, so entering measures which relate to the circumstances in her sister's household should lead to 't' ratios small enough to be judged statistically insignificant. The variable they use to capture interpersonal comparisons is whether the sister's husband earns more than that of the subject. This is statistically significant, with the best estimate of the mean expected impact being a 16 to 25 per cent increase in the likelihood of working outside the home.

The temptation to attribute this differential to envy is hard to resist.

ORIGINS OF ENVY AND JEALOUSY

So reference groups matter to consumption and labour supply. But where do the stimuli come from and why are they translated into actions rather than being merely stillborn as 'cheap talk' grumbling or passive wishful thinking?

Envy and jealousy are complex emotions compared with greed and lust, although there will be circumstances when they are viscerally evoked. We should also note that there are possible gradations within these emotions. One possible schema is to divide envy and jealousy into pure outcome externalities (i.e. where we say directly 'I envy that person for having a bigger car than me') and the 'sour grape' externalities discussed in Elster (1982), where we say 'I don't want what they have and I wouldn't want it even if I could get it'. The term sour grapes is derived from Aesop's fable 'The Fox and the Grapes' in which the fox, after several unsuccessful attempts to jump up and grasp the grapes he strongly desires, walks off saying they were probably sour anyway.

Both pure envy and sour grapes must be distinguished from overt complaints of injustice at the process leading to some reference group individual's allocations, which may be based on resentment rather than a direct craving to have the entitlements. Going back to the sour grapes case, Elster paints a slightly optimistic picture to explain these apparently irrational feelings as reducers of cognitive dissonance. That is, the 'true' preferences of the enviers may be that they do secretly wish to have the items displayed by the envied but the pain costs of the envy have led them into adapting their preferences (what a therapist would call denial) more in line with what they can feasibly obtain. There is a more brutal explanation that Elster does not give much space to. Simply that the sour grape gripers may genuinely not want the high-profile items displayed by the envied but still experience resentment due to the ostentatious display of Veblen (conspicuous consumption) goods being a reminder of the wealth and power that lie beyond their grasp. This particular issue is taken up further below. It is of course possible that the preferences of the enviers might change if they became wealthy and they would then want the items they currently genuinely disavow, albeit this kind of scenario is ruled out in Paretian welfare economics due to the theoretical and political problems it causes.

The presence of these emotions might be taken as indicative that they are in some way conducive to individual survival otherwise they would have been bred out of the species. Thus we move into the world of sociobiology (or evolutionary psychology which is much the same thing) which economist Robert Frank brings into his 1999 book *Luxury Fever* to motivate proposals for envy-reducing progressive income taxation.

Envy/jealousy has its functional roots in competition for survival. In a primitive society, jealousy may be beneficial in terms of success in the market for sexual partners. Someone who is slow to develop a jealous response may fail to be cued in to allocating sufficient resources to vigilance and/or supporting their partner and offspring. Further, where resources are extremely scarce it is logical to be jealous of any competitor for the same resources as they provide a direct threat to survival. Jealousy would then be expected to be functionally linked to survival-related assets, viz. those which suggest a greater command over future resources than that available to the individual. So it is easy to see that in a broad sense jealousy can be useful to the individual and will be strongly linked to command over resources and the possession of facets or items that may lead to such command. This element of usefulness may be what lies behind the comments of Bacon and Smith quoted in the Introduction. In the evolutionary context of adaptive 'fitness' it is also highly rational that people who are strongly in love should be highly jealous, as their love will tend to be associated with various types of investment of emotional energy and resources which may be 'locked in' to the object of love and thus not easily transferred elsewhere. Outside of sexual contexts, the same argument will apply in any case where strong 'commitment' has been made, e.g. the person who feels they have given themselves loyally to a workplace will experience additional envy, over the pure resource-based one, when an outsider is appointed under more favourable terms *ceteris paribus*. The costs to the loser here may be further accelerated by regret due to their commitment having been induced by the signalling games intrinsic to the organizational culture.

Given that survival instincts are seemingly a vital factor in the envious passions, we would anticipate that childhood will be an important factor in determining how they will be managed. This is attested by biologists, psychologists and social historians of childhood. The primary source of jealousy is any threat to the attachment bond to the mother and father [Vernon (1969)] which may give rise to various complexes if it is not allowed to develop appropriately. Gathorne-Hardy (1993, p. 238) reports that in the heyday of the English nanny, many mothers were jealous of nannies usurping them in the child's affections. All of this serves merely to further illustrate that jealousy is a reflex arising from motives to seek security. If it is deeply ingrained in the sexual motives of 'selfish' gene propagation then as with lust one suspects that price-incentives-style regulation may be weak as a means of curbing it. This particularly applies to the progressive taxation (or income)-based measures usually advocated by liberal reforming economists with a concern for fairness.

As we discussed in the case of lust, reduction of the emotion (or at least its expressed volume) faces the dilemma of the dangers of utility loss through repression and the opposing factor that the capitalist system requires them as drivers to high achievement. This is borne out in the much critiqued work of McClelland (1961) [see e.g. Peacock (1975)] which is the only serious attempt to link national macroeconomic achievement to the individual's need to achieve, which he terms the 'n Ach' factor. Using a cross-national sample he applied his story–analysis whereby individuals are given a set of cards depicting a work situation and asked to compose fantasy stories suggested by

them. The resulting fantasies are used to produce scales which are correlated
with national growth rates. McClelland found a statistically significant positive correlation between the two indicators. He argued that the underlying
causes of n Ach are Oedipal, and thus in essence seems to be saying that jealousy is good for entrepreneurship and economic growth. The prerequisite for
high growth is the absence of fathers after age eight or so, or non-dominant
fathers and warm rewarding mothers who promote excellence and self-
reliance.

Well, one might say 'okay, maybe a few highly repressed driven entrepreneurs are needed to spark high-level economic growth but isn't it possible that
in an economically and socially stable advanced capitalist economy jealousy
might be expected to recede as it would be detrimental for a number of
reasons?' For one thing, envy and jealousy can be dangerous as they may lead
to irreversibly costly wrong decisions, i.e. an individual prompted by the
visceral adrenalin rush of jealousy might inflict serious damage on someone
and end up with a severe punishment, in the extreme case execution either at
the hands of the state or from revenge reciprocation. Full rationality requires
that reflective individuals respond to the risk of punishment and the best way
to do this is by curbing the emotions themselves. Whether an envious response
will be processed into a conscious experience of the emotion associated with
the stimuli will depend on 'considerable processing by the conscious mind and
an elaborate exchange of information and the conscious cortical areas of the
brain and the limbic system beneath' [Carter (1998, p. 83)].

Thus we might depart from the early seventeenth century ruminations of
Bacon that envy and jealousy (like love) are continual emotions into the
contemporary position of Elster (1998, p. 70) that they are more in the nature
of temporary preference sets that can be controlled.[1] If an emotion were 'basic',
i.e. purely visceral, then no amount of preaching could ever make a difference
as the individual would not be able to cognitively process a break on their
impetuousness. The only effect of the sin label on jealousy-motivated action, at
the level of the perpetrator, would be to create a demand for repentance which,
as indicated through Chapter 3, is useful for religious organizations in terms of
sustaining their existence. At the social level there may be a demand for punishment as group agency revenge, but from a rationalist perspective there will be
little point in punishment as we discuss further in Chapter 10.

Whether they be visceral or complex, emotions, if admitted into economics, seem to stake a claim to be considered as goods in themselves or bads in
themselves depending on the situation. Let us stick to the cases where envy
and jealousy may be unambiguously a good for certain individuals. Given that
individuals may be led into unwise choices through the power of emotion it
follows that arousing envy/jealousy in a rival (as with lies and deceit in the
next chapter) may be an optimal strategy for a firm in product markets, or a

worker involved in a promotional tournament. The unwise choice can take two forms: one a concrete decision that would not have been taken with the power of reflective hindsight, such as launching a new product too early, and the other the disclosure of information such as endorsing rumours of a discovery or innovation having been made. Here the envy/jealousy, of a rival, is an instrumental good to the invoking (or if you like, provoking) agent from the discounted flow of utility that arises from its consequence regardless of any direct return on a 'malicious emotion' from enjoying the creation of envy in others. The term 'malicious emotion' is used in a game theory text [Rasmussen (2001, pp. 101–3)] in the context of law suits carried out to inflict damages on others, although the context turns out not to be pure (i.e. without origin) malice but revenge or 'righteous indignation' as Rasmussen puts it.

In advanced secularized economies, jealousy and envy are often clearly derivative of greed as a motor of economic growth. Yet, there are two opposing factors that serve to lead to elements of repression and denial of the source of such emotions. Often the repression and denial will lead to these emotions being masqueraded as righteous indignation and cries for justice and fairness. One is the atavistic hangover of earlier, more religious, times that envy and jealousy are frowned on and so we have a tendency to deny feelings which have had the sin label hung on them. The other is the disembodied nature of social science reflective rationality which sees people as unimpulsive reasoners who can attain some sort of perfection as a utility-maximizing engine.

The apogee of this kind of thinking is the neo-classical economic analysis of institutions and customs as mechanisms of group rationality, particularly as portrayed in the works of Becker. Economists, with more of an eye to the independent influence of culture, might make the criticism that such institutions, in a market economy, will have a hard time solving the problem of 'positional goods', to which we now turn.

POSITIONAL GOODS

The term 'positional goods' originates with Hirsch (1976) and, if accepted, moves envy and jealousy up the agenda of economics. As with X-inefficiency, but not to quite such an extent, the original idea has been absorbed and redefined in such a way that its intended impact has been muted. Some treatments of the positional good seem to blur into the ideas which were previously defined in Leibenstein's (1950) version of the 'Veblen good'. Hirsch introduced the idea as one of 'positional consumption' and distinguished between the 'material economy', where democracy operates (through consumer sovereignty) and there can be a continual rise in output without a quality decline to the consumers, and the 'positional economy', in which the products are inherently very scarce and hence subject to congestion and sharp price rises through competition. The core of the idea is that access to the good depends on one's position in some ranking or other, due to an outright limitation on the supply of the 'good', which means that not all can have it. Take the case of desirable residential location: even if we can increase all people's command of material goods and services by productivity gains we cannot readily increase the supply of physically attractive locations. Thus competition for these takes place on the basis of wealth as they are sold to the highest bidder. Their prices will rise sharply but one might be tempted to say: 'so what, this is merely another case of rents on scarce factors as per the movie stars and the supposed case of beauty in the labour market'. Hirsch attempts to add a 'social' dimension to this as he explicitly acknowledges the role of emulation, envy it.

So, the rise in measured wealth may lead to a loss in welfare from the physically limited positional goods as envy-motivated competition drives the prices up still further, thereby inflicting a negative externality of resentment on those denied the product due to the heightened gap between its price and the price of the corresponding good which they can afford (e.g. a mansion surrounded by a wondrous lake compared with a normal semi-detached house). Hirsch sees this as the less important sort of positional externality. For what it's worth, the evidence in the last section suggests that people's reference groups are formed proximately (in terms of wealth and status) rather than distantly, thus supporting a belief that this type of envy does not bring big losses. The more important category, of positional good, says Hirsch, is the 'socially created' one where severe scarcity of positional consumption items is enforced by such things as the dictates of fashion and control mechanisms regulated by various institutions. In such cases, the scarcity itself forms part of the utility gain to the holder as they derive benefits from knowing that other people are envious. In terms of a consumption good, per se, an example of this is the possession of sophisticated or refined items such as vintage wines, high art painting and sculpture, and so on. There are two factors here: one is a feeling of having superior tastes and the second is a comparison of one's own basket of goods with someone in one's reference group who lacks the positional item.

This might tempt indifference, from an analytical point of view, as it is just a revisitation of the snob good model, [Leibenstein (1950)] which we discussed in Chapter 2, which generally leads to a fairly conventional market demand curve. Perhaps the positional goods analysis is more telling when we shift to the positional analysis of (literal) positions, that is titles and status awards. There can only be one Oscar winner for best actress, only one Olympic gold medal sprinter and, more prosaically, only one salesman of the month. Wealth may expand but the number of positions cannot expand, at parity, as by definition the value of positions would be lost if they were widely distributed. Now the three examples just given can, arguably, be related to productivity in the sense that the winner is judged to be the most productive in terms of the trait being assessed. All other things being equal, that might be judged to be a 'fair' competitive process, albeit a non-market one. They are examples of tournaments and there is by now a sizeable literature on rank order tournaments in the labour market which focuses on the efficiency of the process from the viewpoint of the firm. Envy/jealousy can clearly be a beneficial factor to the firm if it leads to an all-round increase in productivity.

Alternative means of allocating positional goods are: auctions such as scarce works of art or legal titles (such as 'Baron') if they were to be thrown open to tender; queuing where the individual pays in waiting time and the opportunity costs of foregone opportunities; screening where the individual is awarded the position on the basis of a credential that they then have an incentive to invest in for position-seeking purposes.

Hirsch concludes that all of these lead to waste (X-inefficiency if you like) where the race for positions is a zero-sum game or a negative-sum game. Thus individually rational behaviour (or at least in the sense of being consistent in its own terms) may lead to unintended socially irrational consequences. One consequence is mismanaged envy and jealousy, which lower the 'true' value of the national output. This is the thorn in the side of well-intentioned liberal reformers such as Oswald (1983) and Frank (1999) [see Brittan (2000)]. The ultimate message of Hirsch's dualism between the material economy and the positional economy is that growthmania induces a high level of desire for material goods which is bound to be unsatisfied in the positional economy. The envy and jealousy that have been exacerbated by the materialism of the material economy are accelerated by the natural and contrived limitations of positional goods.

CONCLUSION

It is clear that envy and jealousy are important in economic affairs. They may lie behind many of the concrete behaviours we deal with in Part III. The lies and deceits considered in the next chapter will, in some circumstances, spring from envy and jealousy, although they will be considered for the most part in terms of their instrumental uses and the problems they raise for rational choice models.

ENDNOTE

1. He does go on to consider love and revenge, in the group context, as more durable. The discussion on love peters out but, as we have implied, if love is highly durable then the associated envy and jealousy would be of similar quality.

6. Lies and deceit

NAMES AND DEFINITIONS

It is probably fair to say that, in most religions, lying is the most frowned upon of the seven deadly sins. Most likely, it is so heavily frowned upon due to a 'contagion' argument that once one starts to lie about anything at all, success in so doing will lead to a slide in morality culminating in turning one's back on the faith and its deity. This is why the tale of the betrayal of Jesus Christ by Judas Iscariot is so central to biblical teachings, to the extent that the name of the betrayer has entered the language as a generic name for all betrayers. Lying and deceit are frequently automatic instrumentalities of the other sins. Those gripped by lust, greed and envy will often be driven into deceit by the desire to vent these emotions.

In 1759, Smith put the case of the accused as follows: 'To tell a man that he lies is of all affronts the most mortal' (p. 530). In the secular world of drama, and other art forms, the lie performed in assistance of other moral shortcomings is brought in for much more condemnation than the largely inconsequential lie. Often, scenarios are presented as if an honest greedy or adulterous person (for example) was somehow less culpable. However, it would in many cases be extremely difficult to satisfy the cravings of such sins of passion in the first place without resort to lying. In part, this is due to the institutional set-up of society: for example, if serial monogamy were not a central totemic value then there would be much less need to lie when engaged in adultery or multiple dating.

No other area of sin has quite so many euphemisms or name variants. Here is a list of phrases used by economists, and others writing on economic subjects, at various times instead of the more blatant 'lies', 'deception' and 'cheating'.

adverse selection (pre-contractual opportunism)
bluffing
cheap talk
chiselling
collusion
corruption

creative accounting
debasing the currency[1]
economical with the truth
false signalling
fiddling
fleecing
gazumping
hidden economy
hidden information
incomplete contracting
insider trading
misinformation
moral hazard (post-contractual opportunism)
opportunism
perks of the job
ring (in trading)
scam
shadow economy
signalling
siphoning
strategic misrepresentation
tax avoidance
tax evasion
underground economy

Another interesting example, although nothing to do with economics directly, is the rise of the term 'professional foul' in ball-based team sports and the fall of such terms as 'dirty tackle' for malintended contact. This, of course, has plenty to do with economics indirectly as the rising salaries in sports, and their performance-contingent component, contribute to the incentive for professional fouling and the downgrading of its moral lassitude by such terminological obscuration.

Granted one can expect some linguistic variation in word usage for technical reasons (some of them legal), such as the need to distinguish the component elements in different types of deception: for example, fraud describes something very different from armed robbery. This does not account for the motley collection of terms above which are due to two major factors. One is defending oneself against legal action when engaged in making public accusations about someone's conduct. The second, which is of more interest to us, is the desire people feel to imbue words with moral gradations. We all know this from the traditional colour and size divisions of lies into white, little white, and so on and in some cases slippage, via jocular rhyming slang, into such

terms as 'porkies' (from 'porky pies') and infantilisms such as 'fibs'. In his
book on cheating at work, anthropologist Gerald Mars (1982) distinguishes
between 'light' and 'heavy' verbal descriptions of otherwise identical conduct,
where the choice of word depends on the position of the attributor in the social
grid. He says that he prefers to use the word 'fiddle' to describe deceptive
practices at work, in order to come in line with general public feelings on the
matter, whereas the police would see the activities as serious crimes of theft
from an employer or customer. Naturally, such linguistic flexibility has always
been with us: a good example can be found in J. Rives Child's 1989 biography of Casanova which recalls how cheaters at gambling, in eighteenth
century Vienna, were known as 'correctors of bad luck' and it was a great
compliment to be known as a skilful corrector of bad luck.

Different categories of activity are involved here. One is deliberate deviation from a contractually specified performance, such as failure to deliver
items which have been paid for, which might in a literal sense be seen as cheating. Closely linked is misrepresentation such as getting a job by dint of a
forged certificate or advertising a product as not animal-tested when it has
been. The final category is the making of promises not backed by any contractual obligations; a sub-species of what economists now call 'cheap talk' (see
below). Not only does the discipline of economics contribute terminology
which, in some cases, 'lightens' the sinfulness of lying and deception, it also
can establish circumstances under which these moral failings can be welfare-
improving. In many cases these are examples of the theorem of the 'second
best' in welfare economics [see e.g. Ng (1983, ch. 9)].

The following is a set of cases illustrative of this.

(a) Mars (1982, p. 167) discusses overcharging, in a hotel bar, with the
surplus going back to the firm which encourages its staff to perpetuate the
fraud. This may appear to be a theft from the customers but it could be beneficial to all concerned if this is the best value hotel in the region at the 'true'
cost (charges plus 'fiddles') but the consumers would desert it for the next
best, due to some sort of myopia or irrationality, if they were choosing on the
basis of all costs being fully reported.

(b) Rose-Ackermann (1999) has analysed corruption in terms of efficient
deceit within all forms of organization. Corruption such as bribes to win
contracts or favourable treatment to those in one's charge (for example ensuring promotion on terms other than those laid down in the codes of the organization) may be a way of overcoming formidable transactions costs that impede
the optimal functioning of the organization. In the job promotion example, the
corrupt promoter of the lower level colleague may be in possession of valid
information that this person is the expected highest productivity alternative for
the post, but is constrained by the problem that transmission of this information through the relevant channels is prohibitively costly. If they then 'cut a

corner', to use another item from the arsenal of moral lightening, to facilitate this promotion then it is possible that all concerned (even those who may seem to be unfairly cheated of something they have acquired the right to) may be better off due to the increase in total output. In a sense, there is a tradeoff between sins here as deceit is used to circumvent the waste due to the X-inefficiency discussed in Chapter 4. But, of course, the argot of moral lightening within the organizational culture may ease the pain of sinning felt by the practitioner of corruption.

(c) If we assume that interpersonal welfare comparisons can be made, then it is a straightforward proposition that some lies and deceit, which transfer income, may be welfare-enhancing in terms of producing a better income distribution. Leaving aside conventional morality, there is no intrinsic difference between this method of redistributing income and that of taxation to improve distribution. The deceit may not involve direct transfers such as fraud or overcharging and could be performed via the theft of time in the shape of leisure breaks in excess of contract for an individual 'fiddler' [Mars (1982, pp. 78–83)]. There are also well-documented group 'restrictive practices' amongst workers in certain industries to slow down the pace of work and thus transfer utility to themselves.

(d) Some writers on the economics of law and order have claimed that bribery of the police may be efficiency-enhancing, particularly through raising police pay and thereby increasing the supply of officers which further reduces the wage paid by the non-bribing citizens. There is also the obvious production gain of a Pareto optimal trade between a major wealth creator on his/her way to work whose work would be impeded if they did not bribe their way out of a speeding punishment. All of this follows from the not surprising fact that economics sees the law in terms of economics not as a body of moral rectitude.

(e) Within standard microeconomic models, once we allow for imperfect information, untruthful advertising may be beneficial. Traditional morality may say that two wrongs do not make a right but consider the following case: two variants of X are for sale with X1 being substantially better than X2. If X2 has inflated claims made for it then the consumer in a state of information asymmetry may buy it when X1 would have been a better option. The better the seller of X1 is at lying, ceteris paribus, the better off the consumers will be if they believe the lies.

(f) Doctors of medicine are in a position where opportunities to lie, to the gain of the patient, arise as a matter of course. Take the case of someone with a short time to live who may be happier in the remaining time if they do not know the imminence of their death (the opposite could be the case however). This case is complicated by the costs of detection falling on the deceived who, if upset at being lied to, may now be worse off than they would have been if told the truth at the outset. If the doctor knows this, then the decision to lie fits neatly into the Von Neumann–Morgenstern utility function of the SEU model. Doctors can also deceive with placebos, which have the effect of making the patient better. This may be a more self-interested form of deception than the last as the placebo is used as a form of 'blind testing' new drugs against a benchmark of non-usage which these days tends to be an irrelevant treatment rather than the sugar pill of the past. This might be an additional source of disutility to the patient if they find out.

(g) People may prefer not to know certain things. Utility depends not just on material goods and services but also on the information one has processed as 'true'. The managers at levels above the corruption enactor in case (b) above might prefer not to know about what went on as they would then face costs of guilt or conscience, and additional anxiety over fear of being held responsible for the procedures at a later point in time if some contingency such as a legal case for employment discrimination is taken. Such 'rational ignorance' (as discussed in Chapter 4) also rears its head when individuals make altruistic transfers to a third party in the hope that substantial waste does not take place. It is an entirely logical experience within the cognitive dissonance model, particularly as costs of information gathering and stress levels rise.

(h) Lying about non-compliance with legally enforced prices such as rent controls and minimum wage laws can be beneficial. Take the legal minimum wage case. If the wage is too high for a firm to stay in business and market constraints are such that the workers cannot find comparable work at the minimum wage then the firm, the workers and its customers will be better off than if the firm complied with the law.

Cynicism about economics and honesty has long been with us: thousands of years ago in the satires of Juvenal we find the claims that 'honesty is praised and starves' and 'In Rome all things can be had at a price'. We find that some economists have even taken this line in proposing that honesty can be valued by estimating contingent valuation schedules for the willingness to lie by offering people money to lie [see Reder (1979)]. Notwithstanding this and the cases discussed above, we can still find thinkers willing to claim that market economies are intrinsically prone to generate honesty.

The germ of this idea is found in treatments, by Kant and Hume, of the duty to honour promises. It was more fully explicatd by Adam Smith in his *Theory of Moral Sentiments* in 1759. Discussing 'propriety of action' he makes a distinction between those in exalted positions whose power is so great that they may be virtually above the law and those in the 'middling and inferior stations of life' of whom it is true (p. 128) that honesty is the best policy as their success 'depends upon the favour and good opinion of their neighbours and equals'. This leads to the optimistic proposition that markets will evolve into places of virtuous conduct. He elaborates on this (pp. 528–33) in discussing others' writings on practical morality. He presumes that there is an instinct to be fundamentally truthful which derives from the desire to be held in high esteem by other people. Thus he feels that even those known to be liars are merely opportunists whose deceit is more the exception than the rule. He makes a rough guess that even the 'most notorious liar' (p. 530) still tells the truth 95.2381 per cent of the time. A rational player in a game theoretic model may well behave like this precisely because he wishes to be believed when he most needs to (at the time of greatest expected gain) and thus needs a reservoir of trust, which others hold in him, so that he does not end up like the boy in the tale who cried 'wolf' so often that when a wolf finally did appear he was eaten because no one believed him.

Smith is assuming a group of individuals with similar tastes and endowments in a small community with low monitoring costs, which is not exactly characteristic of the modern world where asymmetric information [Molho (1997)] is the key to the scope for opportunistic deception. Any situation where one party has more information about some contingency than another contains scope for possible deception. This deception would be limited in the Smithian scenario by 'reputation effects' being easily observed due to the relative stability and homogeneity of the identity of traders and the menu of trades. This, and the modern variants of Smith's position, are explored more fully in the remaining sections.

GAMES PEOPLE PLAY

There are a number of 'classic' areas in economics where some kind of 'cheating' is an intrinsic feature of the situation. The usual approach to this is to attempt to think of mechanisms that might eliminate this feature on the grounds that it is a source of market failure and hence departs from the optimality conditions for social efficiency. The main areas are as follows:

1. The 'lemons model'. Akerlof (1970) introduced this into the literature and a considerably generalized and clarified version is presented in Rasmussen (2001). The term 'lemon' was originally American slang for a defective car, giving rise to the passing of a 'lemon law' to provide redress for the buyer.
2. Collusion amongst oligopolists, usually over price fixing. In such models [Rees (1985)] the focus is on the risk that one of the cartel members defects by secretly cutting prices.
3. Moral hazard in respect of purposive exploitation of the free-riding opportunities in public goods provision (tax evasion is essentially an adjunct of this).

4. Employment contracts. If workers' productivity is not perfectly observ-
    able then scope exists to represent it as being less than it truly is, imply-
    ing 'shirking' by providing less effort than the contract dictates.

Such scenarios are now generally subject to game theoretic treatments which
usually assume risk-neutrality, multiple periods and hence scope for reputation
building, and rational utility-maximization with known preferences. The loss
due to deception in such games is represented as a prisoner's dilemma where
players choose strategies which are Pareto inferior to other combinations.
According to the Gibbard–Satterthwaite theorem [Gibbard (1973),
Satterthwaite (1975)] we cannot, a priori, rule out devious manipulation of the
outcomes in such models when information is less than perfect and the number
of traders is finite. Given the infeasibility of having perfect information and
infinite numbers of agents (without prohibitively increased costs) much of the
literature in these areas consists of suggestions for mechanisms to force
message sending to be closer to the truth and/or for prices and quantities to
move closer to the welfare optimum. Literature in the above areas proposes
various solutions: in the public goods area 'special' forms of taxation are put
forward (such as in the Lindahl model and Clarke–Groves tax); in the labour
market case incentive compatibility through contracts is sought. Ultimately
such solutions are unlikely to work when the degree of 'common interest' is
low and information costs are high. We are then left with the consequences of
dishonesty as permanent excess demand or supply. For example, in efficiency
wage models, unemployment emerges to solve the shirking problem if fully
effective anti-shirking contracts cannot be devised. In the lemons model,
unsold products may be held by the sellers and in the extreme case, with a
continuum of quality levels and homogeneous tastes [Rasmussen (2001, pp.
217–18)], the market collapses.

   What happens in these cases is that we have 'noisy' markets where permanently high levels of excess supply or demand may feature and total output is
less than it would otherwise be. The above cases all feature adverse selection
and/or moral hazard and would seem to involve deliberate deception. Such
problems will arise even if all agents are still intrinsically honest, particularly
in the case of signalling effort. Modern economics is awash with models of
search and information, increasingly couched in terms of game theory. So long
as information is incomplete, and costly to gather, there is scope for opportunistic contracting facilitated by judicious investment in sending out
messages or 'signals'. The scope for benefiting from investment in signals is
compounded as the degree of asymmetry between buyer's and seller's information. In a world of perfect information, including knowledge of one's own
tastes, there is no need to invest in signals.

   The role of a signal is to suggest to the consumer or producer, respectively, the level of utility or productivity that is likely to ensue from choosing the signalled item. Signalling is beneficial to the chooser if the costs invested in assessing the signals do not outweigh the gains in making a better choice than would ensue in a signal-free world. It might appear that the signaller would only invest in signals so long as they generate a net positive return. Unfortunately, in a world of costly and imperfect information they may, as individuals, make ex post losses[2] even if they are not the victim of seriously deluded wishful thinking. In a world of perfect information it would be impossible to lie successfully unless we allowed some people to be more stupid/gullible than others in so far as they cannot use the available information properly. Even in a world of information problems, the case might be made that false signals will not be generated so long as the type of investment involved does have significant positive correlation with the productivity level in the task involved. The correlation does not have to be very strong, in levels of a ratio number, for the buyer as their real concern is with the rank order of the signal levels. For example, let us suppose that an MBA involves training that is totally useless as far as the work of an executive is concerned but nevertheless the rank order of exam scores is perfectly correlated with actual 'on the job' productivity, then the market should sort itself efficiently so long as there are no serious market failures in the educational side of the market. Although the world of this situation is not entirely 'truthful', it does not involve any deliberate deception by the agents concerned.

Once hired such agents are, of course, in a position to be victims of dishonesty or perpetrators of it so long as they face an appropriate structure of opportunity arising from asymmetric information. 'Insider trading' in financial institutions is a good example of this. Here we may encounter the optimistic (Smithian) view that such phenomena may be mere aberrations which the abiding benefits of mutual trust due to 'common interest' will eliminate. This has to be the case in perfectly competitive markets, but it seems difficult to plausibly extract such a conclusion from game theory, in the abstract, without a prior ruse of writing into the game the conditions it was meant to generate. Game theory seems no more capable of establishing the Smithian world of a mainly honest economy than theoretical physics is of resolving ethical disputes about what went on in Hiroshima.

CHEAP TALK

Cheap talk has received a lot of attention in recent papers in economics journals. The term is derived from the old adage that 'talk is cheap', with the implication that only actions count. Take the case of government macroeconomic policy. The claim that strict monetary policies will be enforced to constrain inflation would be highly effective if it were believed, but if the relevant wage and price setters see no signs to convince them that this is the case then they will carry on as if no such policy exists. One then gets into perplexities of whether the government needs to lie erratically in order to 'fool' rational agents who second-guess it, if it is to have any policy effectiveness whatsoever. Cheap talk can then be a form of lying in the literal sense of the word as it involves making claims that one will not back up. The claims might be true but not verifiable. They may also be true but couched in sufficiently vague terms that any failure cannot be laid at the door of the claimant.

A good example of cheap talk is offering to marry someone and then reneging. This is a case of failing to keep a promise which has become a vexatious legal issue. In the marital promise case, no contract is made until a certificate is obtained but expectation of fulfilment sets in motion a number of actions. One of these which forms the stuff of old British folk songs and many novels is the surrender of virginity, with the possible consequence of pregnancy, in reciprocation for the marital promise. If the false promise is sustained there are directly economic costs (expenditures on wedding preparations and so forth) but the jilted party experiences other utility losses including passing over other offers. English common law established three legal bases for an action: expectation damages for the loss of economic and social position, tort damages for anger and humiliation, and reliance damages for being seen as 'damaged' goods on the marriage market. By the early twentieth century more of these cases were brought in America than England, with concern over moral hazard inducing excessive (potentially) nuisance suits leading to the passing of the first 'Heartbalm Law' in North Dakota in 1935 which was a one- or two-sentence statute simply stating that breach of promise to marry actions were not permitted.

In the presence of a Heartbalm statute, a promise to marriage is cheap talk unless some other factors can be used as costs. Social customs can serve in this way. The offer of a ring, of some value, is a form of binding in which the talk is made expensive as the giver may not receive the economic value back and social knowledge of the ring may deter their other prospects. Currently, American courts are wrestling with claims and counter-claims concerning the return of the ring in terms of its status as a conditional gift or an unconditional gift. If it is deemed to be a conditional gift and thence returnable to the giver then promises to marry will unequivocally become cheap talk.

Game theorists take the view that, at first sight, cheap talk might be expected to have no influence on equilibria. Farrell (1995, p. 186) says '. . . one might think that cheap talk cannot be informative' as the lack of effort being shown by the sender effectively means the message is received as 'empty'. However, the cheap talk may be efficacious where there is a degree of 'common interest' between the relevant agents in the trading situation. This optimistic position is reinforced by the proposition that long-run stable 'babbling' equilibria will not occur. Babbling is where the signal is totally uncorrelated with the item the message concerns. Babbling is a form of lying and we might be tempted to take away from the formal models, in the cheap talk literature, the conclusion that cheap lies won't persist under reasonable assumptions [see section 5.3 of Mailath (1998)].

However, the optimistic conclusions of game theoretic models of cheap talk are premised on two fundamental elements of economics that are not necessarily justified other than as convenient simplifications for the purposes of beginning the construction of an analytical framework. The first is rationality in processing information. In the case of false promises the latter element may be circumscribed by such things as unwarranted euphoria and wishful thinking. These elements in choice may create scope for opportunism by those in positions of greater power than the message recipients. The scope will rise as abilities to resolve messages into their true and false components vary across individuals. As the lying cheap talker is essentially a predator of sorts one would expect rational deceivers to sort themselves into niches of the economy where maximum scope exists to exploit the agents [cp. Cameron & Collins (1999)].

Product advertising might seem to have the character of cheap talk when it fails to present a discernible cost, to the advertiser, of falling short of the truth. This applies even when the truth *is* being told. The best mousetrap in the world may have been invented and trumpeted as such but this is cheap talk from an investor's point of view unless consumers actually start to adopt the product and thereby spread knowledge of its superiority by displaying it in use and promoting it through word of mouth. Hence additional factors are included in the sales pitch such as money back guarantees or, in the case of 'lowest price available', advertising the promise to beat the lowest-priced rival by a stipulated percentage.

Economists have long put forward the case for advertising as a means of disseminating information on price reductions and new products. It is thus a 'normal' and desirable part of the competitive process in markets that fall short of perfect competition. In such 'common interest' situations it may, in fact, serve an efficiency-enhancing function. The scope for opportunism in advertising gives rise to very similar forms of regulation in most market economies. That is, the weight of policy is on voluntary compliance by advertisers and complaints by users rather than on direct intervention. The credo that advertising should be 'legal, decent, honest and truthful' seems almost universal. For example in Europe, Hong Kong, New Zealand and the USA this credo is proclaimed in the regulatory provisions. There is a high degree of similarity in the codes of advertising regulation, in that most countries make explicit provision for vetting the conduct of firms' advertising products which may be health-damaging and/or tending to administer to the vanity of the consumer. The specific products usually subject to more heavy vetting than the rest are slimming and alcohol (tobacco products are subject to outright bans in many media in a lot of countries). Slimming products provide a good illustration of the problems in curbing the cheap talk of visual media-based advertising. The regulatory codes can be used to drive bogus science out of the advertisements and to prevent people being encouraged to go on health-damaging regimes. However, advertising standards bodies refrain from operating any censorship on the grounds of subliminal advertising on the premise that it is difficult to sustain any case law argument over such a complaint. Subliminal advertising refers to more than the clichéd 'brainwashing' scenario of inserting split-second hypnotic messages which say 'buy this' in between frames. That could, in any case, be detected simply by slowing down the film of a tele-vision, or cinema, advertisement. The more problematic case of subliminal advertising is the creation of a positive atmosphere, surrounding the product or service, by clever juxtaposition and manipulation of images. In the slim-ming case we may see a relatively thin and fit person engaged in vigorous activity who extols the benefits of a proprietary brand of dieter's meal substi-tutes followed by a picture of the same person as they 'used to be' in a less desirable state. Even if it has been established that the pictures are of the same person, not merely actors posing as slimmers, and further that the person in the advert really did lose the weight, whilst a consumer of the product, the advertisement does not, and cannot, constitute a guarantee for any individual purchaser that they will themselves achieve anything like a comparable weight loss. Nevertheless the warm glow of expectation has been kindled with what is essentially cheap talk, as any responsibility for failure falls back on the buyer and not on the seller.

Advertising routinely contains claims that are impossible to verify. For example, 'new wonderwash now gets whites even whiter than ever' and I have just seen one, in a freesheet paper for an electrolysis clinic which has the phrase, 'electrolysis has been successful for over sixty years' in the largest typeface used in the panel. This is a claim so vague as to be meaningless and the service being advertised is clearly one where success requires escalating amounts of money if the case proves to be difficult. If one reads the guidelines of advertising standards associations, one finds that these sorts of claims are not approved of: for example any advertiser who claims that 7 out of 10 owners said their cats preferred this brand is supposed to be able to produce a valid scientific study backing the claim.

There are a number of reasons why the cheap talk in such claims is allowed to persist without counter-actions forcing it to be removed. For one thing, the intrusion of the market morality into the general current of ideas may mean that rational individuals are expected to be able to see through any such bluff.

If the bluffing causes serious welfare losses then rational losers should seek redress and the public dissemination of a successful action should work in the Smithian way to promote honesty in other advertisers. Thus the regulatory bodies function in terms of monitoring and investigating complaints which will go to industrial regulatory trading bodies if voluntary compliance does not follow. The number of complaints is not that large: for example in the year 2000, in the UK, of 5691 complaints 1648 concerned truthfulness and 990 substantiation, i.e. that claims could be upheld. The rest concerned decency, which to some extent arises from fear of the inflammation of lust.

Such low-wattage policing of the truth reflects once more the moral relativism of the market culture in which, since absolute truth costs money, it can only be preserved if it pays its way in the form of some sort of contribution to social efficiency. In a market, the truth becomes relative if the individual's preferences are, contrary to the introductory economics textbook world of consumer sovereignty, adaptive. If you believe that a product is good for your health or environmentally friendly (regardless of the truth) then, over a period of time, commitment to this belief may grow until it resembles a capital asset. Some cheap talk will then be effective in the sense that it adds value to the existing commitment stock. In a cognitively dissonant individual, positive cheap talk signals concerning a positively valued belief might rationally be accepted whilst a negative signal about a positively held belief may be filtered out. If/when it exceeds the filter level, set by the individual, possibly due to an informational cascade then a utility loss is set in motion unless the set of signals provides compensation in terms of an enhanced belief stock in some substitute product. As cheap talk may make individuals better off it could influence their overall taste pattern. More specifically, positive cheap talk creates upbeat or optimistic feelings and these lead to overall expansionary behaviour by individuals. It is notable that advertising regulation does not allow advertisements which attack the claims or products of others, largely on the grounds that this is unfair competition. For a brief period, in the USA, it was mandatory to screen a quota of anti-smoking advertisements which was proportional to the volume of smoking commercials, but this was a special case which still prevented spontaneous lobbying effort via paid signalling against individual products.

In summary cheap talk is often a form of lying which does have 'real' effects. It is involved in the contractual issues we consider later in this chapter. As far as advertising is concerned (or rather the broader category of persuasion which includes all forms of marketing effort) we refer the reader to the optimistic defence of its usefulness to the economy as a pure information failure salve in the paper by McCloskey & Klamer (1995) as discussed in Chapter 4.

MOTIVATION

I have given many examples above where it is beneficial for lies and deceit to take place and we will have further illustration of this in some of Part III of the present work. Of course, it is not generally deemed acceptable to lie and cheat; indeed even the person doing it may have some form of pathology which is a deviation from rational choice and thus it fails to make them happy. A good barometer of popular opinion is the text of pop songs, and it is very hard to find many of these that actually celebrate lying as a pleasurable pastime. Indeed only a small UK hit by wealthy Swiss dilettantes 'Yello' called 'Of Course I'm Lying' (highest position no. 23 in the 1989 singles charts) springs to mind as such an item that might have received regular radio plays. On an anthropological level, one might see rituals like the tradition of the 'April Fool', and television 'hoax' programmes are a way of expunging any latent desires for such deviance from the 'normal' person who may feel hemmed in by daily code observance. In more 'normal range' cases (to use the language of psychiatric textbooks), even the expense-fiddling worker and the over-charging bar staff may feel a utility loss from dishonesty which is in some cases forced upon them by the culture of their environment. This could be analysed in terms of the simple tradeoffs in models discussed in Chapters 1 and 2. That is, lying and cheating require a compensation in the price or factor payment to make the person tempted willing to participate in deceit. Thus we have the paradox that the 'more honest' the police officer, in example (d) above, the larger is the size of bribe they would be observed to take all other things being equal. Further, so long as there are costs of being caught then the bribe will need to be even larger the more risk-averse the potential bribe-taker is (assuming that a conventional SEU model is applied).

What is our motivation to lie then? In economic terms a lie, or deception, is analogous to the purchase of an asset which may increase utility ex post, even if detected, provided that the discounted punishment costs are suffi-ciently low. As implied in the discussion above of the potential bribe-taker, the rational choice model does not rule out the appearance of a taste for honesty, as a virtue, as an argument in the individual's utility function. Whether it gets there by sheer force of collectively induced habit formation or also has a strong instinctive component distinguishes 'optimistic' from 'pessimistic' rational choice thinkers. Adam Smith, Peter Kropotkin and in modern times Robert Frank (1988) and 'neo-classical Marxists' Bowles & Gintis (1999) fall into the optimistic camp as they discern instinctual yearnings for virtue which are capable of being developed further by a wisely ordained society.

The pessimistic view that all honesty is, for the most part, a contextual contingency has appeared in cynical and nihilistic philosophical writings such as those of Juvenal and Nietzsche. Thomas Hobbes's *Leviathan*, first published in 1641, represents possibly the first formalized system of thought that bears on this. It finds eloquent expression from the mouths of the figureheads of two of the most influential centres of modern economics: Milton Friedman (Chicago) (e.g. 1984) and Gordon Tullock (Virginia School of Public Choice). Optimism or pessimism is a garnish served up as part of the ritual use of the rational choice model [cp. Arrow (1986)]. This undertow of optimism or pessimism seems to derive from a fundamental view of human nature rather than from pure reason or empirical evidence. The pessimistic view that it is a basic instinct to lie and cheat if it maximizes utility arises from the fact that this sin is not an emotion like greed, lust, envy, jealousy or a state of quiescence like sloth; rather it is an instrument for becoming better off.

If the pessimistic or optimistic views are to be further supported from beyond the pure models of the logic of choice then the place to look seems to be in sociobiological models. Biologists who study social behaviour see lying and cheating as 'natural' behaviour which manifests from birth. In *The Selfish Gene* (1976), Richard Dawkins outlines the structure of opportunism which predisposes children to lies and deceit (pp. 148–50). This has its origins in the power asymmetry whereby the child is dependent on the adult who is superior in all ways relevant to the imposition of their willpower. However, the parent is genetically programmed to support the child and therefore needs to know how hungry the child is in order to optimally feed it. Reward signals are issued upon the receipt of the food, such as smiling in human species and purring in felines. The offspring can engage in deception as it may choose to make hunger signals and gratification signals that are out of proportion to its true needs. This tendency will be exaggerated by the presence of rival siblings. Dawkins is at pains to claim that children do not consciously seek to cheat their parents, but that is a mere trifle on the way to his conclusion that 'we may expect to see cheating and selfishness within families. The phrase "the child should cheat" means that genes which tend to make children cheat have an advantage in the gene pool. If there is a human moral to be drawn it is that we must teach our children altruism, for we cannot expect it to be part of their biological nature' (p. 150).

Pessimistic views of honesty are also supported by most modern psychologists as can be seen in the work publicizing the survey on lying carried out by *That's Life* magazine in the UK in 2001. This reported, contra Frank, that lying can be hidden and that some people are much better at it than others. People also reported a very strong willingness to lie: one much noted finding was that a quarter of women said they would lie to their partner in order to get pregnant if this proved necessary. The survival instinct may be further demonstrated in the skill with which one uses the lightening of language to 'programe' the beliefs of oneself and others. Specifically this will be manifested in one's ability to manage the cognitive dissonance ensuant on living in a community which upholds a code of honesty but yet, at the same time, offers returns to dexterous dishonesty. In the limit, these kinds of survival skills could lead to the surprising paradox of the disappearance of hypocrisy as implied in a paper by the philosopher Daniel Statman (1997). He begins from the observation that hypocrites are conventionally seen as morally corrupt, cynical egoists who consciously and deliberately deceive others in order to promote their own interests. From a survival point of view he claims that the initial experience of hypocrisy ultimately leads to self-deception and, therefore, 'real' hypocrites are hard to find. Hypocrisy transmutes into self-deception as consistent and conscious deception of others is self-defeating from the point of view of egotistical hypocrites. The best way for them to achieve their ends would be to believe in the deception, thereby not only deceiving others but also themselves. Thus it seems it might not be impossible to be a hypocrite but a 'true' hypocrite will be hard to find and, under a competitive process, we would tend to the situation where everyone is a hypocrite but nobody knows it. This is another example of adaptive preferences.

Whether a person can be a convincing hypocrite and liar requires more attention to the function of the brain than is given in Frank's account of observable displays of emotion (see below). The brain has to process emotions before they can be experienced. If certain drugs were applied or connections otherwise interfered with in the individual's receptors then the 'relevant' emotion for the action taken would not be experienced. Creating such a schism is what lies behind a lot of military training (and drug administration) which attempts to reduce the amount of overt grief felt at killing people. Lying skills would also be part of this if there were a risk of the person disclosing important information to enemies. A substantial part of concealing physical signs of lying involves the operation of memory which involves several different brain areas for different types of memory [see Carter (1998, ch. 7)]. If one sticks to an evolutionary model then those whose brains are well suited to lying may have a strategic advantage in certain situations where those who are disadvantaged in this area behave truthfully as unsuccessful attempts to deceive are inefficient.

Data may be in constant doubt but nonetheless still drive much of modern economics especially in policy areas, so it behoves us to review the 'hard' evidence on the motivation to lie and cheat. It is difficult to isolate the motivation of economic agents from the environments they find themselves in and there is the further problem of the difficulty of obtaining suitable data. By its nature deception will tend to be hidden and therefore statistical records are invariably misrepresentative of its extent. Work on the 'hidden' or 'underground' economy uses such things as gaps in the national income accounts and unexpectedly high volumes of large-denomination notes in circulation. Such studies claim to find substantial amounts of officially unreported economic activity. A major world-wide comparison of the share of the shadow economy in GDP was performed by Schneider & Enstel (2000). The lowest shares are in the more prosperous developed economies: even here the share is about 8–10 per cent. At the top end of the range for OECD countries we find Greece, Italy and Spain in the range of 24–30 per cent, which is similar to the estimate for Eastern European countries. Latin American economies generally have a share in the 40–60 per cent range, whilst by far the greatest extent of shadow economy activity is found in some African economies where the top-end estimate is 76 per cent.

As we are more concerned with motivation than the size of the loss it seems appropriate to consider the evidence in studies of tax evasion [see Elffers (1999)]. Work in this area began with the rational choice model in its SEU variant, but many other decision-making models have been applied. The biggest departure from the mainstream is in studies which look at underlying personal differences in the tendency to observe the norm of (near) full tax observance irrespective of the levels of punishment and returns to evasion. These suggest that the factors mentioned in Chapter 5 are relevant to tax cheating: that is people observe the rules as a function of how reasonable they think the system is in terms of fairness, the use made of the tax revenues and the behaviour of those in the reference group to which the individual belongs. All of these will go to make up the level of the internally imposed feeling of guilt costs that an individual experiences if tempted into evasion. Elffers (1999, p. 559) points out that this may lead to evasion being deemed acceptable, even desirable, in some contexts and downright sinful in others.

For economic theorists seeking 'clean' tests of their models there has been an increasing resort to experimental research where subjects are paid to play (usually computer-based) games under rules controlled by the researcher, thus approximating the laboratory conditions of natural sciences. A notable area of such work has been on the question of contributions to the provision of public goods. In an experimental game setting this corresponds to a simple model of voluntary taxation. The chief research question here is: how serious is the free-rider problem? I would not [as Molho (1997) does] classify the free-rider problem, per se, as lying or cheating. If I decided not to give to the Public Broadcasting System (PBS) in the USA at all but still watched its broadcasts there may be little deception involved as I might be perfectly willing to admit to the free-riding that is going on. Deception arises in such situations where there is a deliberate strategy of over-reporting the amount one would be willing to contribute. This will have no effect if the provider does not trust the revealed intentions enough to proceed with a level of output corresponding to the expressed sum of marginal benefit curves. However, the presence of multiple periods of contracting means that the individual dissembler could offer higher levels of support early on in order to promote output, but then strategically withdraw contributions in the expectation of the gap being filled by enough expansion from other people to increase their own utility.

Experiments on voluntary provision of public goods are surveyed in Carter & Irons (1991), Ledyard (1995) and Holt & Laury (1998). These games tend to show high levels of voluntary contribution in early rounds but by the end most people are free-riding, possibly due to a contagious cascade of retaliation against the early movers in free-riding. Studies also tend to find that people who have studied economics act in a more self-interested way than others. The focus of such research is on co-operation and unfortunately for us it does not (as is also the case for ultimatum games and dictator games) build in a full-scale allowance for dishonest signalling. This is dealt with to a much greater extent in experimental research on moral hazard, which has been provided in a number of studies by DeJong et al., starting with a paper in the *Journal of Accounting Research* in 1985. The analysis of the properties of the outcome was based on the assumption that all players are risk-neutral. The experiment consisted of several players in the role of principal and agent, interacting over a sequence of periods. This multiperiod feature allows players to build reputations over their conduct which may influence the conduct of others. The players were fixed throughout the market experiments and kept to the same rules. Treatment of the experiments differed by allowing some trials to permit principals who had experienced adverse outcomes to pay a fee in order to discover the true quality level of service provided by agents. This was extended in some experiments by allowing the principal to collect liability payments from the agent. Each market experiment ran for two and a half to three hours. Subjects were paid for participation. When liability and fees for revelation of true quality were not in place the agents displayed substantial moral hazard in delivering the lowest quality in order to maximize profits by deceiving the principal who is unable to foretell the quality received. This would seem to reveal an underlying motivation to lie and cheat whenever possible, as Hobbesian analysis and economics of crime models would seem to imply. Consistent with such models the introduction of punishments for deception decreases its incidence. Reputation has some effect on reducing deception but for it to be a fully effective curb on dishonesty, the punitive sanctions also need to be in operation. In an ideal world, of Smithian optimism, where people told the truth, total output would be higher and hence welfare greater, other things being equal. But one of the things we are assuming to be equal is the amount of motivation an individual displays in real markets (as opposed to university laboratories) which might well vary due to greed, envy and so forth influencing people's effort levels, particularly when they have scope for gain through opportunistic indulgences in deceit. This takes us neatly to the next section.

BUSINESS ETHICS

On the face of it, it is hard not to envisage a conflict between free market economics and ethics, as normally understood in a philosopher's lexicon, given that telling lies and perpetuating deceit may be a means of increasing profits. We have already encountered this view with Mandeville, in 1704, and the sociologist Ross, in 1907, the latter fulminating against this fact and the former waspishly celebrating it, both at times of a shift in gear towards an ever more business-driven culture. Despite this, we find an increasing interest in American management schools and amongst other academic researchers in the potentially oxymoronic field of 'Business Ethics'.

Whether this is a genuine attempt to square a problematic circle, or merely self-serving rhetoric to prevent business culture being plagued unduly by ethical criticism, it seems essential that we look into the heart of this particular enterprise. Business ethics is, of necessity, a branch of applied philosophy dealing mainly with issues of right conduct and responsible action. Like most academic areas it is prone to vogues which sweep across its frontier. Anyone undertaking a 'keyword search' of the business ethics literature 15 years ago would only infrequently come across the word 'virtue'. Today virtue, which we note is a word with wholesome connotations, is the main stamping ground for the business ethicist notwithstanding that the leading contemporary proponent of virtue ethics, namely Alasdair MacIntyre (1984, 1988), argues the Mandeville–Ross line that virtue has no role in business.

Attacks on the deployment of virtue within business ethics have been greeted with hostility. A paper by Stark (1993), 'What's The Matter With Business Ethics', that appeared in the *Harvard Business Review* provoked intense hostility at a meeting of the Society For Business Ethics (SBE) in Atlanta, culminating in an angry 'letter to the editor' of *HBR* from the SBE, which argued that 'It is unfortunate that a distinguished journal allowed such an uninformed and largely unsubstantiated indictment of serious professionals and their field to be published in its pages . . .' [Duska (1993, p. 10)]. It would be hasty to jump to the conclusion that this is prima facie proof that the SBE has something to hide. It might be claimed that such furores are indicative of a research field being at a 'young' stage: after all it is doubtful that anybody in mainstream economics is ever going to get as excited ever again as they did over the 'Cambridge Capital Controversy' in the 1960s and 70s or the host of contentious issues in the 1930s and 40s (the Keynesian revolution, imperfect and monopolistic competition, the socialist planning debate).

As the philosophy element in business ethics is the cause of the recent disputation it would seem likely that its practitioners would turn ever more in the direction of economics, in order to refine and define the field in a more impregnable way. At ground level, this takes the form of bringing back Adam

Smith's proposition that virtue can grow, in a market setting, as it may be conducive to profitability. Firms can reap significant profits from building reputations for such attributes as social responsibility or trustworthiness. Swanda (1990), for example, notes that '[t]he value of the firm's moral character . . . can result in a market value of the firm that is greater than the firm's net assets' (p. 752). He conjectures that 'even in the short run one can argue that the firm with an excellent ethical reputation can have a special economic advantage' (p. 753). An extremely visible manifestation of this, in only the last few decades, is the mushrooming of environmentally responsible business ventures encompassing ethical investment trusts and firms which proclaim their virtuous nature in terms of avoiding sinful activities of their competitors such as animal testing of cosmetics and sourcing materials from Third World workers 'exploited' by sweatshop conditions.

In a world of imperfect and costly information, there are likely to be cascade effects which lead to the building of negative and positive reputation capital. Reading the paper by Jennings & Entine (1998) on 'green business', one sees that firms which have established themselves as 'ethically sound' have a first-mover advantage not unlike the first adopter in the standard models of research and development in the industrial organization literature. Rivals will experience lower returns to promoting such an image in a particular market niche regardless of the veracity of the claim. The deceitful 'business with a soul' can cover its tracks by sourcing tainted inputs via third parties and then protesting that these were purchased in good faith with they, themselves, being the victims of deceit, rather than perpetrators of it. Under such circumstances, if we genuinely wish to preserve honesty, then we fall back on the need for sanctions and regulation. These of course face the problem that they bring deadweight costs of their own which will expand if the agents being regulated evolve deceptive strategies which, in the limiting worst-case scenario, involve capture of the regulators. If the consumer of the New Age brands touted by supposedly soulful businesses is, like the charitable donors in Tullock's (1966) model, simply basking in the warm glow of an atmosphere of self-righteousness, then they will exhibit rational ignorance (or cognitive dissonance if you prefer) in the form of deliberately avoiding information which upsets this view.

There are two ways forward from here: one is to take the optimistic route of believing that humans have the potential to transcend purely instrumental ethics and the other is to justify instrumental ethics as unavoidable pragmatic correlates of complex decision-making environments. The economist who most epitomizes the optimistic stance on human virtue, Robert Frank (1988), defines a truly ethical act as something higher than the purely instrumentally grounded profit motive as it implies a motivation in which 'satisfaction from doing the right thing must not be premised on the fact that material gains may follow; rather it must be intrinsic to the act itself' (1988, p. 254). In his 'commitment model', Frank argues that acting in one's material self-interest need not be anti-thetical to acting ethically. He claims that the unethical pursuit of self-interest often fails because of the consequent commitment problems (1988, p. 258). These will undermine the scope for devising efficient contracts, hence giving rise to some of the X-inefficiencies of Chapter 4. Frank claims that inherently trustworthy agents will be unable to hide their false trading signals as other emotional signals (facial expressions and body language) will give them away. Thus on average, in the long run, principals will not be deceived by their agents. This being the case rational agents will realize the folly of rent-seeking decep-tion and therefore will enter a set-up of trust and co-operation rather than conflict. Thus some form of 'moral' code arises naturally in a competitive market system as agents realize the economic advantages of co-operation.

This is ultimately still an instrumental model rather than one where busi-nesses are ethical in the original meaning of the word. It is the Smithian opti-mistic version of the spontaneous evolution of a 'natural order' (*à la* Hobbes) with the extra driver of false signalling being assumed to have a low produc-tivity for vaguely grounded biological reasons. It seems hard to see why a world of Frankian business ethics should be the dominant outcome in a multi-person, multi-period game, even with reputation effects. A number of factors may lead to other less ethical equilibria, some of which may be prisoner's dilemmas that cannot be escaped unless the endemically eroded trust is some-how restored. If there is asymmetric costly information and some traders are in fact risk-lovers the gains to deception may increase. This cuts both ways: a risk-lover may be more likely to believe a lie and more likely to take a chance on a lie being true. If they can engage in predation in markets or niches of the economy where other traders have different risk-preferences then the scope is increased. They may engage in chameleon-like behaviour which is highly rational, that is, entering a trading arena until fully detected and thus nullified and then moving on to another where information from their last set of activ-ities is not readily known. Even if all traders are risk-neutral they may not have the same levels of productivity in detecting the bodily signals linked to false messages. Thus, the more cunning exploit the less cunning. The more cunning may also have higher levels of investment in deception-specific capital. This can take the form of human wealth such as training in the techniques of deceit. There is also the factor of technical progress giving rise to enhanced deception opportunities. At a down-to-earth accounting level, honesty cannot be capital-ized in a firm's balance sheet as its only influence is through registering as an instrumental concern in the form of profit potential. Without this, a reputation for honesty in business is not worth the paper it isn't printed on.

Let us turn now to the second way in which the business ethics circle might be squared. On a cynical level this could be described as using economics of transactions costs to 'explain away' what looks like dishonesty. A good example of this is to be found in a paper in *Business Ethics Quarterly* by Dees & Cramton (1991). They observe that 'good negotiating skills' as normally understood are those of deceiving people by bluffs over preferences. A good agent (for example in house sales) is seen as one who successfully dupes the other party into more favourable terms for their clients. This is mainly bluffing about a settlement price, and the fact that we call it bluffing shows a moral lightening that places it below, say, selling people an item which is of much lower quality than they were promised (probably likely to be termed a 'rip-off') and indicates its low position in the hierarchy of modern sinfulness. The small innocent-sounding word 'only' plays an important role in relegating business deceit to the status of minor moral failings. For example, we might hear the expressions 'It's only a game' and 'I'm only doing what everybody else does as we all know that bluffing goes on and nobody takes it seriously'. This takes us into the 'self-defence in an imperfect world' gambit, which lay behind a lot of the cases given in the first section of this chapter. This would not be a sufficiently sophisticated means of justifying moral imperfections for the business ethicist so we come to the economic argument. This is that bluffing is a means of eliciting information in a risky costly environment. It is a cheap talk that works. As long recognized in bargaining models, the key elements in determining the outcomes of bargains are the discount rates of the traders. If both are fairly certain that a deal will be struck at some price (or other terms) there will still be uncertainty about the range of prices. If both parties knew each other's discount rates (and other relevant information) at the outset, then the deadweight costs of delay and resource usage in communicating messages could be avoided.

One's discount rate being unknown may be strategically advantageous; hence the incentive for bluffing arises in so far as the other trader may make a biased estimate of it. If the bluffers are risk-neutral, equally well-endowed and equally skilled we regress to the position that bluffs should shrivel away to a minimal element which may become a mere hollow ritual. But, of course, the major bluffers might be expected to be risk-takers. The most extreme case of this is in the entrepreneurial (in the purest Austrian sense) role of assembling a large number of disparate spot contracts for a unique, highly risky product. This is found in the entertainments industry, particularly film and television productions where obtaining one contract may be contingent on the procurement of another and hence we have misrepresentation of the probabilities of certain events happening as well as bluffing over prices.

CONCLUSION

It is an open question whether honesty can be reconciled with market economic systems. This is not to say that a command economy could necessarily effect a tradeoff of lower national output for greater honesty as, without suitable cultural norms of restraint, such a system creates opportunities for corruption as an alternative mechanism of resource allocation [cp. the results in Schneider & Enstel (2000)]. For all the claims of economists, of the optimistic persuasion, it is hard to sustain the idea that markets have any inherent tendency to evolve honest conduct. There is no grand sweeping mathematical proof of this proposition and the available empirical evidence does not particularly support it. Optimists who are aware of this fact end up proposing that the cases we list early in this chapter are dismissable 'exceptions to the rule' and then going on to propose an instrumental use of moral precepts as a rule of thumb to solve problems of trading optimally in a world of imperfect information and scarce cognitive processing ability. To illustrate my claim, here is the conclusion of Parisi (2000, p. 618):

> Evolution assures that practices which are socially inferior (in the sense that they do not make a cost-justified contribution to human wellbeing) are less frequently adopted because they are labelled as immoral, socially inappropriate, or ethically wrong. Of course, evolutionary processes are never completed, and their task is only stochastically accomplished. Still, the strong correlation between activities and institutions that are efficient, and the community's moral approval of them, should not be underestimated. Many activities that are generally considered immoral (for example, stealing, cheating, lying, and so on) are also inefficient in that they dissipate human wealth. While counterexamples exist in which 'morally condemned' behaviour actually contributes to overall human welfare, social norms and moral principles of the type described above should be considered 'rules of thumb' principles of conduct for individuals who operate in a world of imperfect information and limited cognitive competence.

But such an instrumental means of justification takes us right back to the criticism made of Frank, in respect of business ethics, that this is not really moral behaviour after all. Ultimately technology, markets and institutions entwine to select in favour of certain sorts of dishonesty. The favoured sorts will tend to be blessed with the most morally 'light' names. The regular bestowal of a morally light name on a piece of economic deceit reflects a certain communal confidence that the contagious effect of specific dishonesty is not fundamentally destabilizing to society as a whole.

ENDNOTES

1. The practice of sweating and clipping coins [see Jevons (1910, p. 73)] to cheat people out of the declared precious metal content is now long gone due to coins being intrinsically worthless.
2. In the SEU model this tendency will be exacerbated if the signallers are risk-preferring, albeit this is an assumption unlikely to be found in formal game theory models.

PART III

7. Matters of life and death

INTRODUCTION

The intentional deprivation of life has been widely regarded as one of the most sinful acts a person can engage in. This chapter will mainly focus on cannibalism and capital punishment, but we must first clarify the nature of life-depriving acts and intentions. As ever this discussion is rooted in economics; a detailed philosophical treatment of the issues in this chapter can be found in Glover (1977). The right to life seems initially to be a simple concept; however, we quickly get into problems of what it is that any such right entitles one to. According to two economists writing on the relationship between economics and philosophy, the libertarian view is that 'The right to life . . . is a right not to be killed, not a right to be given subsistence' [Hausman & MacPherson (1993, p. 703)]. Such a view rules out the death of individuals, through poverty caused by the greed of others, as a sin on the part of the 'others'. As phrased, it is ambiguous on the contentious areas of euthanasia, abortion, artificial insemination/surrogacy and all attempts to 'create' life by scientific means. The sustained interest in Mary Shelley's 1818 tale of Dr Frankenstein's monster suggests that opposition to such tinkerings with life is rooted in the 'not natural' idea of sin discussed in our first chapter. The crucial distinction, in secular humanitarian and 'moderate' religious thought, is between taking away something that exists and denying the conditions for something, which does not exist, from coming into being. In more dogmatic religions which are heavily 'naturalistic' the distinction tends to evaporate, i.e. all of the above forms of tinkering with life would be condemned as sinful, as would the use of contraception in sexual intercourse and also attempts at suicide. However, this tends to be combined with endorsement of revenge murders such as biblical endorsements of the 'eye for an eye' principle of just punishment. The ultimate formulation of this is to be found in the case some writers make for capital punishment.

With the advance of technology, the possibility of sinning via assisting 'unnatural' life creation arises. In the secular world of libertarian rational choice economists the topics of artificial insemination and surrogate motherhood can all be analysed from a relativistic point of view in terms of marginal costs and benefits without any need to especially highlight sin. Standard econometric studies exist in many of these areas [see e.g. Medoff (1988), Lester & Yang (1994), Cameron & Welford (1992)]. In the case of surrogate motherhood, partners pay for another woman to bear a child from the male partner's semen. Economists have not carried out any studies in this area, although the allocation of time model yields predictions. We would expect higher-wage women to cost more to hire as surrogates. Younger women would also be expected to command a premium because of greater expected fecundity. If the surrogate feels some stigma costs in the nature of sinfulness then they will, in the standard economic model, have to be paid more all other things being equal. Artificial insemination by donor (AID) is carried out with an anonymous donor. In the UK the donor receives a very small payment indeed and is matched as closely as possible to the male partner in terms of height, weight, ethnic origin and so on. At present there is a shortage of black donors. Lesbian participants do not have an existing father figure to match donors to. In a totally free market they would buy the best package of characteristics on offer. Cameron & Welford (1992), in the only study of AID by economists, estimate a willingness-to-pay schedule for semen as a function of profession of donor. As in the surrogate mother case we would expect the high value of time donor to cost more than others. Cameron & Welford show that the higher the profession of the hypothetical AID subject the greater is the willingness to pay for semen. It is also found that higher-income women will pay more with the income elasticity of expenditure being 0.77. A willingness to pay more for higher-quality sperm was found amongst heterosexual as well as lesbian women.

Two objections have been raised to AID [Buchanan & Prior (1984)] which also apply, broadly, to surrogate motherhood. The first is paternalistic: donors may put themselves at risk. For a man selling his genetic material there is no risk as sperm is an easily replenished bodily tissue. The second argument concerns the resulting child. The sale of sperm does no damage at the point of sale. One might argue that a person born of the exchange may suffer psychological pain later when they find out the origins of their birth, not least as they may feel tainted at being produced in a 'not natural' sinful way. Buchanan & Prior (1984) argue against this also on the grounds of there being no evidence in its favour and the children recognize the transaction was essential for them to be born.

One of the main facets of perception of these sorts of activities as sinful is the involvement of money probably on the grounds that greed is entering into a relationship that should be based on spontaneous biological urges which are in some sense not themselves tainted with greed. This worry also surfaces in discussions of selling children for adoption such as that in Radin (1996, p. 257, fn. 10) where the case of a couple who tried to trade their child for an $8800 secondhand Corvette is discussed. The car dealer eventually declined as 'it would be wrong not so much for the expense of it, but what would this baby do when he's not a baby anymore? How could this boy cope with life knowing he was traded for a car?'

The objection here is that the biological bonds of kin are being usurped by market forces. If kinship bonds underlie general feelings of respect for others then their erosion by financial incentives may ultimately lead to a deterioration in the status of the right to life. This is an archetypal point of conflict between lay ethics and economists, as price theory promotes the notion that the use of the price mechanism is the 'natural' way to solve problems of resource allocation. For example, if there is a shortage of sperm being donated, in specific desired demographic groups, then offering a higher price should cure the shortage as donors will come forth in response to such inducements. The usual basis of such life creation is to fill a gap where an existing person or relationship dyad cannot reproduce for whatever reason (for example a partner may be infertile, or for lesbians there will be ideological objections to traditional means of reproduction). Within more lenient religious traditions this might be defended against allegations of sinfulness. However, there is still the contagion argument which crops up in most areas with some aura of sin around them. That is, paying higher prices for scarcer ovaries or reproductive fluid might lead to a totally market-led form of breeding. Recall the movie stars in Table 5.1; how much might their sperm be worth to someone who is infertile or simply wishes to commit test-tube adultery? In such cases we have the dual sin of denying the right to life to some in favour of the creation of life for others which ultimately leads into the area of eugenics which was, to some extent, a movement, paradoxically, motivated by the desire to have a less sinful population.

The remainder of this chapter is exclusively focused on life-deprivation activities rather than those of life creation.

MURDER AND CAPITAL PUNISHMENT

Capital punishment is now mainly seen as a deterrent for murder, although it has always been in existence somewhere for other crimes as well. In early nineteenth century England it was a sentence for many minor crimes of theft, but was frequently commuted to deportation. Whether or not it is actually carried out, the application of a death sentence is symbolic of the high sinfulness of the activity. This is one possible explanation of why it is presently applied to offences of the consumption/sale/smuggling of addictive substances in nations with strict religious observance. I will divide the remainder of this discussion into three parts: the analysis of the decision to commit murders; attitudes to the use of execution; and the welfare economics of capital punishment.

The Supply of Murder

Economists have modelled the performance of crimes in general, and murder in particular, as just another rational choice decision. In the more complicated models, time allocation is taken into account. The simple case is to extend the SEU model as follows:

$$EU = (1 - PCON)U(C0) + PCON(1 - PE)U(C1)$$
$$+ PCON(PE)U(C2) \tag{7.1}$$

where:

EU = expected utility
$PCON$ = probability of a murder conviction
PE = conditional probability of execution given a murder conviction
$U(C0)$ = utility of the individual if not convicted of a murder
$U(C1)$ = utility of the individual if convicted and not executed
$U(C2)$ = utility of the individual if executed

In such a model, a murder is like purchasing an asset. If it is instrumental to some other gain, such as killing a security guard during a robbery, then the utility if not convicted goes up as the expected gain from the robbery rises. Economists have been constantly prey to the objection that many murders are not of pecuniary orientation, but in fact the outcome of interpersonal disputes where the death was often the accidental outcome of a dispute and thus devoid of all premeditation [Glaser (1977)]. In the extreme limit this leads to the claim that murder is largely an irrational act and therefore not susceptible to economic analysis. To some extent this has been reflected in the processes of law where intention is taken into account in sentencing decisions, particularly in terms of allowing clemency on grounds of temporary (or permanent) disturbance of the balance of the mind.

Lack of rationality on the part of the murderer implies an absence of sin under most moderate religious precepts and thus suggests that execution serves little purpose other than giving some people satisfaction from the observance of moral retribution. However, one could argue that the moral demand for punishment may be a veneer for the latent demand of the general citizenry to exercise the power to forcibly remove an existing life; that is, vent their own latent demand for murder. Thus it becomes a case of licensed murder by the state which is a further addition to sin rather than being a means of atonement.

Most economists see deterrence as the main argument which could be used in favour of capital punishment. Deterrence does not operate if individuals are not exhibiting some degree of rationality in contemplating future punishments or at least responding in an instinctive way that looks 'as if' they did calculate the costs and benefits of action. To keep this element of the capital punishment decision on the agenda, economists resort to the argument that the individual in an interpersonal dispute who may be about to strike a fatal blow to their partner's head will subconsciously estimate the probability and costs of being executed and thus be deterred if these figures are large enough. Viewed in this way the individual is also a sinner as they are allowing the anger which may have arisen from other sins of jealousy, lust, greed and so on to drive them into this ultimate sin.

The vast majority of work by economists on this subject focuses on the quantification of the relevant elasticities of deterrence: the Ehrlich model of Eq. (7.1) predicts that there should be a strict ordering whereby the greatest deterrence effect is from execution followed by the conviction rate and the arrest rate. Statistical models included further control variables to measure wealth, poverty, demographic factors and so on. The type of data available dictates that attitudes to taking a life cannot be included in the model, although a sense that killing people is wrong because there is a sanctity of life will help to deter murders through influencing tastes in the supply of murder function. Before economists entered the capital punishment debate the prevailing thesis was that variations over space and time in rates of murder and violence are explicable in terms of a 'culture of violence'. For example, Sellin (1959) argued that the southern states of the USA had high rates of murder and assault due to the culture. Extrapolating the importance of culture implies that capital punishment may not deter very much, and might in fact even produce the perverse (as in unintended) consequence of *more* murder and violence due to a 'brutalization' effect [which is explored fully in Bowers, Pierce & McDevitt (1984)].

A similar argument was made in Chapter 6 of the present work where we argued that controlling lust via price-type signals, such as taxes or punishments, is going to be comparatively ineffective and requires considerable back-up from 'social capital'. For the workaday economist, the issue of which explanations are more valid resolves into the performance of the relevant hypothesis tests on the coefficients of a regression equation. From the mid-1970s economists produced a flood of such studies [see the survey by Cameron (1994)]. These supported the idea that capital punishment is a highly effective deterrent and also the prediction of the rankings of the relative magnitude of the deterrence elasticities. Not surprisingly these studies met with considerable criticism from non-economists but also from the highly respected econometrician Lawrence Klein [see Forst et al. (1978)]. In response to such criticisms, econometric studies have tended to pour on increased levels of sophistication in formal testing of the propositions of the supply of murder model. It is probably fair to say that most economists who work in this area still hold to the notion that capital punishment is a highly effective deterrent.

Ultimately, statistical work relies on the quality of the data which ideally should come from an experimental design or some source which can be controlled artificially by statistical techniques in order to approximate an experimental design. The wave of econometric studies of capital punishment was heavily dependent on a few data sets: for the most part, US time series from the 1930s to the 1970s with occasional use of UK and Canadian time series and cross-sections of American states for 1940, 1950 and 1960. This is a limited range of data in several ways. One problem is that there have been very few executions in developed economies since 1960 as most countries abandoned execution totally. Abatement in the USA began in 1968 due to a ruling that it was unconstitutional to have capital punishment, but the moratorium ended in 1976. Since 1976, there has been a sporadic return of capital punishment in a growing number of states to the point where statistical analyses are now appearing which incorporate these data [e.g. Dezhbakhsh, Rubin & Shepherd (2001)] and show some support for a negative statistical association between executions and murders.

However rigorous such studies may be, a serious and very elementary problem, which most economists are reluctant to face, remains. That is, the data that have been used are severely limited in that very little variation in the rate of execution occurs, which makes it dangerous to infer that the rate of responsiveness of murders to executions would persist at the same level as the estimated magnitudes if we substantially increased the rate of execution. Even assuming that the marginal adjustments of standard price theory are taking place, it may well be the case that increasing the likelihood of execution brings rapidly diminishing returns once we move beyond the range of probabilities observed in the data. Beyond this, it may be that a standard SEU model as per Eq. (7.1) is not the most appropriate representation of the decision-maker's behaviour in a life and death context. If cognitive dissonance is a more appropriate representation, for example, one can envisage circumstances where increments in the risk of being executed have little effect. A potential murderer may work, in such circumstances, in terms of simply deciding whether the risk is 'high' or 'low' enough to make the act worth their while. This might be in the context of a multi-stage process rather than a simple decision to kill 'on the spot'. Take the case of a robbery: the participants will know that if they arm themselves there is a risk of being pressurized into fatal use of weapons which, ideally, would enable them to obtain the proceeds purely by threat. A 'low' probability of execution following such a contingency, when there is a high expected payoff, may continue to be perceived by a specific individual even when substantial rises in the objective risk have been effected.

Table 7.1   Support for capital punishment in the UK

Year	Percentage in favour
1937	47
1947	69
1955	73
1962	70
1964	70
1965	70
1970	61
1979	71 {for premeditated murder}
1981	83
1983	63
1984	66
1985	66
1989	89

Sources: 1937–1970 and 1981 Gallup polls; 1979 Capital Radio/Marplan survey; 1983–1985 British Social Attitudes Survey; 1989; Oracle teletext phone-in poll.

Attitudes to Capital Punishment

One index for the sinfulness of murder and/or its reciprocation by the state in the form of capital punishment is the support for the latter offered by the public. Table 7.1, adapted from Cameron (1993), shows some historical data on this for the UK.

The notable feature of this is the majority support in favour of the penalty during a period when it has been in abeyance. In the USA, poll data [Zeisel & Gallup (1989)] show support rising to a peak of 68 per cent in 1953 but declining to below 50 per cent by 1960. The bottom of this decline was 42 per cent in 1966 but by the late 1980s support was running at over 75 per cent until it peaked at 80 per cent in 1994, whereafter it declined steadily to the 2001 level of 65 per cent.

There is a broad degree of positive association between these movements and the amount of murders. A cross-national study by Ray (1982) found majority support in a number of countries. The opinion poll data are of course subject to a number of caveats about the dependency of answers on the question asked, the demographics of the respondent, the information held by the respondent and so forth. These factors are amply illustrated by the independent studies of legal scholars and social psychologists reviewed in Cameron (1993). Nevertheless the overall thrust of the evidence suggests that individuals do not consider it a sin to execute a person found guilty of murder whether this be motivated by deterrence or moral retribution. Or, at least if they do consider it a sin then they seem quite willing to tolerate it as a necessary evil.

Scholars who take such evidence as valid are sometimes prone to wander into casuistic endeavours to reconcile the conflict between the high level of support and the low level of utilization of the death penalty. Ray (1982) claimed that the fact that South Africa had a death penalty shows that it is more democratic than the UK, USA, Australia, etc. because it gives the people 'what they want'. Still, we are left with the puzzle of why people are so keen on something yet show so little enthusiasm for pursuing its restoration. Noted American legal scholar Hugo Bedau (1982, p. 68) suggested that:

> One might hazard the hypothesis that the average person seems convinced that the death penalty is an important threat, abstractly desirable as part of society's permanent bulwark against crime but that he or she is relatively indifferent as to whether a given convict is executed. . . . To put it another way there is no evidence that the two-to-one majority in favour of the death penalty for murder is also a two-to-one majority in favour of executing right now the hundreds of persons currently under death sentence.

It is notable that Bedau seems to consider only the instrumental justification in terms of deterrence rather than the retribution argument. Yet, the retribution argument couched in terms of sin might explain the attitudes to capital punishment in countries where the dominant religions are primarily based on the Bible whose 'eye for an eye' dictates lurk in the moral consciousness of citizens even if they engage in comparatively little overt religious observance.

Welfare Economics of Capital Punishment

Supposing we could collate a body of reliable and unambiguous evidence on attitudes to capital punishment, its costs and deterrence effects could be fed into the applied branch of welfare economics in the shape of cost–benefit analysis [see Hoffler & Witte (1979)]. Only when we do this can we decide whether the supportive results for deterrence, from murder supply functions, justifies the implementation or increase of capital punishment. This point seems to be neglected not only in non-economists' contributions to the debate, but also in the economic papers. Doubtless this is due to the fact that establishing deterrence effects seems to be a prerequisite for making a case for any/more executions if one is not engaging with the debate on retributive grounds. Hence, the empirical economist can claim to be absolving himself from value judgements, whilst he gets on with generating useful input information for those who are qualified for full-scale normative discourse. However, according to some controversial papers by McKee and Sesnowitz

(1976, 1977), the empirical evidence is totally irrelevant to the debate about whether capital punishment should be readily available to legislators. They say that capital punishment cannot be justified on welfare economics grounds as the argument 'does not survive the logical application of economic welfare criteria' [McKee & Sesnowitz (1977, p. 217)]. In McKee & Sesnowitz (1976) they base their position on Kaldor's test for potential Pareto improvements without bringing in the subsequent well-known literature on reversal paradoxes and so on [see Ng (1983)]. They cast the execution problem in terms of two states of the world: (i) a convicted murderer is not executed and we have a probability of being murder victims of $pm1$; and (ii) a convicted murderer is executed and we face the probability of being murder victims of $pm2$ where $pm2$ is less than $pm1$. Here we may gain from the removal of the murderer, the savings on costs from their confinement and the deterrence of murders by others. These gains can be represented as a finite sum of money regardless of any problems concerning the accuracy with which they can be estimated. But what of the losses? In a simple-minded economic framework we lose the potential output of the executed person and, in a cost–benefit framework, one might also want to take into account the 'psychic' costs of pain and suffering to their relatives and intimates and also to those who may experience distress at processing and completing the execution. Again this collection of items will amount to a finite sum of money that may or may not add up to less than the benefits (leaving aside the complicated issue of discounting the time stream of both amounts). So far, I have neglected to consider the loss of welfare of the criminal. McKee & Sesnowitz claim that this is infinity and so must by definition exceed any gains thereby ruling out any use of capital punishment whatsoever.

This claim is not made (well at least not overtly) on the grounds that killing people is sinful no matter who does it, but rather on the grounds of standard willingness to pay measures of the value of life. McKee & Sesnowitz (1976, p. 46) say that 'there is not likely to be any sum of money sufficient to compensate an executed individual for his life'. Not surprisingly this position was subject to severe responses. These have been on two fronts: first as Reynolds (1977) points out the standard position within welfare economics is that life can be valued and is not infinite. Many studies in cost–benefit analysis place a value on life through such things as measuring variations in risk-taking, which again is premised on the SEU model. There is now a large body of 'forensic economics' which values lives for the purpose of arriving at settlement costs in court cases where loss of life is involved. Such literature does not of course condone killing people on purpose in the context of a transfer of the money for the privilege, but it does reduce the status of life to a market transaction. For example, the decision not to spend more on crash barriers on high-risk road areas is effectively condemning a certain number of anonymous individuals to death. Capital punishment can be seen as part of this continuum of decisions.

The conclusion of welfare economics then is the unsurprisingly undramatic one of 'it all depends'. Sometimes capital punishment will be at the corner solution of zero and at others not, depending on movements in the key variables. For example, suppose means were to become available of gaining massive productivity gains in useful work performed by prisoners on life sentences, then the likelihood of capital punishment being of net benefit greatly decreases. By the same token, economics seems to say that, all other things being equal including future output contributions, then there should be a greater predisposition to execute the young than the old. This is boldly stated in a formal paper by Shavell (1987, p. 109) which concludes that the death penalty is 'more likely to be optimal when j is large since then society will save more in imprisonment costs' (where j is the number of periods of life left to the individual offender).

The second criticism made of McKee & Sesnowitz, that some criminals do not have a right to life, highlights problems in the economics of crime and punishment models of the constituency of the welfare function. Becker's pioneering 1968 paper on the subject included the criminal with an equal weight to everybody else. This has a certain appeal, in a rational choice framework, in terms of consistency as we are all regarded as ex ante capable of criminality (including murder) if the payoffs are suitable. Nonetheless a number of economists [see e.g. Stigler (1970), Skinner & Slemrod (1985), Reynolds (1977)] chose to argue that the criminal is not in the social welfare function. To raise such a claim beyond the status of a mere personal opinion requires some philosophical underpinnings.

Reynolds (1977) attempts to give these on the grounds that economics should be rooted in contractarianism, although he does not fully develop the idea. Under a contractarian system the murderer forfeits the right not to be murdered because of breaking an earlier accord in which murdering rights were traded for something else such as being murdered. Some economists object to such a politically abstract theory on account of the fact that individuals do not get the chance to negotiate a social accord other than the one they were born into. Nevertheless, even would-be murderers might be expected not to vote for an anarchistic system where there are unlimited rights to kill. Potential output losses in such a free-for-all are enormous. Thus we may come down to the position that state killings are a necessary evil in a world threatened by the unstable brutish nature of man, to which persistent wars pay further testimony.

CANNIBALISM

On a cynical note of pessimism, one might argue that the persistence of murder and the desire to avenge it with yet more murder may represent an attenuated form of latent anthropophagic impulses. Such impulses would represent sins in terms of the image of man usually held up in religious and secular humanist discourses.

Exception to a Rule?

One way of dying is to be eaten by other people. The most controversial view-point on this is that it is a natural lust which people will revert to given half a chance. It certainly seems to be the case that the more one studies the subject the more one is likely to take this view as evidenced, for example, in William Graham Sumner's monumental 1906 *Folkways* world-wide collection of customs, mores and morals. Sumner gives examples where human meat does, in fact, enter the marketplace in regular trading. He takes the position that there is no real rhyme or reason to the pattern of taboos on foods: there is no more essential logic to forbid the eating of some animals and insects than others, yet great revulsion is instinctively felt at the thought of eating slugs or peacocks in contemporary developed nations. Human flesh falls into this cate-gory as 'just another' irrational prejudice. He seems to conclude that the issue of the sinfulness of eating human flesh has not been adjudicated on: 'It is not forbidden in any religion because it had been thrown out of the mores before any religion was founded' (ibid., p. 341). Yet, such extreme taboo resonance might be regarded as a solid basis for sinful status.

Hogg (1958, p. 26) attempts to explain the behaviour of Fijian islanders in terms of them having a strong inherent, hard to control, taste for human flesh and blood. After all, the lust for flesh from livestock seems hard to eradicate from the human (and many of the nearer human) species. Hogg surveys many other tribes and in some cases is willing to attribute blood lust as the cause, whilst in others coming down on the side of different motives such as revenge (but even so one wonders why revenge should not just stop at killing without eating). Anthropophagy has been held up for popular entertainment in movies about the crisis situation of plane crashes in a desolate location and in the behaviour of pathological deviants within a culture which does not involve any endorsement of cannibalism as in the novels and films involving the char-acter of Hannibal Lecter. The pioneering work of Krafft-Ebing in 1897 reported a number of cases of cannibalistic efforts by those with acute sexual neuroses.

Plane crash fictionalizations have been 'straight' dramas. Yet the taboo on flesh eating is often the subject of macabre humour and thereby an index of our discomfort about the subject. Several variants of this exist, such as the blood lust of the Dracula films, Jonathan Swift's 'modest proposal' for eating children, the turning of people into pies by Sweeney Todd, the demon barber of Fleet Street (even becoming an award-winning musical by Stephen

Sondheim in 1979) and the Swiftian satire of restaurants, along the same lines, in the films *Eating Raoul* and *Eat the Rich*. These satires generally derive their pith and humour from being addressed to economic problems such as over-population, unemployment and feelings of inequity. Actual, near and metaphorical cannibalism is also a persistent motif in the works of Shakespeare, although in tragic rather than humorous contexts.

Evidence on the history of cannibalism comes from many sources. The stereotypical image of its use in primitive societies originates from the accounts of Christian missionaries. Other accounts come from commentators and anthropologists with the results of archaeological excavations. There has been a tendency to rule out anthropophagy as an aberration found only in indi-vidual deviants, crisis situations (the famous case of the stranded 'Donner party' in mid-nineteenth century USA and various modern-day plane crashes)[1] and primitive tribes rather than an inherent trait of humanity. The apex of marginalizing our possibly latent people-eating tendencies was reached when Arens (1979) attempted to claim that there was very little evidence that canni-balism had ever been practised anywhere. His proposition was that most sources quoted as authoritative could be traced back to repeated quotation of a very limited pool of sources which were patently unreliable. Anthropologists contested this position severely [Brown & Tuzin (1983)], to the point where the widespread existence of non-crisis resort to cannibalism was largely agreed, amongst them, to be a fact. Nevertheless the debate rages on, as can be seen in the current reading given in the appendix of Gardner (2000) who advances the claim that anthropologists have a vested interest in believing in pervasive anthropophagic activity, although he does not make it entirely clear what it is their interests are vested in.

The supporting evidence suggests that it was a feature of Greek society, with Herodotus in 450 BC reporting the eating of the old which is something with a clear 'economic' basis (cp. the literary and filmic satires mentioned above). Reports exist from Burgundy, France in 1621 where a famine induced the eating of grass and people. Easter Island by 1722 had widespread canni-balism due to disastrous ecological mismanagement. The collapse of the Russian economy in 1921 is said to have induced cannibalism. World War II has also given rise to reports of cannibalism, solely from Germany. It is reported that many of the inhabitants of Belsen were eaten or at least attempted to be so prior to gassing due to the extreme starvation of the captives. In 1942 German troops were under strict orders not to come back from certain battle sites, and allegedly resorted to eating dead soldiers as a means of prolonging the campaign. These instances in civilized societies are all of the 'desperate measures' variety, and thus might be claimed as exceptions to the rule that people do not bristle with sublimated urges to eat each other. Nevertheless, one might claim that people always have the alternative of resigning themselves to their fate in a crisis situation and dying with dignity. This taste might be displayed in the above situations by some portions of the community who are, of course, on average likely to die sooner and hence will be eaten with those who are (in lay thinking) thought to hold the exceptional taste.

Cannibalism as a Rule?: The Aztec Debate

The main documented instance where regular economically motivated canni-balism (i.e. it is a 'normal' part of everyday life) has been alleged is in the Aztec civilization [Smith (1996), Ortiz de Montellano (1978)]. The basis of the argument is that dietary poverty leads to a rational recourse to cannibalism as a supplement, as in the crisis scenarios of famine, air crashes and lost explorers. This is an argument that ought to appeal to any economist not blinded by revulsion. In the late 1970s Harner propounded the thesis that the Aztecs resorted to sacrifice due to the problems of their environment which has a shortage of animal meats, water for crop cultivation and agriculture which did not produce complete proteins (as maize is deficient in this respect).

The thesis of 'cannibalism as rational food policy' garnered a great deal of media attention, but has been discredited by professional anthropologists. Ortiz de Montellano (1978) calculates that human meat could only have been providing a very meagre portion of the total nutritional requirements. Further to this, the sacrifices did not correspond to the peaks and troughs of the agri-cultural cycle in the manner required by the 'economic necessity' thesis. Harner's thesis found acceptance difficult due to the weakness of the empiri-cal evidence and the prevalence of ritualistic and ceremonial elements in the process of consumption, which might suggest that the purpose of the act was primarily due to magical thinking rather than an efficient economic develop-ment policy. For example, the connection between the agricultural cycle and human sacrifice statistics suggests that they were ritual magic offerings to attract the favour of the gods. Those eaten were from enemy tribes captured in wars. There was no evidence of the 'farming' of fellow humans for consump-tion purposes, which has been attributed to various tribes in the Congo basin, or of hunting expeditions, outside the context of war, to look for human meat. Many farmer–hunter tribes have few ceremonial elements in their cannibalis-tic consumption, which is suggestive of pure lust and/or economic motives. Additional support for such a claim can sometimes be found in the scarcity of edible animals in some locations.

Still, one can find standard microeconomic theoretical propositions against the efficiency of farming and hunting so long as labour productivity, at the margin, is sufficiently high in other activities. Farming may be inefficient (depending on available vegetative food supplies) as the costs of fattening up the victims may exceed the efficiency gains of eating them, not least as incentives to work for the captives will be low given the fate that awaits them. Hunting expeditions are risky in terms of risks of loss to predators, and diseases, on the way. Such search activities also involve opportunity costs of foregoing production activities.

Anthropophagy: Economic or Cultural?

It is not necessarily easy to make a distinction between the economic (rational choice) and cultural (symbolic engrained or intuitive response) explanations of human behaviour. Nevertheless it is worth maintaining this here as it fairly represents the way in which the debate on Aztec cannibalism was framed. Let us take the cultural argument first. The cultural argument has many components, mainly related to ritual and grounded in magical thinking. These can be divided into reasons for eating one's own community and for eating one's enemies. One's enemies may be eaten in celebration of the victory, but also from the magical belief that the strength of a rival can be captured by consumption of their relevant organs/limbs and/or blood. Eating a human sacrifice (of any provenance) may also be an instrument for raising magical powers in spell casting. In such contexts it is a step forward from mere killing. The magical invocation of fertility rites is the source of sacrifices, from within a community, to appropriate gods. This could be done without actually eating the subject, however, across many systems of thought from the creation of the borfimor amongst the 'Leopard societies' of Sierra Leone [Hogg (1958, ch. 6)] to certain elements of Voodoo, cannibalism is required.

Not only can both motives exist simultaneously and powerfully, but also the ceremonial activity could be a front for the economic motivation. For example, at times of regular war, resource scarcity is exacerbated and thus eating the dead increases in its usefulness so it is beneficial to have a culture develop where eating dead enemies is the norm. Ceremonies of revenge and triumph over the dead and magical beliefs that eating them transfers their power may, in such a context, be useful survival traits, however irrational they may seem to us. Their social usefulness partly derives, as instinctive 'cues', from the reduction in costs in decision-making about how to deal with a crisis situation. If there is a positional good element in consumption of the sacrifices (for example only certain high-status people can eat it at all or alternatively only be allowed the choicest or most magically empowering portions) then it may induce a generalized increase in effort levels leading to higher long-run average community income.

In the here and now, people-eating is a taboo activity and there is also a taboo against eating companionate animals (pets) amongst the majority of non-vegetarians. The widespread prevalence of meat-eating in human societies across cultures and environments suggests that there is a strong latent drive to meet this lust. The general tendency of species to prey on different species rather than consume each other[2] may be explained on a number of (socio)biological grounds. The desire to propagate one's genes should lead to the evolution of tastes *not* to eat one's own species as that would lead to depletion of the gene pool. This drive suggests substantial limitations on the gains from anthropophagic farming and hunting, but it does not eliminate the beneficial eating of the naturally and accidentally deceased, although the risk of disease transmission would put something of a brake on this practice.

There is nothing in neo-classical economics, per se, to rule out cannibalism. It might be argued that it violates the Pareto criterion because those eaten are worse off, or alternatively one might propose the libertarian view quoted at the head of this chapter which would rule it out as the right to life has to be violated if one is going to be eaten. However, if one permits the right to trade away one's own life then this need not be the case; some may freely choose to be eaten if they were adequately compensated. Hence welfare-maximizing cannibalism is a possibility. Compensation could be donated to heirs or enjoyed by those to be eaten in a 'grace period' before death. This grace period occurs in the case of anyone nominated to serve the 'sun king' role of being selected as a sacrifice to fertility gods. Sun kings need not be eaten, but the documentation on the subject suggests that this is a common feature of the role.

In an economy of free exchange, with tradable rights to life, one can envisage the sun king system being instated as a means of Pareto-improving income redistribution. Let us suppose there is a group of very wealthy individuals who exhibit tastes for human flesh as a special delicacy, for rare celebratory occasions, which therefore becomes one of the positional goods of Chapter 5. The income generated by this demand could be pooled to fund a better life for people who would otherwise be poor, which is designated to end at some point through termination for the purpose of being eaten. The individual who volunteers to enter the sun king (or indeed sun queen) pool is making a very similar decision to the person who consumes harmfully addictive drugs or engages in dangerous leisure pursuits (high-speed driving for example), that is the expected date of death is being moved forward in a tradeoff for higher utility in the present. Thus those most likely to be eaten will be those with the highest discount rates, which may even be beneficial to the stability of the economy.

One could argue that cannibalism has declined due to downward shifts in the supply and demand curves, arising from growths in wealth (including the shadow price of time) and technology, leading to the collapse of the market. Symbiotic relations between the ritual culture of the act and its ease of sustaining lead us to the conventional 'civilized' equilibrium of the Akerlof model (see Chapter 2), where the code of not eating people is, in the main, both believed and observed.

CONCLUSION

The sins in the previous three chapters have, at various times, been referred to as ultimate sins, but this is probably premised on the assumption that a 'reasonable' person will not be operating as an agent in matters of life and death on a regular basis. In contemporary thinking, if justifications can be found for ever intervening in matters of life and death (including execution and people-eating) they seem to be decidedly 'economic' ones in that they would be defended on efficiency arguments that derive from the rational choice model.

ENDNOTES

1. The legal opinion in such cases is discussed in an analysis of the hypothetical future crisis faced by the Speluncean explorers in d'Amato (1980).
2. There is evidence on cannibalism in animal species which takes the exception to the rule position for the developed primates.

8. Addiction

INTRODUCTION

> ... the process of weaning one's self from the deep bondage of opium, by many people viewed with despairing eyes, is not only a possible achievement, and one which grows easier in every stage of its progress, but is favoured and promoted by nature in secret ways that could not, without some experience, have been suspected.
>
> [Low (1911, p. 64)]

So wrote Thomas de Quincey, nearly 200 years ago, in his *Confessions of an English Opium Eater*. De Quincey is one of the few (perhaps the only) to have written publicly about the anatomy of drug addiction and the highpoints of the prevalent economic theory of his time. Indeed, shortly after the passage quoted he goes on to explain how working on his critique of Ricardian political economy, which appeared eventually in the form of a Socratic dialogue, helped lift him from the sloth encountered in a serious 'down' phase of his addiction. It might be claimed that addiction is intimately connected with the sin of lust. Lust may lead to addiction which in turn leads to the promotion of further lust in the form of an unbearable craving which may over-ride the rational choices that a person would make in the absence of the drug. The trend in general thinking has been to see addiction as a biochemical misfortune brought on by specific elements contained in a consumption good. Such goods range from those currently seen as non-sinful such as chocolate, tea and coffee (which were not always seen as non-sinful and certainly coffee is still sinful in certain religions) up to the usually legal drugs (alcohol/tobacco) and illegal drugs such as cocaine. Clinically it has been recognized that consumption of a chemical is not necessary for addiction: for example, gambling can exhibit addictiveness due to the brain stimuli from the elements of risk and exaggerated expectations. The most visible recent signs of placing the cause of addiction inside the person rather than the activity are the much publicized internet addiction and the 'sex addiction' first heard of in the therapeutic treatment of movie stars which has now spread into general usage. A good index of the spread of the addiction label to seemingly almost any activity is the following list of addictions from a Christian website (http://www.wholeperson-counseling.org): Alcohol, Sexual, Romance, Exercise, Nicotine, Work, Entertainment, Power, Drugs, Thrills, Food, Gambling, Television, Internet, Religious, Occult, Music, Shopping, Success.

Economists have also gravitated to the position that addiction is more widespread than the mere collection of goods which have identifiable biochemical addictions embedded in them. This has come through another of Gary Becker's contributions to the economic explanation of social behaviour: the 'rational addiction' model which is dealt with below.

Only a few biochemically addictive goods have been fully integrated into the legal market economy. In general they have been subject to toleration interrupted by waves of severe regulatory attempts (or rather sometimes severe policy-maker rhetoric in lieu of action). The typical regulatory framework is to have spatial and temporal zoning with additional person-based exclusions, most commonly age limits. Tea, coffee, alcohol and tobacco were initially popularized by their consumption in designated public spaces such as salons. This model has been extended to the current cannabis market in Amsterdam. Club-, bar- or café-based consumption as the main mode of delivery can also bring informal zoning through fashion, fad and herd elements in consumption. Enforcement agencies may also impose some zoning by selecting certain sectors of the population for more tolerant treatment.

Drinking alcohol to excess has long been regarded as sinful, with the canonical text on this being the tale of Noah, in the book of Genesis, becoming the first drunk, leading him to neglect his duties and thereby become a victim of sloth. Throughout the Bible there are numerous condemnations of the drinking of wine and beer and the idea of being drunk is used as a wider indication of exalted mental states: in Revelations there is a reference to a woman being drunk with the blood of the saints. This extension of the notion of being elated 'artificially' by stimulants has carried on in such ideas as people being drunk with power and so on. One instance of this is the borrowing of the term 'workaholic' from the root of alcoholic and we also hear, jokingly, of chocoholics and so forth. Alcohol has been tolerated in moderation and even encouraged in some religions; that is the mere act of drinking at all has not been seen as sinful.

Alcohol has been present in all parts of the world since time immemorial but tobacco did not establish itself as a pervasive commodity until the seventeenth century, primarily as snuff, or smoked in pipes, in organized social gatherings such as taverns. At this time it was the opinion of doctors that smoking was actually good for the health. Once tobacco had established itself, King James I, various Popes, other leaders and a variety of pamphleteers explicitly condemned snuff [see Corti (1931)] and smoking as sinful. In the late eighteenth century in the military academy in Stuttgart where tobacco was forbidden the pupils called the items they had smuggled in by the name of 'sins' [Corti (1931, p. 219)]. It is not clear exactly why this view was taken. There is no pretext in the religious literature for such condemnation. Much of early anti-tobacco concern arose from the fire hazards created by smokers. This is not a sin per se although, of course, social codes of perceiving an activity as a sin might emerge as a means of internalizing risk externalities. The first wave of attacks on smokers claimed that they looked silly and had lost control of their minds. Essentially then this points to a fall from grace into foolishness, where a person falls short of the potential that God has gifted to them.

It may be that such attacks on those who revel in addictive goods derive from envious resentment by the inhibited of those who are able to escape restrictions into a life of hedonism. Calvin condemned all enjoyment of luxury as sinful, and we might reasonably perceive an addict who is in control of their addiction as leading a life of luxury. Presently there are Christian websites, such as http://www.wholeperson-counseling.org, willing to condemn addictive commodities as tools of the devil and/or evil spirits devised to lure weak individuals from the path of righteousness. Within such thought systems we encounter also the idea that most addictions are sinful because the practitioners are doing something which is 'not natural'.

Ultimately, some of the condemnation of addictive goods as sinful might reflect the fear that work effort, and human capital formation, would fall. Take the case of periodic anxieties about adolescent fixations with arcade games, and now computer games. If these were pathologically addictive, in the sense of total control failure, then education would be neglected. The 'loss of output' concern has been variously voiced about smoking, heavy drinking and new fads in gambling and illegal drugs when they are introduced. However, once a new addiction establishes itself on the menu of social vices and demonstrates that it is not a threat to the social and moral order, we then enter the phase where it becomes ripe for sumptuary taxation and/or revenues from the sale of state monopolies. Commentators such as Goethe [Corti (1931, p. 218)] also condemned it as a waste of money which could be put to better use. However, as we have emphasized throughout this book, the trend of twentieth century economics gave short shrift to such a view. Rational choice theory, in mainstream microeconomics, rules out judgements about any type of consumption being more useful than any other unless there are serious negative externalities. Macroeconomic arguments have also been found, in terms of multiplier effects, that far from being wasteful such consumption is job-creating [Chase Econometrics (1977) presents estimates of this for the tobacco industry]. Certainly in Anglo-American culture there is a strong perception of smoking as harmful, sinful and the producers in the sector, as being sinners. Nevertheless, an analysis of the differential rates of taxation by state, in the USA, showed that there was some degree of tradeoff by legislators between the employment-creation effects and health-damaging effects [Cameron (1989b)]. States with high job creation from the industry levied lower taxes, but increases in the rate of smoking-related diseases were associated with higher rates.

DEMAND

Once the theory of demand had been rigorously formulated, economists were still prepared to allow exceptions for addictive commodities. If individuals were addicted, in the total loss of control sense, then the good would exhibit a very low price elasticity of demand. This might seem to be supported by the legacy of many centuries of failed attempts to control addictive goods by taxation and punishments [Corti (1931)]. From the public finance point of view then addictive goods would become very attractive items for sumptuary taxation which would, in essence, become a means of redistributing rents from producers and/or addicts to the rest of society. Many economists, working in the crime area, have shown a particular interest in heroin demand [for references and summary see Maynard & Wagstaff (1988, ch. 5)], coming to the conclusion that there are vertical segments on the demand curve over a fairly wide range of prices, but when prices are relatively 'high' or 'low' we switch to a conventional demand curve. At the low-price region this happens because the addict is tempted by income and substitution effects to allow their maintenance dose to drift up to the new customary level. In the high-price region the demand falls mainly because of income effects: that is, the addict is now expending so much of their resources on procuring the drug that they need to switch towards other goods. The proposal of an 'extreme seeking' approach [Barthold & Hochman (1988), Averett & Hochman (1994)], premised on indifference curves with concave segments, tries to provide a foundation for the vertical segment in terms of individuals having 'preferences that are structurally inconsistent, over some range, with the conventional axioms of demand theory'. These extreme seekers have indifference curves which are negative, as in the conventional case, but with concave and convex segments so that marginal rates of substitution are increasing in some ranges. This generates corner solutions; i.e., in a two-good model only the addictive good is consumed and it is extremely unresponsive to relative full price changes. The segmented demand curve described above, where two conventional demand curves are joined together by a vertical section, can be linked to the general dynamic model of consumer demand proposed in the pioneering 1960s econometric work by Houthakker & Taylor (1970) who applied it to data for alcohol and tobacco. Here consumption depends on a 'stock of habits', which is a function of past consumption and the depreciation rate in the stock of habits.

In the last ten years or so the myopic approach has almost completely dropped out of studies of addiction demand as the 'rational addiction' approach has become the dominant research paradigm. Rational addiction is the term used by Becker [see Becker & Murphy (1988), Becker (1992)]. It is important to return, at this point, to the issue of definitions of rationality. The work reviewed in the previous paragraph was an attempt to explain seemingly irrational behaviour (people being less well off than they could be) in terms of them being trapped in some kind of inertia in the manner of the X-inefficient agents of Chapter 4. The decision-makers are still assumed to be operating in a rational manner, so it would not be strictly correct to call these 'irrational' addiction models. The key difference in the Becker models is that the addicts have a much higher degree of foresight (indeed in the formal models it is perfect foresight) in the shape of a willingness to act on the basis of the knowledge that their habits are not a 'given' but are rather endogenous to the level of consumption. For what it is worth, this seems to be exactly what Thomas de Quincey is saying in the quote with which we started this chapter. Accounts of the withdrawal problems of his contemporary Samuel Taylor Coleridge are not so sanguine, but it could be claimed that the latter's torture was due, in large part, to a lack of knowledge on the nature and operations of opium.

Becker & Murphy (1988, pp. 675–6) make no distinction between goods in terms of their pharmacological properties as 'people get addicted not only to alcohol, cocaine and cigarettes but also to work, eating, music, television, their standard of living, other people, religion, and many other activities'.

This is a very similar list to that on the Christian website given above and it chimes with recent trends in psychiatric practice. The crucial feature of addiction, in this sense, is that the marginal utility at a point in time depends on consumption in other periods; it does not matter whether this interdependency has a chemical component or is simply learned habitual behaviour. A fully rational individual plans for the sequential dynamics brought about by the intertemporal non-separability of consumption arising from addiction. The distinctive feature of the model is that, under certain assumptions, it gives rise to a linear demand equation in which price, income-led consumption and lag consumption enter. This is a general formulation which nests the myopic Houthakker–Taylor model as a special case in which the coefficient on the lead term is zero. It is also easy to work out the estimated discount rate from such a model by applying the relevant formula to the coefficients on the lag and lead terms. These types of equation are now commonplace in health economics and general economics journals, and we even have the spectacle [see Chaloupka et al. (1999)] of behavioural psychologists using baboons, rats, etc. to estimate rational addiction equations from laboratory studies where they provide addictive drugs to these animals. Many studies in the Chaloupka volume review the same evidence on the range of magnitudes of the own-price elasticity of drug use and also present their own. Broadly speaking the overall impression is of a figure in the –0.5 to –1.0 range.

An interesting, but neglected, question is the differential addictiveness of women. As smoking in conjunction with the contraceptive pill greatly increases the risk of heart attack or stroke [Jacobson (1986)], and babies of smokers, in developed countries, weigh on average 200 grams less at birth

[World Bank (1993)] than those of non-smokers, one would anticipate that women have greater incentives not to become smokers. This generally applies to other addictions also. In the UK, female smoking (measured in cigarettes per day per adult) rose steadily from 1956 to 1973 against a background of fairly stable male smoking rates. This took place in the context of a general anti-smoking environment. Reports of 1953 and 1962, from the Royal College of Physicians, drew considerable attention to the health–smoking link. In 1965, broadcasting of cigarette advertisements, on electronic media, was banned. These measures were not followed by any decline in female tobacco consumption but rather the reverse. Whilst per capita female cigarette consumption fell after 1973, the fall was less dramatic than that for men. From 1976 to 1994 the percentage of adult males smoking fell from 48 per cent to 28 per cent whilst the corresponding fall for females was from 38 per cent to 26 per cent [ASH (1995)]. US experience of trends in male–female smoking has been similar to the UK; in 1955–1966, against a background of anti-smoking information, male smoking fell whilst that of females rose. In contrast, in Taiwan only 3 per cent of women smoke, despite a heavy growth of advertising from multinational firms and a strong male smoking habit, whilst in South Africa, smoking amongst women has been low because of 'cultural traditions' [Mandela (1993, p. 99)]. There does not appear to be any country in the world where adult female tobacco consumption outstrips that of males to a significant degree.

Evidence on differential, by gender, price elasticities in cigarette smoking is somewhat mixed. The evidence on male–female differential responsiveness, from work on other addictive goods, is inconclusive. Some studies of the demand for alcohol exhibit a larger price elasticity for women [Kendell, de Romanie & Ritson (1983), Kenkel (1993)] and a study of 1834 injecting heroin users in Oslo [Bretteville-Jensen (1999)] finds that the female sample is more price-responsive than the male and also has a higher drug intake level. In contrast, a study using the discount rate criterion in a rational addiction approach to illegal drugs [Pacula (1997)] finds women to be more addictive. To further confuse the picture, a recent study by Saffer & Chaloupka (1999) using the National Household Survey of Drug Abuse finds few significant male–female differences in price responsiveness for cocaine, alcohol, marijuana and heroin.

Some additional results are available, in the econometric work on non-price factors, which seem to imply that women are more addictive than men in terms of responding to health scares [Atkinson & Skegg (1973)]. Leigh (1995) finds a deterrent effect of anti-smoking ordinances (bans on smoking in public places) on the probability of smoking, although Chaloupka (1992) using a similar analysis finds no effect of these ordinances on the amount that women smoked. One econometric study [Viscusi (1992)] using telephone survey data for 1985 deals with the issue of sex differences in the perceived risk of smoking. He finds that the perception of health risk from smoking is higher for women (p. 73), which implies they should have higher price elasticities and be more likely to give up, in the face of other deterrents, if there is no sex differential in addiction.

Clinical studies of individual smokers indicate that women have much greater difficulty quitting than men, suggesting that they may be more addicted. Jacobson (1986) reports that the Royal College of Physicians in the UK, in 1983, found that it was twice as difficult for women to remain committed non-smokers. Gender differences in quitting are also well documented in the USA [Pierce et al. (1989)]. A study in California in 1990 [Kaplan et al. (1993)] found that, amongst former smokers, women were more vulnerable than men to relapse in the second year after quitting, although there were no differences in quit difficulty *ceteris paribus*.

The main message of rational addiction models is that the old-fashioned view that addict consumption will not be very responsive to prices is misguided. This has the corollary that revenues from sumptuary taxes will be very sensitive to tax increases. We should also expect that high-level rationality should mean addicted consumers will be very responsive to anti-use ordinances and (valid) health information which is provided to them at low cost. Although Becker appeared to soften the Chicagoan insistence on treating tastes as given, in his well-known Nancy Schwartz lecture [see Becker (1992)], he still seems to treat the non-addicted as fundamentally similar to the addicted, except that some random variable has caused them to hold off falling into the 'trap' of addiction. He remarks that 'demand for addictive goods tends to be bifurcated: people either consume a lot, or they abstain because they anticipate that they will become "hooked" if they begin to consume. Smoking is a good example of bifurcation, for 70 per cent of adults in the United States do not smoke, while persons who do smoke generally consume at least half a pack a day' (ibid., p. 329). One problem with such observations is that the only reliable statistics available are from legalized goods and it may be that cannabis consumption, for example, in many countries is not bifurcated as extremely as that for cigarettes.

In recent presentations Becker, and those who follow his line, argue that addicts may lower their lifetime utility because the rational addiction model is predicated only on a degree of 'foresight' rather than omniscience. Supposedly the failure to optimize lifetime discounted utility comes about through an endogenous discount rate whereby substance abusers acquire an unfortunately inappropriate discount rate because of their substance consumption. This must surely lead to the bifurcation remarked on above. There is a worry about the distinction between cause and effect when we deal with the issue of bifurcation and addiction. Can a product be addictive and not lead to a bifurcated

demand? Presumably it can if there is a 'high' level of consumption for everyone (a rectangular distribution) or a spread with a peak such as a normal distribution. Addiction is a somewhat pejorative value-laden label (despite Becker's
claims on beneficial addictions) and it seems that a social code of regarding a
good as 'addictive' is unlikely if it is widespread in usage. Nevertheless, much
consumption has a thick tail of low/zero users and an opposing tail of heavy
users. No doubt we can all agree that fine-cut marmalade is not an addictive
good, even though it probably has a bifurcated user profile in many countries.
But how do we arrive at this conclusion? Is it on intuitive grounds that
marmalade does not lead to endogenous changes in the discount rate? If so is
this not merely derived from the knowledge that no addictive chemicals are
present and that no serious health damage is likely from 'high' usage? If addictive chemicals present in goods are forcing a person into sub-optimal choices
by altering the discount rate then the word rational is surely being somewhat
strained.

Not surprisingly, Becker's approach has met with criticism from well outside
the 'hard core' of American economics [e.g. Tomer (1996, 1998), Cameron
(2000a)] and from slightly nearer home [Akerlof (1991), Winston (1980),
Gruber (2001)]. Most critiques have to stop short of claiming that addicts are
totally irrational lest they cease to be regarded as 'economics' in the first place.
The theory gap is filled with some notion of meta-preferential choice or a modi-
fication of Festinger's cognitive dissonance [Festinger (1957) as treated in Gilad
et al. (1987)]. A time-honoured problem arises with the alternative approaches,
viz. however much more plausible they may seem, it is difficult to operational-
ize them. A number of papers have sought to refine and extend the rational
addiction model to enhance its resistance to criticism [Orphanides & Zevros
(1995), Coutoyannis & Jones (1999), Jones (1999), Suranovic, Goldfarb &
Leonard (1999)]. In general such refinements of rational addiction models tend
to take the route of incorporating adjustment costs into the process in the pursuit
of greater realism. For example, Orphanides & Zevros model the demand-side
process entry to addiction markets as a stochastic process so that people can
become accidentally 'hooked'. Ultimately the rational addiction model is just an
extension of the principles of discounting utility to a situation where some goods
exhibit temporal complementarity whilst others do not. It has certainly encountered considerable problems in estimation. Becker, Grossman & Murphy (1994)
gave highly statistically significant results, albeit with an implausibly high
discount rate in terms of 'rational' behaviour given that the implicit discount rate
in daily decision-making is usually under 15 per cent. Some studies have even
found negative discount rates.

An alternative approach is to focus on a purely static conceptualization
drawing on the more behavioural approaches to choice discussed in Chapter 2.
This takes into account the risk and social context factors that pure rational

choice models neglect. Initially I shall assume that the good has biological addiction properties, i.e. it contains chemicals that are directly delivered in the process of using it. Behavioural addictions with no chemical content will be discussed afterwards.

Let there be two goods: one (X) which is 'normal' in the sense that it does not deliver any chemical alterations to the brain state nor is it imbued with any learned components; and another (Z) which delivers chemical 'hits' to the brain, through the bloodstream, and also provides utility from being a constituent of 'scripts' (M) [Van Raaij (1990) pp. 168–9)]. A script is a scenario of interlocking consumption elements which have a reinforcing quality. We can distinguish between private and social scripts. In the private script one might be drinking or smoking alone as a reward for completing a solo work task, or simply because one finds an alcoholic drink relieving on a hot day, or to alleviate feelings of loneliness or tension. In the social script, the tension and excitement of the presence of other people are factors in generating the desired level of alcohol consumption. The social script element is enhanced by the impact of alcohol on lowering inhibition or cigarettes in easing the process of conversation for a stressed or nervous individual. The basic idea of the script is that the image of the consumer becomes intertwined with the experiences which are temporally joint with the consequences of the bodily absorption of the relevant chemicals. Over a process of time, these mental associations (or imaging) may be a non-separable element of the utility from the psychopharmacological processes. The mental process of association may engender brand loyalty as the style of bottle, name of the product, etc. can potentially become part of the overall pleasure.

The individual utility function is:

$$U = U(H, S, X, W) \tag{8.1}$$

where H = 'hits', S is the volume of 'scripts' in which Z features, W is the perceived stock of health. There is assumed to be an exogenously given menu of scripts which the individual can work his/her way through. The delivery of scripts, hits and health is through the following production functions:

$$H = H(M, S) \tag{8.2}$$

$$W = W(Z, X, k) = \&(k)W(Z, X) + [1 - \&(k)]W(X) \tag{8.3}$$

where

$$\&(k) = \begin{cases} 1, & k \geq k^* \\ 0, & k < k^* \end{cases}$$

k is a filter variable to represent cognitive dissonance [Gilad et al. (1987)]. If $k*$ is exceeded by the flow of messages, indicating that drinking is a serious health risk or anti-drink driving messages, then it will be curtailed as the switchover in Eq. (8.3) works through Eq. (8.1). This model is similar to the 'flip-flop' utility function formulation of Winston (1980), who emphasizes the problem of self-control, but does so without incorporating hits or scripts.

The '$k*$' filter will be exceeded by events which make the risk more 'salient', such as witnessing at first hand the details of drink-related deaths, illnesses and accidents. If there is a switch in perceptions, the smoker could simply reduce alcohol unit intake by drinking less volume per se, or for example moving to weaker lagers/beers. The market has an incentive, as Winston (1980) points out, to provide devices to assist self-control. Hence the emergence of 'light' cigarettes, lower ethanol content and even alcohol-free lagers. Clearly such devices cannot change the underlying preference structure viz. the latent demand function for hits and scripts. Thus there is the problem of backsliding. The smoker who is apprehensive about personal health could backslide to an old higher danger brand or stick with the 'safe' brand and consume more to keep up the steady state dosage level of psychopharmacological effects. There is a possible distinction here in terms of scripts, that is volume of units of the addictive good taken is mediated by the social situation. For someone who manages a switch to a safer brand (or perhaps type of alcohol), whilst staying within a social context where the relevance of chemical stimulation is low, it may be more likely that pure alcohol intake can be reduced compared with a private drinker or one whose social scripts are heavily dependent on the psychopharmacological element, e.g. to overcome shyness, stress, lose inhibition and so forth. The script for an addictive good may be a private 'escape valve' response to social pressures occasioning stress, such as the reported case of very low-income single mothers maintaining cigarette expenditures to cope with stress [ASH (1995)].

A major determinant of k is general attitudes to risk management and health. Although there are a plethora of extremely sophisticated models of decision-making under risk [Viscusi (1992), Machina (1989)] they are not greatly relevant here as we would see risk as not being the subject of marginal responses but rather embedded in a switching of levels of risk (high/low) through the filter.

What of addictions not delivered in direct chemical form from the good? In many cases these have low levels of social interaction in the traditional sense of face-to-face contact. Many people use internet services, pornography, gyms, go shopping and so on in a socialized context, but the 'problem' users who would be labelled addicts tend to have a mainly private repertoire of scripts. Leaving aside maladjustment neuroses, such as bulimia and anorexia, the defining characteristic of these addictions is low direct health risk/low sociability and the importance of a fantasy element. We can illustrate this in terms of the Becker–Lancaster goods characteristics/time allocation model of household addiction. The aggregate fantasy production function can be written as:

Fantasy output = f(time, fantasy-related goods, fantasy energy
supplied, imagination, random error)   (8.4)

Individuals may substitute between different fantasies according to the relevant prices and shadow prices. In the specific case of pornography the goods are magazines, videos or subscriptions to web pages, all of which may be fairly time-intensive if fantasy output is to be created. For an internet fantasist, other than a porn user, posing as somebody else or the cultivation of some fixation with the life of 'star' personalities is the fantasy output.[1] Gambling and shopping escalated to obsessive levels may reflect fantasies of being incredibly wealthy.

So far this is just putting the commonplace into economic garb, but is there any economic logic which suggests that such a set-up has addictive tendencies given that there is no direct intake of chemicals involved? Fantasy goods may be very time-intensive, relative to other goods, which would seem to go against high-level consumption unless a person has enforced 'idle' time available to them through some constraints of market failure or, in the opposite case, high levels of income. On the other hand fantasy may have the unusual (for a consumer choice model) property of substantial zones of increasing marginal utility, and better still (or worse still depending on your point of view) increasing returns to some of the fantasy production function inputs. This strange effect has been previously remarked in a piece on collecting by Troilo (1999), which also points out that early research on collectors tended to paint them in a stigmatized light as persons with problems of mental adjustment, as in the traditional stereotype of addicts. The collector may have an increasing marginal utility for items in the collection if the sequence of acquisition is appropriately structured. Fantasizing may have a similar quality in that there is a complicated synergic and lexicographic relationship between the goods used that creates zones of increasing marginal utility. Even if we don't want to call this kind of thing addiction it will look like addiction from an empirical point of view and also in terms of Becker's model.

Before moving on to supply, I briefly consider some perspectives on addiction from outside the rational choice economics model or the 'pure sin' concept found in many religions. Humanistic psychologist Eric Fromm treated addiction as derivative of neurotic cravings:

To crave that which is harmful is the very essence of mental sickness. Every neurosis thus confirms the fact that pleasure can be in contradiction to man's real interest. [Fromm (1944, p. 180)]

We should add that to crave that which is not harmful may also be symptomatic of an underlying sickness. Postage stamps are not harmful per se but we
might still be concerned about the welfare of someone whose life is dominated
by collecting them. Neurotic cravings are seen as different from 'normal'
tastes. Becker ignores the process leading to cravings, treating them as a by-
product of a standard rational choice process. In mainstream economics it does
not make sense to say that 'pleasure is in contradiction to one's real interest'
as one's real interest is the pursuit of pleasure.

Some therapists [see e.g. Mahony & Waller (1992, pp. 173–5)] regard
addiction as emanating from a narcissistic disorder. Narcissistic conflicts arise
where an individual blocks or internalizes aggressive impulses towards love
objects under pressure from a frustrating environment. Such feelings are
trapped in the non-verbal stage of development and may require non-verbal
(therapeutic) regression to the stage of fixation in order that they be explored.
In terms of multiple preference models, such individuals in normal circumstances are not able to be overtly conscious of the 'self' which is associated
with the ideal set of preferences. Their experience is one of conflict between
actual preferences and the knowledge that they are not the preferred state. A
cycle of addiction is here different from in the Becker model. It would represent a build-up of tension and aggression spilling over into frustration at
inability to discover and enforce 'true meta-preferences'. In the psychothera-
peutic literature, problem gamblers are generally seen as suffering from
neurotic aggression [see e.g. Bergler (1970)]. They do not choose to gamble
on the basis of maximizing subjective expected utility, rather they secretly
wish to lose as a confirmation of their own failure to get what they want in life.
This reflects a failure to escape from the mind state of early childhood where
every wish is granted.

In the case of neurotic behaviour, or simply more 'normal range' stress
responses, we see addiction (whether it be to gambling, eating or drugs) in the
sense of an inability to break out of a cycle of activity which would not be
freely chosen as the preferred pattern if the individual were in full control of
their choices. Those deemed to be neurotic, or in some sense disordered, could
be absolved from sin on the grounds that they are void of the capacity to
choose to be bad. The 'rational addicts' of current economic analysis could be
sinners in their own eyes if they are trading off intertemporal pleasure management against some negative utility from the negative sin capital[2] they have
inherited. But with this observation we come round in a circle as it seems to
place us back in the myopic world of Houthakker–Taylor demand models and
discontinuous heroin demand schedules. The self-adjudicated sinner could

surely obtain higher lifetime utility if they were to invest in negative sin capital reduction. If they do not then we seem to be in the X-inefficiency world of prohibitive transactions costs, excessive risk perceptions and so on. Indeed, one of the strategies of organized religions is to imprint a heavy emphasis on the negative utility of trips to purgatory and hell on the mind of the individual in order to make a total exit from the belief system somewhat problematic.

SUPPLY AND PRICE

The same factors would be expected to influence the supply of addictive goods and services as others, the main one being the rate of return in the sector. Differences between supply in this and other sectors are mainly due to the regimes of regulation or tolerance that are in place as is also the case for prostitution, as discussed in Chapter 10. The degree of legality and regulation influences the amount of risk attached to expected returns and the competitive nature of the industry along with the size distribution of firms. The fully legal sale of addictive goods would seem naturally inclined towards high levels of sectoral concentration, as addictive goods seem to offer scale economies in advertising and production. This is borne out by the highly oligopolistic nature of the alcohol and tobacco industries.

It is hard to think of a case where other allegedly addictive commodities have the same orbit of commercial freedom as the general run of goods. People may claim that since 1996 Amsterdam has had an overtly legal cannabis trading economy (as opposed to the prior de facto legal tolerance) and that the more 'liberal' economies have variously given legal status to alcohol, tobacco and some areas of pornography. However, in all these cases the growth of the size of the industry is hampered by lack of full access to means for expanding demand, such as advertising, etc. Control and tolerance of illegal goods seem to push individual firm size towards being small in these kinds of circumstances.

Illegality, however, sets in motion a number of factors enhancing any innate tendency to concentration. There are entry barriers of illegality deriving from the risk of the enterprise. Larger organizations benefit from scale economies in a number of ways:

i.   being able to absorb costs of fines and prison sentences when punished;
ii. preventing these costs arising in the first place through bribery and corruption;
iii. preventing these costs arising in the first place through camouflaging the illegal activity and its profits by laundering them in legal enterprises;
iv. preventing competition from rivals via intimidation or episodic resorts to entry level 'limit' pricing.

The role of organized crime in the supply of drugs, gambling and pornography was first brought to the attention of economists by Thomas Schelling (1971) and, with more provocative policy-oriented rhetoric, by Nobel prize winner James Buchanan (1973), which we consider further below. This kind of work has been largely speculative until the pioneering work by Chicago economist Steven Levitt and sociologist Sudhir Alladi Venkatesh (1998), who looked at the account books of a street gang over a four-year period largely involved in crack cocaine in the eastern United States. The structure of the firm was highly organized. It had a leader and three officers, followed by 25 to 75 'foot soldiers', with an additional 60 to 200 rank-and-file members who paid dues to the gang in return for protection and a reliable supply of drugs. The gang was one of about 100 in a multi-state organization. Like franchisees, each gang paid the parent group about 20 per cent of its take for exclusive rights to its turf. The rank and file earned substantially less than minimum wages and the leader made what would be a reasonable middle-level executive salary [alternative, and sometimes contradictory, evidence on the earnings from drug dealing can be found in Cairncross (2001)]. Levitt and Venkatesh also discerned textbook firm-style behaviour in the form of pricing below cost during periods of gang warfare. Such commercially archetypal behaviour is likely to be even more pronounced in cases where multiple products are dealt with and has often been documented in organized crime research without being pinned down to testable economic hypotheses.

EXTERNALITIES AND POLICY

With an addictive good there can be an epidemic in which associated externalities spiral to dangerous proportions. This accounts for the moral panics over self-inflicted health risks and danger to the health of others via dangerous use of transportation, burning, infectious diseases and so on, that sweep nations when new addictions first float to the surface of public consciousness.

Ironically many of these social *bétes noires* start life as wondrous new health-giving treatments. Tobacco smoking first hit mass world markets in the context of the belief that it was beneficial to health and protective from dangerous infections. As recently as 1992 the drug MDMA, soon to become night clubbers' current favourite drug Ecstasy, was being touted as a drug which would heal human relationships and make 'us all feel the way we wish we were anyway' [Albery (1992, p. 45)]. Earlier LSD, first synthesized in 1943, was consumed as a restorative and enhancing form of therapy with its advance in consumption coming from lofty-minded and elite persons such as Aldous Huxley and Cary Grant.

Positive effects are still claimed for some legal addictions by labour econ-omists. In a number of papers [e.g. Heien (1996), French & Zarkin (1995), Zarkin et al. (1998), Cameron & Ward (2000)] a statistically significant posi-tive relationship was found between earnings and alcohol consumption, for moderate drinking generally around a 5–7 per cent differential over the non-drinker. The returns to drinking for women are generally found to be statisti-cally insignificant. Drinking may be a proxy for other personality traits which do not have similar effects for men and women's respective earnings: for example recent papers find [see Bowles, Gintis & Osborne (2001)] that measures of aggression have significant positive effects on male earnings but significant negative effects on female earnings.

I turn now to the more widely enumerated negative effects of addictive goods. A number of studies come to the conclusion that smoking lowers the hourly wage rate by an estimated 4–7 per cent [see e.g. Levine (1997)]. This gap could be due to many things, such as discrimination against smokers, risk-preference variation in that people who smoke and drink may have greater risk-preference than others, and lower productivity due to health damage and/or interrupted work patterns. Addictions are also blamed for mental health damage and social ills, such as crime pursued to feed the addictions and infringements on the welfare of children. Pornography, although not a deliv-ery mechanism of addictive chemicals, is generally attacked by its opponents in terms of the risk to children and the possible third-party damage to others from the depraved mental state of users. This is reflected in legislation which has generally been on material which 'tends to deprave' rather than specific items due to the difficulties of defining pornography from justifiable 'erotica' [see O'Toole (1998)]. Early concerns over pornography's effects culminated in the 1968 appointment of the United States President's Commission on Obscenity and Pornography which was charged with understanding of study and testimony, the Commission concluded that pornography had no discernibly harmful effects on society. Similar inquiries in the UK have come to the same conclusion [Howitt & Cumberbatch (1990)]. Those who are found to be violent criminals are not generally particularly imaginative, so there is little indication that porn has the power to inflame them beyond their inherent danger levels. The direction of the evidence points towards 'the safety valve' benefits being dominant. Nonetheless in staunch religions, pornography (including all that might be deemed erotica) would be condemned, whatever the evidence, on the grounds of being both lust manifestations and inappro-priate uses of the images of those who should keep their bodies private.

Conversely, as a sin becomes or stays a sin in an evolutionary rational choice economics model because of its negative effects then the question arises as to what types of policies can be implemented to optimally regulate addictive goods. The liberal utopia where we can engineer a 'good' society, where detrimental stresses from work, family and so on are absent, and so individuals can engage in whatever dangerous pursuits they like, will never come. So the pragmatic issue is, in crude terms, legalization versus a highly criminalized system where government bureaux are seen to strive to stamp out addiction reinforced by 'free' dispensation of education and information on health and other risks. Such a black and white dichotomy is an abstraction for didactic purposes. The blurring of the distinction between legal and illegal is explored in more detail when we get to Chapter 10 which deals exclusively with prostitution.

Economists operating out of fairly similar systems of thought and ideology have, paradoxically, come to the opposite positions of broad advocacy of legalization and the maintenance of an illegal system.[3] Rational addiction might be thought to drive us powerfully down the road to legalisation as rational addicts are best left without paternalistic restrictions on their freedom of choice. Further, rational dealers in harmful addictions may have powerful incentives not to drive their customers over the edge. Providers of illegal substances can potentially be under as much pressure as the dealers in legal goods (see Chapter 6) to maintain a good reputation, particularly in view of the uncertainty surrounding the quality of the product. Small numbers oligopoly may also, but not automatically, enhance any such pressures. Milton Friedman (1972) put forward a concise case for the controlled legalization even of the most feared 'hard' drugs on the basic economic grounds of net benefit from reduced health costs, law enforcement outlays and so on [see also Stevenson (1997) for a review of this claim with commentaries from the opposing view]. In the case of organic drugs, as opposed to laboratory 'designer' drugs, the enforcement costs may well escalate due to the difficulty of detecting and deterring importation (via low-income, high-risk-taking 'mules') from countries with no viable alternative in terms of agricultural crops. So, for Friedman the case for legality comes from a simple pragmatic cost–benefit analysis: he carries with him no residues of his own value judgements on what is, or is not, sinful. In 1991 he restated his case firmly:

> There is no chance whatsoever in the near future or the distant future of getting what I would really like, which is a free market. As a first step on the right road, I believe the right thing to do is to treat drugs, currently illegal drugs, the same way you treat alcohol and tobacco. Not because that's the best way, not because that's the ideal arrangement, but because it's an arrangement that people know, that is in existence.

Commentators from the 'rational addiction' perspective would no doubt make the same claim about their thoughts and yet they significantly do not discuss the legality issue or, when they broach it, veer towards the view that the statistical results imply that legalization of drugs is undesirable because it would lead to large increases in the consumption of drugs as the nominal and 'hedonic' (risk- and quality-adjusted) price would fall [see the contributions in Chaloupka et al. (1999)]. However, if addicts are rational then large consumption is surely their own free choice not to be subject to paternalistic intervention by others. Arguments may be made that externalities of dangerous proportions would follow from legalization, but no one has yet demonstrated that they exceed, in value, the savings identified by Friedman. Currently, increasing emphasis seems to be laid on endogenous discount rates in rational addiction models and this could be another plank in anti-legalization thought. Yet it seems to take us to the point of claiming that addicts are not rational if they have harmful discount rates, in the sense of lowering them to X-inefficient welfare levels, caused by their addictive consumption. This also begs the question of how price elasticities could remain relatively high for serious addicts with the distorted high discount rates. We should also point out that estimates of price elasticities available are from a restricted range of observed demand curve positions, with the exception of the experimental studies in Chaloupka et al. (1999). These may back up the claims of early rational addiction work, but it is highly debatable if we can base public policy on the rational choice of baboons and rats being force-fed hard drugs.

James Buchanan (1973) advocates tolerance of an illegal situation rather than controlled legalization. His premise is the same as Friedman's:

> Resources involved in enforcement may be freed for the production of alternative goods and services that are positively valued; the taxpayer has additional funds that he may spend on alternative publicly provided or privately marketed goods and services. (p. 402)

Further, he produces the economic version of 'two rights do make a wrong', which we discussed in Part II, in the 'theory of the second best', to come to the conclusion that organized crime can be beneficial. He pastiches Adam Smith's remark about the irrelevance of altruism by butchers in determining the social efficiency of the meat market as follows:

> It is not from the public-spiritedness of the leaders of the Cosa Nostra that we should expect to get a reduction in the crime rate but from their regard for their own self-interests. (p. 407)

Buchanan's basic point is that criminal monopoly is good because the monopolist will restrict output thereby restricting the external 'bads' associated with it. He makes sweeping remarks about the pervasiveness of negative externalities from various types of sin, but mainly prostitution. From this, he arrives at an asymmetrical, if not downright inconsistent, position of advocating tolerance of criminal monopolies, but *not* promotion of them, by law enforcement authorities. This must then be the claim that the situation at the time of writing was a Pareto optimum, or else it is a reflection of a fundamental Panglossian belief about American institutions, in which case it seems to be an instance of the importation of non-essential ritual elements to the rational choice analytic framework as noticed by Arrow and discussed earlier in Chapter 2.

CONCLUSION

Addiction has been another site to be conquered in the ever-expanding empire built by rational choice economists of the Chicago persuasion. Ostensibly their work neither condones nor condemns it as sinful. However, with the exception of Friedman, few economists are willing to countenance widespread tolerance of addictions. Paternalistic and externality-based arguments inevitably buttress this position. Perhaps innocently, orthodox economists are inevitably biased towards punitive responses to problems of incompatibility of behaviour in society due to their rigorous schooling in the metaphor of the market and its (in an ideal world) efficient price signals. The whole of the economics of crime emerged in this way to advocate increasing the likelihood of detecting and punishing criminals and/or rises in the size of punishment as means of solving the problem. This kind of thought is consonant with much of the implicit thought framework of society in general, although there we find added layers of explicit moralizing. The advanced capitalist economies constantly replay the rhetoric of 'wars' on drugs, various types of porn and so on with media portrayal of the two poles of the sinning spectrum: the weak and feeble-minded 'victim' in thrall to the sinister, malevolent dark forces of organized crime intent on sacrificing moral considerations to the lure of profit.

ENDNOTES

1. The internet is full of many sites which seem fixated with what various people had for break-fast and all other conceivable *minutiae* of their lives.
2. Positive sin capital might exist of course. Binge drinking is known to be not just a simple bifurcated consumption phenomenon of the type Becker adduces to support his model. It is not randomly distributed across demographic and cultural groups: for example, it is notably concentrated in Roman Catholic and Celtic persons. In a purely formal theoretical model it is entirely possible that such persons have a higher level of utility because of the feelings of sin, as the guilt and recrimination might make them better off than if they were uninhibited in the first place. This links back to the discussions of Marcuse and Lyotard, in Chapter 4, on the possible inability of humans to find true rational choice in a condition of freedom from conditioning.
3. Granted the 'public choice' school of economists which Buchanan leads differs from the Chicago economics of Friedman and Becker in terms of the emphasis on non-market processes and institutions. Nevertheless from the perspective of anyone outside economics they are coming from roughly the same place.

9. Adultery

You know of course, that the Tasmanians who never committed adultery are now extinct.

W. Somerset Maugham, *The Bread Winner*, iii

PUNISHMENTS

Adultery is forbidden in the ten commandments of the Bible which proposes stern punishments for adulterers. Punishments are a partial index of the sinfulness with which a transgression is viewed. Table 9.1 is a summary of some historical instances of punishment for 'adultery'. The term adultery is used, for the moment, although the terminology of the act is discussed further below.

In modern times, in liberal economies, the main punishment for adultery has been divorce instigated by the 'victim' as this has been one of the major grounds for divorce to the extent that it was faked when divorce was hard to obtain and the partners wanted to separate for other reasons. Although legal punishments have been rescinded, in liberal economies, the implicit punishments remain of private justice from the wronged individual in the form of revenge assaults and property destruction. Further, in the spirit of the models of Chapter 2, there is the use of social exclusion to punish code (fidelity) non-observance. The evidence below suggests that adultery is widespread, however it is not approved of as reasonable or normal behaviour in most circumstances. For example, standard male/female 'country and western' duet song 'Dark End of the Street' admits that the act is a sin and that both parties know it is wrong and yet they are unable to desist. In terms of the Akerlof model then practice conflicts with the stated code of conduct (for example the wedding service has not been respecified to allow for the likelihood of adultery). This suggests that the punishments have weakened. Social and legal punishments give us some insight as to why the activity has been frowned upon.

Individuals are programmed to revenge acts for sound biological reasons as they may have actual or intended genetic investments in the adulterous partner. Apart from potentially losing their breeding partner, the cuckolded male might also end up wasting resources on someone else's progeny. The granting of a divorce serves to somewhat defuse the disruptive power of revenge which

Table 9.1 Punishments for adultery[1]

Punishment	Period/source	Notes
Man pays cuckolded husband varying amounts	Medieval England/Germany [Alamans & Franks]	In England man pays marriage price
Prison	Medieval England	Only if adulterer is a holy man with the sentence rising with his position
Flog × 100	Koran	
Whipping and wearing the letters AD	Plymouth, New England, 1641 [Ecclesiastical Records]	
Woman is driven into the street in a loin cloth for the public to punish	Chaldea	
Nose slitting	Roman Law	And the woman is divorced but the man is not
Nose removal	Virgil's *Aeneid*	
Justifiable homicide by the cuckolded	Plato's *Laws*	
The brother or father of the woman involved in adultery had the right to kill the offender	Visigoths	
Burning	Byzantium	
Death by stoning	Deuteronomy – Bible John – Bible	
Killing	Papua	
Killed and eaten	Bataks	

Note: If no explicit comment is made on the matter it appears that men and women received the same punishment.

Sources: Sumner (1906), Laiou (1993), Isaacs (1993).

could (cp. the discussion on lust in Chapter 4) undermine economic activity, as resources would be wasted in contesting property rights in sexual partners. Under the capitalist mode of production, the property right was assigned to the man with the main burden of costs of adultery if detected falling on the woman. There is of course the alternative and opposite solution to the problem of lustful conflict of communal living, where partner access is shared, which we discuss below.

WORDS AND FIGURES

Let us now address the issue of terminology. In the popular media, the common usage is 'adultery'; for example the front cover of *Newsweek* on 30 September, 1996 was 'Adultery: A New Debate About the Oldest Sin'. An article in the *New York Times* [Norman (1998)] was entitled 'Getting Serious About Adultery: Who Does It and Why They Risk It'. On the other hand the relatively 'low-brow' UK weekly paper the *News of the World* ran its special feature on the topic (30 August 1998) under banners with 'Affairs' in the heading. Some argue that adultery is a pejorative usage, to be equated with betrayal and infidelity, implying immorality on the part of the participant [Vaughan (1998)]. To an extent this is due to the associated sin of lying being involved where exclusive pair-bond marriage is the norm. The social science community usage appears to tend towards 'extra-marital affairs' in a quest for value-neutrality: for example, the database of the survey archive of the ESRC (Economic and Social Research Council) in Colchester, England does not permit the search string 'adultery', requiring instead the phrase 'extra marital affairs'. However, this is a little inconsistent as the survey, which such a search should lead you to, was written up by its researchers using the term 'adultery' as the dominant concept employed to describe the phenomenon under consideration. 'Extra-marital affairs' was the term used by Fair (1978) who is the only economist to have written on the subject. The report on the major American sex survey uses the term 'infidelity' on the book jacket of Gagnon (1994a), whilst the index heading is 'fidelity' and there is no entry for adultery: the only related heading is 'extra-marital partners' which simply says 'see fidelity'.

As it stands, adultery is a technical term which refers to sexual intercourse with someone from outside of a legal marriage. The term 'paramour' which Fair (1978) adopts in his formal modelling is simply archaic French for the same thing. Whilst it might be desirable to avoid the term 'adultery' when analysing behaviour, the term 'extra-marital affairs' is also becoming problematic in the context of the increasing tendency to cohabitation: for example, in 1995, in the UK, 70 per cent of women had lived with their future husband before marriage compared with 5 per cent in the mid 1960s [source: *Population Trends* 80 (1995)]. From a purely conceptual point of view, the difference between these states (as far as economics is concerned) can be minimal, as both signify some form of specialization in exchange towards 'sole trader' in sex (as a commodity) status. Hence, the distinction between extra-marital and extra-cohabitative partners may lie more in the degree of costs associated with detection than being one of kind. An economic use of the term 'affair' can be defined as 'partner outsourcing', where one is engaging in sex and/or future relationship capital formation outside of an established marital or cohabitative set-up.

The advance of technology further blurs definitions. E-mail and internet chat rooms have made cyber outsourcing a possibility. It is now a commonly reported event that relationship partners have become jealously aggrieved at significant internet others distracting their partners from them. It is physically impossible to have actual intercourse electronically, so strictly speaking there is no such thing as cyber adultery. However, it seems feasible to claim in terms of the model presented below that electronic relationships can involve 'partner outsourcing' as both sexual and companionship benefits are traded in this way. Statistical studies focus on the presence of sexual intercourse during the 'affair'.

A study sponsored by the Robert Wood Johnston Foundation used the 1992 data on the sexual conduct of Americans in the National Health and Social Life Survey, which is a face-to-face survey of 3432 adults [Gagnon et al. (1994b)]. This is part of the General Social Survey conducted annually since 1972. As well as relying solely on face-to-face information gathering, this survey resorted to very direct questioning; for example, the measure of extra-marital sex was garnered from an upfront question on whether or not you had had sex with someone other than your partner during the relationship. The results showed that 1/4 of the men and 1/6 of the women admitted to having had an extra-marital affair. More recent data, from the 1996 survey, have shown corresponding figures of 22 per cent and 14 per cent.

Writing in 1993, Reibstein & Richards concluded that 'admittedly flawed studies', of a one-off nature, showed between 50 per cent and 75 per cent of men and only slightly fewer women reported having had an affair whilst still married. A later work by Vaughan (1998) again reviewed these one-off studies of sexual activity, many of which have been heavily criticized for selection bias, such as the Kinsey Reports, the Shere Hite Reports and the work of Halper (1988), coming to the conclusion that lifetime participation, in the USA since World War II, has been a majority activity as the reported involvement exceeds 50 per cent, and on occasions men have self-reported at over 80 per cent.

In marked contrast, the reportage of *Sex in America* [Gagnon et al. (1994a)] plays down the prevalence of affairs, saying:

marriage is such a powerful institution that, essentially, married people are nearly all alike – they are faithful to their partners as long as their marriage is intact. . . . Once married the vast majority have no other sexual partner; their past is essentially erased. Marriage remains the great leveler. (p. 105)

This assertion ignores the possible presence of an upward cohort trend effect and the possibility that people are inclined not to tell the truth in ways which are not invariant to the design of the research on their behaviour. The large sample surveys conducted in 14 countries, since 1996, by the Durex corporation [Durex (1998)] permit international comparisons of cumulative infidelity as shown in Table 9.2. This adopts a broader notion than outsourcing from a legally contracted bond as the question refers to 'having more than one sexual relationship at a time'.

Table 9.2 shows America leading the way at 50 per cent incidence, but none of the other countries falls below 20 per cent. In the UK, the Oxford University magazine *The Cherwell* [Anon. (1997)] discussed Kay Wellings's work, laying great stress on the statistical finding that higher education in general and university degrees in particular are positively and significantly associated with adultery. Wellings was not able to obtain a direct question, relying instead on a consistency check based on concatenating questions on the length of the

Table 9.2   Percentage admitting to ever having had more than one sexual relationship at a time

USA	50
Australia	37
Great Britain	42
Canada	34
France	36
Germany	40
Hong Kong	24
Italy	38
Mexico	40
Poland	28
Russia	43
South Africa	33
Spain	22
Thailand	39
Average of 14 Country Sample	37

Source: 'Global Sex Survey 1998'. Available in downloadable pdf format from http://www.durex.com

172 *The economics of sin: Part III*

relationship and the number of sexual partners during a designated time interval. Fair (1978) used two sources of data. The first is taken from a survey for *Psychology Today* in 1969 and consists of 601 observations for which the pooling of male and female is done through a male intercept dummy which is not statistically significant. The second is from the magazine *Women Only* consisting of responses from 6366 readers. The dependent variable, for both samples, is a proxy for time spent with extra-marital partners (or 'paramours' as he terms them) based on how often, during a year, individuals claim to be engaged in such activity. The explanatory variables are occupation, education, marital happiness, age, length of marriage, presence of children, degree of religiosity plus the aforementioned sex dummy. The overwhelmingly significant variable is the (negative) marital happiness scale. There are significant negative effects of age and religiosity. The children variable is not significant and the results for education and occupation are rather patchy.

NON-ECONOMIC ANALYSES OF ADULTERY

The debate on the prevalence of adultery has been dominated by extensions of biological analogies via sociological twists in the shape of sociobiology [Wilson (1975), Barash (1979)] and psychological twists in the shape of evolutionary psychology [Wright (1994), Miele (1996)]. These derive fairly directly from the accepted interpretation of Darwinism as shown in the following quote:

> The fundamental theorem upon which evolutionary psychology is based is that behavior (just like anatomy and physiology) is in large part inherited and that every organism acts (consciously or not) to enhance its inclusive fitness – to increase the frequency and distribution of its selfish genes in future generations. [Miele (1996)]

A desire for a variety of partners follows logically from such arguments, as weaknesses in one gene pool are more likely to be compensated for when breeding is spread across a diversity of partners. Anthropologist Symons (1979) argues that the relative investment level of men in producing children steers them towards a preference for polygyny, whereas women may be equally happy in monogamous or polyandrous relationships. A cross-cultural study reported in Miele (1996: source not cited) of 853 societies came to the conclusion that 83 per cent of them are polygynous. Further supporting evidence is adduced from the revealed preference of men for younger women in cross-cultural studies [Buss (1994, pp. 49–60), Symons (1979, pp. 187–200)] which is confirmed in an econometric paper by Cameron & Collins (1997). Anthropologist Helen Fisher (1992) examines divorce in 62 societies around the world, finding that the peak divorce period is from 2 to 4 years. She claims that this correlates remarkably well with the period of human infancy. Her argument is that once a child has been brought beyond the initial phases of rearing it may now be optimal to diversify through finding a new mate. This is a driving factor from the female side as the underlying male incentive is to constantly find new partners due to the low cost of male genetic inputs to reproduction. English biologist Robin Baker's much publicized work [Baker (1996), Baker & Bellis (1995)] is complementary in arguing that the propensity to engage in partner outsourcing is much greater for women than is commonly supposed. Having an affair with a partner with better quality sperm, within the context of a stable relationship, is fitness-enhancing. Baker's contention rests on evidence that, when women do have affairs all their behaviour at that time tends to maximize the chances of pregnancy. Further, he claims there is a literal survival of the fittest as a woman can have intercourse with two men, during a week, and retain the sperm of both, whereupon the most competitive will 'win'. This of course permits the above strategy of passing off any child as that of a committed stable mate. In support of this, blood group studies have shown that about 10 per cent of children were not fathered by their legal fathers. The strength of the female urge to diversify genetic investment is also attested to by Norman (1998) writing in the *New York Times*, who says:

> In Atlanta, Frank Pittman, a psychiatrist who has written often on the subject in books and magazines, estimates that he has treated some 5,000 couples in the last 38 years. Lately he has noticed 'women seem to be having more affairs than they did 20 years ago, 10 years ago,' in part because as they travel more for work, they have more opportunities for affairs far from home, he said. 'I've also started to see a few female philanderers,' he added, 'married women who have casual affairs in what used to be the old male pattern of find 'em, bed them, forget them, the kind of sport men used to brag about.'

It may of course be that personality 'type' determines the probability of infidelity. Buss & Shackelford (1997) interviewed recently married subjects at home about willingness to engage in six levels of extra-marital interest. They found that 'narcissistic', i.e. self-obsessed personalities, of both sexes, were more likely to give higher-level responses than others. This could be connected with a number of preference attributes: for example the variety-seeking that Fair identified as an economic element in infidelity is known to be a feature of narcissistic individuals [see Millon et al. (2000)].

ECONOMIC MODELS OF 'ADULTERY'

One motive for adultery would be to extract financial support for oneself independently of the production of any offspring. This was certainly a feature in some noted mistresses of the past [Griffin (1999)] but has dwindled in the modern world. In what follows we assume that this is not a motive or consequence of the 'partner outsourcing'.

Having sexual congress outside of an established relationship appears to be extremely rife judged by the materials reviewed above. There would seem to be ample scope for economic analysis here. For example, neo-classical theory might lead one to predict that the risk and transactions costs would engender the appearance of specialist brokering firms. Indeed, this has occurred in the UK, in the form of a dating agency specifically targeted at the would-be philanderer. This is called 'Loving Links' and has its own website at: http://www.lovinglinks.co.uk where one can view scans of its accumulated press coverage.

In the only explicit economic analysis of partner outsourcing, Fair (1978) utilized a time allocation model to identify predictions relating to the effect of key variables to the time spent in affairs rather than the incidence of them. Fair also mentions, in passing, the role of variety in human desire [cp. Scitovsky (1976)], and expected punishment costs. Scitovskian variety is just the utility from change per se as opposed to the intrinsic genetic drive for partner variety discussed in the previous section. It is expected to exist for all production and consumption activities as a basic fact of human nature, particularly aversion to boredom. Becker, Michael & Landes (1977) suggest that an important factor in the breakdown of contractual serial monogamy is divergence between *ex ante* and *ex post* utility from partner characteristics. This can be regarded as a failure of the partner search mechanism. Starting with Gale & Shapley (1962) [see also Bergstrom & Bagnoli (1993), Burdett & Coles (1997)] it has been considered that partner search might be an intrinsically efficient process, but divergent notions have since appeared. Frey & Eichenberger (1996) argued that people search too few partner prospects for too little time, with the high prevalence of divorce in Western societies being adduced as support for this. Harrison & McCabe (1996) argue that mismatch is endemic due to strategic misrepresentation of preferences to gain an advantage. Reviewing the general literature on search/matching problems, Todd (1997) argues that the models put forward suppose an infeasibly large number of partners to be evaluated for an infeasibly large amount of time. His solution to this is to propose 'satisficing' rather than optimizing approaches to partner selection. This is likely to lead to stability in partnerships so long as key variables do not change rapidly over time. For example, a 'satisficing' choice of partner may well remain optimal until new opportunities are opened up by wealth, technological change or serendipity.

An alternative perspective on partner outsourcing could be found in the economic theory of clubs introduced by Buchanan [see the survey by Sandler & Tschirhart (1980)]. Suppose the existence of an individual who is deemed

to be highly desirable in terms of their partnership characteristics; this individual could be regarded as equivalent to a fixed asset, like a swimming pool
or golf club, which could be shared among many users. Although this is widely
observed in the animal kingdom such as the case of bees and cats, it is generally circumscribed in Western society by the legal institution of monogamous
marriage. However, in some cultures, it has, on occasions, been formally
accepted, e.g. Mormonism and the harem of Muslim potentates. To some
extent a club good approach is implied by the analysis of polygamy by Becker
(1991a). This was foreshadowed by the nineteenth century French Utopian
social thinker Charles Fourier [Beecher & Bienvenu (1975)] who argued that
the most desired individuals in society should share some of their endowments
with the least desired on an occasional voluntary basis. Multi-partner clubs are
currently practised in San Francisco, USA by a group of 'advanced practical
scientific Utopians' who publish a journal *Kerista* detailing their theory and
experiments in polyfidelity, which is basically a sexual commune structure.
Fuller details on the case made for this and all the other forms of 'polyamory'
can be found at: http://www.sexuality.org/polyamor.html.

Communal sexual consumption is also observed in the case of Eskimo society. Freuchten (1961, ch. 4) details the partner-swapping rituals of the
Eskimos and also reports cases where men are 'loaned' the wives of other men
to go on hunting expeditions. It would be a mistake to equate the Eskimo codes
with the sexual promiscuity advocated in the 'swinging' sixties (and at times by
Fourier). The partner-sharing that goes on is still circumscribed by moral rules
and someone who attempted to divert someone else's partner full-time to themselves would meet with social censure. Undoubtedly the normality of partner-
sharing in the Eskimo communities is a reflection of the property rights
structure consequent on their difficult economic circumstances. Adverse physical conditions and the need for difficult hunting to provide food makes people
highly dependent on each other. Women were comparatively scarce in the areas
studied by Freuchten due to the destruction of female births on account of the
greater economic value of men. Apart from occasional lending and swapping
of wives this also occasioned a fair degree of polyandry. In all cases, men were
seen to be the owners of their wives and romantic love was scarcely apparent.

The caveats we have applied to Eskimo partner-trading can also be made
for the 'swingers' (beloved of television documentary makers) of advanced
economies. Organized swingers essentially trade partners purely for sex on an
occasional basis, one suspects, largely to satisfy the variety drive. There is no
upfront betrayal or infidelity involved. Exchanges may be unequal due to
imperfect markets for obvious reasons. Undoubtedly there are pockets of society where swinging is seen as a sin to some extent on the grounds that it is
'not natural', because a pair-bonded heterosexual family with children is the
'natural' way to live.

The extremum of the club good arrangement can be found in some forms of prostitution. It could be argued that so-called adulterers are people with strong drives or a high need for variety who are forced into infidelity, or the paid sex market, because of the unavailability or unacceptability of a harem-like club good arrangement. Of course such individuals could opt out of contractual monogamy in favour of informal serial monogamy, polygamy, polyfidelity or whatever. However, there are a number of incentives in most market economies which offer inducements to enter into, and remain in, the state of marriage:

i.   The tax system is tilted in favour of marriage.
ii.   Studies of earning functions indicate that there are returns to men from the state of marriage of the order of 5–15 per cent [Daniel (1995), Waldfogel (1998)] and further controlling for other family factors associated with marriage shows that there is also a net labour market gain to women [see e.g. Cameron & Ward (2000)].
iii. Social esteem and advancement may be accelerated by having a visibly 'good' marriage as is shown in the case of politicians who are, in the UK at any rate, usually forced to resign as a punishment for being discovered as partner outsourcers.

THE EXIT-VOICE MODEL

We now outline an exit-voice model derived from the pioneering ideas of Hirschman [see Hirschman (1970), Williamson (1975, 1976)] and the Lancastrian (1971) model of consumption. Following this we comment briefly on how it encompasses the various economic and non-economic approaches above. To set up the exit-voice model we first present the extension of the basic ideas of Becker [(1991a), see also Grossbard-Shechtman (1982, 1984, 1995)] into an 'economics of relationships' by Cameron & Collins (1999). Individuals are assumed to maximize stable underlying utility functions, for interaction with partners, subject to constraints. A partner must first be selected from the available pool, and once their willingness to engage in evaluation of the product (i.e. the potential relationship) is established, search is then conducted over their attributes. The underlying utility function may be characterized as follows:

$$U = f(S, M, X) \qquad (9.1)$$

where there are two types of services supplied by partners, S = sexual services defined broadly to include any sexual arousal or gratification received from interaction with a partner and M = companionship broadly defined to include non-sexual exchange. X is the composite variable representing all other things, which obviously spans private goods and public goods which might bring scale economies in sharing. This is a general formulation of mate search which encompasses homosexuality and has, as the extreme case of public goodness in X, the production and rearing of children, whether or not these are genetically linked to the partners. We assume continuous substitutability and convexity between S and M, at least over certain ranges of the utility function. The constraints are primarily related to time and search costs in procuring S and M. A rudimentary diagrammatic exposition is provided in Figure 9.1, which is a simple indifference curve presentation. There will be an equilibrium choice of partner where the marginal choice of substitution between S and M equals the marginal rate of transformation, given by procurement costs. We assume that the individual utility function is invariant with respect to intrinsic endowments of the searcher. Utility may alter with age due to biological transformations in individuals, however, we adopt a Becker–Stigler (1977) type assumption that individuals know about this in advance. Having chosen in such a context, individuals enter into formal or implicit long-term commitments with one individual who has the S–M combination pertaining to the static equilibrium in Figure 9.1. Supposing there is an unanticipated decline in S or M then, if the relationship–commodity analogy holds up, a rational individual should simply

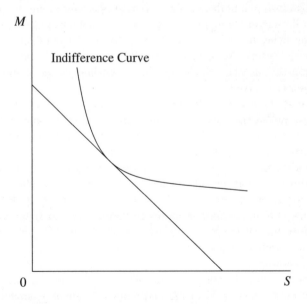

Figure 9.1   Choice of partner in terms of S *and* M

exit to a rival supplier. However, the presence of potentially substantial exit costs and the 'experience good' dimensions raise the prospects of a preference for the use of 'voice' to renegotiate supply conditions. The voice mechanism, within marriage, requires a combination of bargaining and communication skills along with responsiveness of the partner. If it fails to function properly then there will be a decline in the quality of the relationship [see the literature review of Karney & Bradbury (1995)] over time which will equate in our framework to an unanticipated fall of the quantities of S and M from the levels at the point of contracting into the partnership. There may of course be an exogenous decline in the quantity of S or M due to intrinsic biological imperatives. As with labour markets, individuals could exit into a pure search phase, that is leave their partners without any outside sourcing being involved.

The following presentation attempts to capture the salient features of the partner outsourcing decision in the context of a model in which there is possible exit, at the period end, due to the tradeoff between the formation of exit capital, during an affair, and a decline in the effectiveness of voice. The following assumptions are made for the purposes of simplification:

i. Individuals maximize utility, over a fixed single period, which is part of a known remaining lifetime.

ii. The choice over this period is between the existing inside partner and M and zero or more outside partners where there is no intent to quit this relationship until the end of the period. We refer to this as 'juggling'.

iii. At the end of the period, exit may or may not take place with this decision being recursive on whether or not the juggler is detected by the inside partner. We make no attempt to deal with this node.

iv. Transactions and search costs in procuring outside partners are exogenously given.

v. There are exogenously given probabilities of detection (p) by, and punishment (D) from, the inside partner. An additional component of guilt may be factored into costs from the psychic cost of the pain at hurting others [cp. Drago (1995), Kahneman, Knetsch & Thaler (1986)] or a stigma cost from social disapproval [cp. Akerlof (1984)].

vi. Whilst the outside and inside partners may both supply non-zero amounts of S and M, we will assume that they generate different varieties of S and M; hence the inside partner (1) will supply $S1$ and $M1$ whilst the outside partner (2) will supply $S2$ and $M2$, and so forth.

vii. The varieties of S and M are continuously substitutable in the utility function.

viii. The varieties of S and M are not substitutable in production viz. partner 1 cannot generate $S2$ or $M2$ and partner 2 cannot generate $S1$ or $M1$. This could be a strictly technical limitation within the time frame, or it could be due to the blockage of voice in that the agent has no mode of communicating to their partner, in a way that is not prohibitively costly, that will effect the desired change.

ix. The consumption of $S2$ and $M2$, over the period, will result in an amount of 'exit capital' (XK) being formed, as a joint product, for use at the end of the period. This may arise from learning relationship or other skills, but may also involve things like an increase in self-assessment of one's value in the partnership market.

x. We are treating the amount of XK as an exogenous by-product of consumption of the outsourced S and M, that is 'learning by doing' rather than a purposive choice for maximizing a lifetime-discounted utility stream.

xi. The exacting of punishment (D) only takes place at the end of the period.

xii. XK and D are mutually independent.

Given the above assumptions, we are adopting a somewhat quasi-rational or behaviouristic approach. This is imparted by using a satisficing framework bounded by assumptions (ii)–(iv) and (x)–(xi) and pre-constrained by the scenario of Figure 9.1. The utility function is therefore (making the further assumption that only one outsourced partner is on offer):

$$U = Uf(S1, S2, M1, M2, X) \qquad (9.2)$$

where it is convenient, in formulating the decision criterion (9.4) below, to treat $U(S1, M1)$ as separable from $U(S2, M2)$ even though $U(S1)$ may not be separable from $U(M1)$ and $U(S2)$ may not be separable from $U(M2)$. We further introduce a function where the depreciation rate (r) of marital satisfaction is an influence on the value of D. The precise parameters of this function will depend on the efficiency of the exit-voice mechanism in the existing relationship:

$$D = f(r, G) \qquad (9.3)$$

G is a vector of the value of other goods which may be available to be lost from punishment, such as wealth and access to children.

The decision function as to whether to engage in an affair thus becomes:

$$U(S2, M2) + U(XK) - pU(D) > 0 \qquad (9.4)$$

As we are eschewing the question of time substitution between the 'in' and 'out' partners and using a recursive current period satisficing framework there is no maximization problem involving choice between relative time inputs to 'in' and 'out' partners. Rather, the problem reduces to whether there will be non-zero amounts of $S2$ and $M2$ in Eq. (9.3) as solved by the agent, i.e. whether an individual is a juggler or a sole trader in implicit and explicit partnership rights. For the purposes of carrying out statistical work, the amount of $S2$ must be non-zero even though the amount of $M2$ may be zero for there to be any apparent outsourcing. In practice, individuals may be engaging in out trades with zero $S2$ and non-zero $M2$ but this would, in this context, be classified as 'flirtation', although it might be labelled as infidelity in the cyber-adultery context.

Rearranging Eq. (9.4) thus indicates that outsourcing will take place if the following expression for the magnitude of p is satisfied:

$$p < \frac{U(S2, M2) + U(XK)}{U(D)} \tag{9.5}$$

The likelihood (L) of statistically observed outsourcing is thus:

$$L[S2 > 0, M \geq 0] = L\left[p < \frac{U(S2, M2) + U(UK)}{U(D)}\right] \tag{9.6}$$

which suggests the following relationships (ceteris paribus):

$$\delta L/\delta p < 0 \tag{9.7}$$

$$\delta L/\delta U/\delta S2 > 0 \tag{9.8}$$

$$\delta L/\delta XK > 0 \tag{9.9}$$

$$\delta L/\delta r > 0 \tag{9.10}$$

$$\delta L/\delta G < 0 \tag{9.11}$$

I now comment briefly on three areas of the non-economics literature that can be illuminated by the above model. Firstly, let us consider relationship scholar Steve Duck's ruminations on the end of relationships [Duck (1998, pp. 87–93)]. He notes the asymmetry in the comparative social prominence of the process of romance versus the neglect of the process of ossification and stagnation of relationships. He goes on to say:

A crucial point made by La Gaipa (1982) is that every person who leaves a relationship has to leave with 'social credit' intact for future use: that is we cannot just get out of a relationship but we have to leave in such a way that we are not disgraced and debarred from future relationships. . . . It is socially acceptable to say 'I left because we tried hard to make it work but it wouldn't'. It is not socially acceptable to leave a relationship with the cheery but unpalatable admission 'well basically I'm a jilt and I got bored dangling my partner on a string so I just broke the whole thing off when it suited me'. (p. 90)

Here one sees a clear exit-voice nexus lurking and the notion of social credit can be equated to part of exit capital. A curious feature of Duck's standard text on relationships is a total absence of any discussion of money as a feature of relationship problems. A report in the *News of the World* (1998) reports the feelings of a woman, with three children, who has been flirting with the prospect of an affair where she identifies the problem as having come after the birth of the second child when she was pressurized into working and found that her partner supplied little input to the child-rearing process. Asymmetry of exchange was further compounded by her feeling that she was being forced to give in to demands for sex when she was not interested. This is a decline in marital quality for the woman in question (that is an exogenous increase in r) due to marriage being an incomplete contract in the face of uncertainty. Her behaviour represents, in our terms, an initial search for more/different M, which may turn into a demand for conjoint S (that is $S2$) ultimately leading to the formation of exit capital. That is, even if exit did not come with the first affair prospect being screened the formation of exit capital therein leads to an increased probability of exit at the next nodal point. Taking all of the above into consideration, we could put forward a 'market failure' alternative to Helen Fisher's 'infancy hypothesis'. That is, the length of time taken for the risks of affairs and/or divorce to peak may correlate with the process of learning about the partner, which leads to a rise in the marital quality depreciation parameter and thus precipitates the exit-oriented events, rather than a biological variety imperative.

I have estimated a logit equation for (9.6) using the 1990–1991 UK National Survey of Sexual Attitudes and Lifestyles which has a large sample and a wide range of variables. Full results and details are in Cameron (2000b). The NSSAL survey was carried out, by professional market researchers, in the UK in 1990/1. This was a rigorously conducted survey of 18,876 adults of ages from 16 to 59. Technicalities involved in tracking a population in which extra-relationship sexual activity can be estimated resulted in a further reduction in the samples to 4044 for men and 4490 for women. Given that the questions were answered at home, sometimes with family members or partners nearby, it is not surprising that low estimated rates of outsourcing were found. The estimates were 8.93 per cent and 3.94 per cent for men and women. The probabilities of outsourcing were linked to a number of possible determinants.

The quickest way to summarize the findings is to indulge in the 'most likely to' game. So, for women, those most likely to are those Roman Catholics recently moved into the area, working long hours and/or away from home at times, with past homosexual experience, whose first sexual intercourse was at age under 15, who are not highly afraid of AIDS, who have had a past live-in relationship and whose partners do not work long hours. The men most likely to are wealthy, highly educated, black, young, Welsh, non-church-going Roman Catholics, with past homosexual experience who had their first sexual experience at age under 15, who are not highly afraid of AIDS and who have had a past live-in relationship whilst being at an early stage in this one. These statistical results show the influence of opportunity, risk and cultural restraining factors which may make the activity taboo.

CONCLUSION

In this chapter we have looked at an activity which arises from some of the sins, and gives rise to others, particularly lying and deception. Rational choice modelling neither condones nor condemns partner outsourcing. Nevertheless, it is hard not to conclude that if we start from the premise that people wish to maximize their utility, then following lustful impulses which involve violating explicit and implicit relationship contracts seems like 'normal' rather than aberrant behaviour. At some times it has been labelled as socially deviant behaviour because markets[2] and quasi-markets have evolved the norm of companionate monogamous heterosexual marriage as an efficient form of organization in terms of ensuring continuous labour market effort of the present generation of workers, and via parenting, the future generation of workers. Still, given that there is a latent variety demand we might wonder why it cannot be met through a formal market recourse to outsourcing. This is the subject of the next chapter.

ENDNOTES

1. Anti-fornication laws will serve as anti-adultery laws but they are seldom enforced in advanced economies.
2. Overt market processes may serve to promote or retard partner outsourcing depending on the power position of those searching for the outsource. An aspiring corporation man who seeks to sleep with his superior's wife may be deterred by the threat to his income stream, whilst the same does not apply in the reverse situation. The marketization of entertainment services (acting, singing, etc.) provides enhanced scope for outsourcing (in the form of one-off trysts with 'groupies' as well as all-out affairs), with there being many well-documented instances of it being tolerated by the full-time partner.

10. Prostitution

INTRODUCTION

As with most things sexual, and otherwise, the progress of technology has made the process of definition somewhat harder than it was. The most restrictive definition of prostitution is to regard it as paid sex where there is an expectation that full physical intercourse (copulation or anal intercourse if we wish to encompass non-heterosexual prostitution in the definition) is part of the menu of services. A lot of activity is not covered by this, which falls into the broader definition of services sold in the 'paid sex market' including such things as lap dancing, strip shows, internet interactions and indulgence in the fetishes of customers by paid sex workers which do not involve copulation. At the latter point the distinction becomes blurred as the client may obtain full sexual release for the exchange of money. Words have been used other than prostitute, such as whore and harlot, but these have not persisted with any regularity into modern times where hooker seems to be the most prevalent demotic alternative. The archaic term 'whore' seems sometimes to be used by those campaigning for the rights of prostitutes in order to give an edge to their message.

The term prostitute has escaped from its occupational sphere to become a wider form of condemnation. We commonly hear of people 'prostituting' their morals or their talent in the sense that they are exploiting something, of intrinsically higher moral worth, for the mere pursuit of income for its own sake. This reflected stigma derives from the notions emanating from religion and the 'romantic love' era of capitalism, that sex is a sacred act to be saved for the person's partner. In the strictest religious views, prostitution is the tip of an iceberg of sexual sinning. Apart from any absence of love and presence of money, it involves sex outside marriage which is a sin in itself. On top of this, it involves sex for purely recreational purposes which can be construed as sinful on the 'not natural' grounds that it perverts the status of procreation ordained by God. Given the presence of money it should be higher in the tariff of sins than the adultery of Chapter 9 or masturbation as discussed in Chapter 4.

In more theoretical terms we might claim that one's sexual services, like one's blood, are inalienable rights which should not be traded. As with blood, the sexual trade may reflect an enforced case of unjustly unequal exchange where individuals are driven by poverty or some other power imbalance into surrendering their inalienable rights. This takes us to the Marxist–Feminist position that marriage has been, in many times and places, a form of prostitution hidden behind a veil of respectability. That is, with property being concentrated in male hands often to the extent that wives are legally treated as the property of the husband, women are forced to sell their sexuality in order to obtain support. The radical view is that there are two systems of prostitution co-existing rather than a primary market for sex (marriage), which is consolidated in the serially monogamous form due to transactions costs and the commodity benefits of 'locked in' child-rearing inputs, that is then supplemented by a secondary market. The secondary market view follows from the analysis already encountered in Chapter 9. This implies that the primary market (marriage and 'ongoing' serially monogamous relationships) may fail due to constraints on meeting the needs of the male partner for variety/unusual practices, etc. In Chapter 9 it should have been clear that this also applies to any partner, however the use of paid markets to adjust to a disequilibrium in internal 'relationship' trades has historically been a mainly male preserve.

Prostitution, like the other activities in the present section of this work, has been widely regarded as sinful in many times and places but has been tolerated. Prostitution is commonly labelled as the oldest profession, indicating its intrinsically economic character. There is a plethora of historical research on the subject. Timothy Taylor (1996, pp. 205–7) reports that there is considerable evidence of female sex professionals in the Iron Age. On page 206 he reproduces drawings of the symbols on Roman brothel tokens which had long baffled archaeologists. These contain drawings which indicate the tariff of charges for different sexual acts. Their wide acceptability meant that a fully regularized sex economy was established at least as early as markets for other goods. The Roman professional prostitutes were either slaves or full-time employees in brothels in which men controlled the revenues.

One fact which strikes the lay reader of historical research is the presence of communities where prostitution is treated as virtuous rather than sinful. The profession afforded considerable esteem to women when in ancient history it was sanctioned by, and housed in, religious temples, e.g. the hetaerae of Ancient Rome [see Griffin (1999, pp. 36–40)]. Before we go on, it should be emphasized that the higher status of prostitution in ancient civilization was not based on free market economics or sexually liberated thinking which would form the arguments for such a system today. Rather [see Frazer (1993, pp. 330–331) and Ryley-Scott (1996)] it was premised on magical thinking such as the sex being an offering to the gods or that sex, by the appointed harlots, with a stranger would confer benefits on the community from wider cosmic forces.

With the suppression of magical thinking as a major factor in social codes we find tolerance, alongside sinful status, as the major prevailing attitude. Toleration has generally derived from the 'lesser of two evils' position. In older times the belief was that male lust was a raging torrent that had to be satisfied and therefore prostitution served to protect 'decent' women by siphoning it off. This necessity was clearly recognized by Mandeville [Harth (1970, pp. 127–8)] who remarked that:

> Where Six or Seven Thousand Sailors arrive at once, as it often happens at Amsterdam, that have seen none but their own Sex for many months together, how is it to be suppos'd that honest Women should walk the Streets unmolested if there were no Harlots to be had at reasonable Prices? (capitals as in original)

A modern analogue to this was found in the proposal to establish sex zones in out-of-town industrial estates to cater for the needs of incoming fans for the duration of the Rugby World Cup in Wales.

St. Augustine [Ryley-Scott (1996, pp. 20–21)] had earlier endorsed this view also on the protective grounds of preventing rape and adultery and thus reducing the threat to marriage, i.e. the 'secondary market' view expounded above. Thomas Aquinas defended the acceptance of prostitution as a necessary evil, the extinguishing of which would lead to the prevalence of the worse sin of sodomy. Various risk externalities have led to the evolution of more organized tolerance of the secondary market for male lust. A major one is the fear of the spread of infectious diseases which has inspired various forms of quasi-regulation in military [Fels (1971)] and nautical contexts in order that the fighting fitness of the men be maintained. In commercialized sex centres we encounter the use of mandatory health checks as a condition of the operators being relatively free from stricter official interference.

Tolerance of prostitution has also sometimes been posited on other 'secondary market' grounds. In terms of welfare economics we are dealing with its role as an externality abatement technology. Two chief defences spring to mind, both of them particularly rife in Europe at the end of the nineteenth century. One is that the prostitute can be used to help cure someone who has sexual problems, such as the inability to achieve orgasm other than through indulging strange and dangerous fetishes. This view is amply illustrated in Krafft-Ebing's case notes, the twelfth and last edition of which was published in 1897, where he frequently recommends trips to prostitutes in the hope of overcoming problem behaviours. The second argument springs from the notion of an ideal marriage being one where the man was highly sexually experienced yet the woman was a blushing virgin. Equilibrium in a market with such a code can only be obtained if there are secondary markets where the man can acquire this marriage-specific human capital. This could be met by a segment of the potential partner supply who have higher promiscuity or who can be coerced into sexual activity. Regular prostitution, servants, slaves and mistresses from the existing group of married women can serve this function. A moderated version of this second benefit is the use of prostitutes to, at the very least, remove a male of his virginity so that he is not embarrassed and disadvantaged with his first major partner in the informal market. For example, the noted French philanderer and novelist George Simenon took his son to a prostitute for this reason [see Bressler (1983)].

Tolerance has generally taken place within a context of illegality or very attenuated legal status. There has been a remarkable variety of laws in the piecemeal process of dealing with the issue. In many cases ancillary activities, like causing a public nuisance, have been the basis of prosecution rather than the selling of sexual services per se. It is difficult to establish the precise policies in operation, in any given country, as the legal statutes are subject to local interpretation which is hard for the scholar to discern in the abstract. Paradoxically, one can find a more liberal sex economy in places where it is technically illegal than in others where it is legal. The best source of information, on formal legal status and informal practice, is the World Sex Guide published on the internet which provides many reports by customers who have travelled in the countries discussed. I have attempted to summarize the information, as available at July 2001, in Table 10.1.

Some judgement had to be made in summarizing the information into a workable table. Where there are blanks in answers to the headings or a one-line summary is given this is because further information was not available. Clearly it is not that easy in practice to tell the difference between countries which have legal prostitution and those which do not. In terms of the Akerlof models of Chapter 2 we have some economies where behaviour and observance are concordant and some where it is discordant.

It would be a great mistake to suppose that those regions with a legalized system do not still have an illegal system in operation. There are several reasons why illegal prostitution, in terms of unregistered and non-health-checked workers, will continue to be supplied alongside legal prostitution. For one thing, they may stand to gain from tax evasion and offering higher-risk premium services (i.e. no use of condoms) which are prohibited in the legal market. Further, the prostitute who has failed a health check is now under pressure to work illegally to sustain their income. Organized crime might also continue to provide prostitutes from a selection of workers against the general tendency in Table 10.1 for third-party financial gain to be unacceptable. They could sustain this market form due to scale economies and pre-existing holdings of coercion capital with which to enlist sole traders in their ring.

Table 10.1 Legal status of prostitution in various countries

| Country | (a) Countries with 'legal' prostitution | | | |
	Allows third-party gains	Tax paid	Health checks	Zoned
Aruba	[Dutch colony regulated as Netherlands (see below]			
Australia		yes	yes	yes
Austria	yes	yes	yes	yes
Costa Rica			licences and ID cards	
Cyprus	unconfirmed; seems to be legal in both parts			
Czech Republic	no			
Denmark	no			
Dominican Republic	yes			
Estonia				
Finland	no	not formally regulated but generally contacted via magazines as 'daytime coffee service'		
Germany	no	yes	yes	yes
Honduras		yes (ID cards)		
Hungary	no	yes	yes	
	(legal since 1992 and are treated as private entrepreneurs)			
Iceland	no			
Israel	no	(but law on brothel-keeping widely flouted)		
Italy	no	no		
Latvia				
Luxembourg	legal in principle but most is illegal			
Netherlands	no	yes	no	yes
	(zoning is up to individual city governments which may also impose health checks in some cases)			
Norway	no			
Poland	tax is being mooted: no explicit regulation			
Portugal				
Singapore	yes*	yes	yes	
	(some Singapore brothels give benefits)			
South Africa	fully legalized in 1997			
Spain	no			
Switzerland	yes	yes	yes	yes
Taiwan	regulated with licences			
Turkey	no			
	(reports of coercion of women to service soldiers in government brothels to work off fines and prison sentences they cannot pay)			
	(b) Countries with illegal prostitution			
Albania	Allegedly thrives at low prices since end of communism			
Bahrain				

Table 10.1   continued

	(b) Countries with illegal prostitution			
Country	Allows third-party gains	Tax paid	Health checks	Zoned
Bangladesh				
Bulgaria	Tolerated mostly in hotels and bars			
Canada	Pimping and running or working in a bawdy house and soliciting are the offences as prostitution is not strictly illegal			
China	Police do not enforce law and hotels are used			
Cuba	Widespread and actively promoted			
Egypt				
Hong Kong	Run by organized crime using legitimate business fronts			
Ireland	Widespread use of escorts			
Jamaica	Must be caught in the act to be charged			
Japan	Technically illegal but ignored by police			
Kazakhstan	Streeet girls pay fee to organized crime			
Mongolia	Widespread under fronts of hotels, etc.			
Nigeria	Tolerated			
Pakistan	100 lashes anti-fornication law is used but paid sex can be obtained through difficult covert operations			
Philippines	Despite illegality has health checks and registration			
Romania				
Sweden	Fines are used: the only country in which buying or offering to buy is punished but selling or offering to sell is not			
South Korea	Designated red light districts (RLDs) exist			
Tanzania	Tolerated			
UK	Like Canada			
United Arab Emirates	Widely available and almost tolerated			
USA	Except in certain parts of Nevada (where it is legal) generally like Canada			
	(c) Countries with ambiguous systems			
Belgium	Illegal with similar set-up to Canada but the regulated system abolished in the 1950s has been unofficially reinstated in parts			
Mexico	There are regulated zones in bigger cities and prostitutes must pay for their own health checks. There is also some tolerance of third-party gain			
New Zealand	Described as 'nearly legal' yet is advertised on radio			
Portugal	Status unknown but prostitution is widespread			
Russia	Not specifically regulated or prohibited			

DEMAND

The theoretical treatment of demand, in this area, is closely linked to that for the adultery of Chapter 9. Below is presented a simple economic model of the decision to use prostitution services. Its characteristics reflect a focus on the determinants of moving off the corner solution (zero prostitution usage) rather than determining the interior solution (how many hours to spend with a prostitute). This is a static presentation which ignores the possible 'threshold crossing' problem that may be faced by entrants into this market on the demand (and also the supply) side. That is the person may face a dramatic switch in their preferences once they make their first trade in this market. Some individuals who might obtain net benefits at the margin may be held back from a form of negative capital which could consist purely of feelings of sin but might have broader elements of resistance in terms of stigma or simply a self-identity which thinks 'I am not the sort of person who does this'.

Utility-maximizing behaviour is assumed with the functions being twice differentiable and continuous. The utility function for a male is:

$$U1(S11, S21, M1, X) + (1 - p)[U2\ (S21, S22, M2)] - pU(D) \qquad (10.1)$$

This characterizes the decision on engaging in paid sex, as satisfying the axioms of the Von Neumann–Morgenstern utility function. $S1$ and $S2$ are two distinct types of sexual activity. The male has the choice of one relationship partner (1) and/or one paid sex partner (2). $S1$ and $S2$ can of course be zero quantities from either supplier. M is the companionship utility introduced in Chapter 9 but here we assume it to be generic and obtainable from either the paid or unpaid sex partners. From the consumer's point of view, the presence of non-zero amounts of M from the paid sex partner can blur the extent to which the seller is regarded as purely a prostitute. Higher-priced services tend to involve more M and thus are subject to the moral lightening of name changes into 'escorts' and 'call girls'. Even outside the premium markets, the boundary between outright prostitution and 'something else' is sometimes blurred in the mind of the consumer. Reports of the 'sex tourism' of Cuba indicate that there is a sub-species of 'backpacker' user who may associate with a woman for the duration of the stay on a quasi-informal basis and gives them money but not as a direct transaction based on any specific services provided. Although this veers towards the 'temporary wife' phenomenon found in cultures of economic austerity, such as the Eskimos, it is essentially a form of prostitution.

X denotes other sources of utility from a relationship partner, e.g. child rearing. The probability detection p is exogenously determined. D is the damage function associated with engaging in paid sex and is given by:

$$D = G + CO + RDC + MP + PDC \tag{10.2}$$

where G = guilt, CO = community opprobrium, RDC = relationship disturbance costs, MP = monetary punishment and PDC = personal damage costs
(chiefly health capital depreciation through diseases). The guilt function is
given by:

$$G = G(R, F, SU) \tag{10.3}$$

where R = religiosity (intensity of religious observance), F = faith and SU =
social upbringing. It is assumed that community opprobrium is exogenously
determined.

RDC is given by the function:

$$RDC = RDC(X) \tag{10.4}$$

PDC is given by the function:

$$PDC = PDC(S12, S22) \tag{10.5}$$

Substituting Eqs. (10.2)–(10.5) into Eq. (10.1) yields:

$$U1(S11, S21, M1, X) + (1 - p)U2(S12, S22, M2) - pU[G(R, F, SU)$$
$$+ CO + RDC(X) + MP + PDC(S12, S22)] \tag{10.6}$$

Looking to some key parameter influences we may note that, in the
presence of strong variety demand, there would be a greater tendency to non-
additivity in the S (sex) arguments of the utility functions. Risk-taking disposition will be reflected in the responsiveness of PDC with respect to its
arguments. Disease probability, social stigma and punishment costs inflicted
by partners will deter individuals more the greater is their risk-aversion.

In such a model there can be, in the utility function in the S elements, a
number of distinct drives as implied by Chapter 9. One is genetic variety-
seeking arising from procreative impulses; that is the individual seeks to mate
with a wide range of partners in order to expand the pool of genes available to
their offspring and thereby maximize their fitness. Granted, prostitutes'
customers do not seek them for breeding purposes, but they may still be influenced by these impulses albeit reined into a recreational sex mode of behaviour. There is also Scitovskian variety. This is variety for its own sake not for
any sociobiological purpose. Paid partners may be an easier means of obtaining variety than non-market ones, due to lower transactions costs so long as
the costs of paid partners are not extremely high. Throughout history certain

individuals may, on account of their stardom, be offered so much variety at low transactions costs (from 'groupies') that the incentive to meet this need from prostitution does not exist unless the prostitutes available are of much lower health risk than the 'free' supply. In the moral universe of non-economists this type of activity has sometimes been regarded as little more than 'amateur prostitution'. Ryley-Scott (1996) constantly refers to the threat to the trade of prostitution from the 'amateur prostitutes' of the promiscuous society believed to be operating in the 1960s.

Paid sex markets, in general, may form the primary sexual release market for some individuals who are unwilling or unable to have a non-paid sexual partner. Likewise some individuals may have a partner who is totally unwilling or unable to meet the volume or nature of their sexual demands.

A common assumption in sociobiological and economic analyses [see Posner (1992)] of sexual behaviour is that men have a marked preference for younger partners at least as their purely sexual needs go. It may be much easier to get younger partners through the paid market than the informal market of regular dating (or adultery) as this is, *ceteris paribus*, likely to be rising in search and other costs. For example, the older the man, relative to the women, the greater may be the level of wealth needed to attract them (and also the fraction of it that needs to be spent). This proposition has been quite strikingly demonstrated, for the informal market, in an empirical analysis of personal advertisements by Cameron & Collins (1997). Substantial anecdotal evidence on the high negative elasticity of prostitute age in the consumer utility function can be found in the accounts published on the World Sex Guide website (http://www.worldsexguide.org) where report after report shows considerable emphasis on small variations in age, even over the age range where sexual functioning is not biologically diminishing for women.

Generally, the extreme of this youth orientation is found in the desire for virgins. A regular partner cannot be a virgin once the relationship has been consummated thus, if there is a taste for sex with virgins the paid market may be a more efficient source of supply than the unpaid informal market or resort to coercion (rape). Further the primary informal market virgin demander faces formidable obstacles in terms of the seriousness attached to breaches of the age of consent which, in many nations, is extremely high relative to the age at which (purely biological) sexual maturity is normally reached. Some scholars are puzzled by tastes for virginity per se. There certainly was once a strand of magical thinking on the bogus idea that the consumption of virgins would regenerate the health and vitality of an older man (this is found in the biblical story of Abishag). Such was the demand for virgins in eighteenth century Europe that 'fake' supplies were created by false blood letting and thespian subterfuges by young, but experienced, prostitutes.

Statistical evidence on the influence of various factors on the demand for prostitution services is rare due to the lack of fully tolerant legality and the presence of stigma. An analysis of the 1990/1 National Study for Sexual Attitudes and Lifestyles (NSSAL) in the UK by Wellings et al. (1994) came to the following conclusion:

> The factors associated with ever paying for sex in bivariate analysis were examined in a logistic regression model that includes age, marital status, social class, work away from home and a homosexual partner ever. Age and marital status exerted the dominant effects in the model with the odds ratio for commercial sex increasing rapidly with age. Men who were cohabitees or widowed, separated and divorced were significantly more likely than married men to report contact with prostitutes. After controlling for other variables in the model, single men did not differ significantly from married men in the odds of reporting experience of commercial sex. This contrasts with the bivariate models, which suggest a lower prevalence among single men. The difference in effect is due to confounding by other variables in the model, particularly age. Working away from home was sustained as an independent effect in the model. A history of a homosexual partner ever was associated with significantly raised odds of commercial sex contact. [Wellings et al. (1994)]

Cameron & Collins (2000b) estimated a logit equation based on the economic model of demand using the same data set. This shows the importance of situational opportunity by confirming the significance of the working away from home variable. It further demonstrates the significance of risk attitude with other measures of risk-taking, in potentially health-damaging activities (including the perceived risk of HIV/AIDS), proving to be positively associated with reported use of a prostitute.

SUPPLY FACTORS AND FEATURES

Given the role and status of prostitutes in modern society they are clearly not selected for this profession. In the days of sacred/magical prostitution they might be picked at 12 years of age. Nor do they, presently, self-select via information and training given in schools and careers advice services. So it is an occupation usually arrived at via failure to enter another, discontent with an existing choice, or loss of support whilst not actively seeking work. Hence it is, in current circumstances, probably judicious to take an asymmetrical theoretical perspective on the rational choice elements in the prostitution market. That is, the demand choice seems reasonably treated in the rational choice manner. The participation decision on the supply side (whether to or not) seems to be less prone to the assumption of long-run foresight than the issue of supply behaviour once in the market. In support of this we may point out that the sources of supply have tended to be skewed towards particular segments of the population which experience outright poverty or relative deprivation in terms of an unanticipated inability to meet expenses. In late nineteenth century Europe dismissed servants were a source of supply. Currently the quasi-legal status of prostitution makes it a repository for many with poor access to other labour markets, such as chronic drug addicts, single mothers in welfare traps due to tax and benefit systems and migrant workers, often of illegal immigrant status, who are sometimes misinformed about the jobs, wages and conditions available to them by those instrumental in their movement.

At first sight, a rational choice utility-maximizing perspective on supply decisions might seem to imply that punishments such as fines and imprisonments would be an effective means of curbing the activity as per Becker's model of the economics of crime. However, there is good reason to suspect that this is not the case for the low-income sectors. Those who lack alternative job opportunities, and are in poverty, are most likely to go straight back to prostitution to attempt to pay their fines and to atone for the loss of income whilst detained. There may also be very weak deterrence even for those working above the street prostitution level. The deterrence prediction presupposes that the individual is at the margin of allocating time between the punished occupation and some other uses. If the prostitute is highly specialized then the only alternative is to take more 'leisure' when expected punishment rises. However this need not arise if the income effect of punishment outweighs the substitution effect.

The types of market structure that have evolved in the industry can be defined from the supply side being allowed to drive the form which trading takes in the absence of any coherent long-run 'sex economy' framework plan emanating from governmental policy. The base-level spontaneous form of supply arising to meet latent demand is that of sole traders with little other capital inputs than their own personal attributes. The absence of any need to pay taxes and otherwise keep accounts promotes this situation. The purest form of sole trader is the street prostitute who neglects to use their own premises, or a rented room as a capital input to the sexual trade. The use of a public wall, or the customer's car, as the site for the transaction leads to lower prices due to this reduction in physical input costs and the associated time inputs required to set up the trade. Getting off the street requires certain investments for the sole trader such as contact methods, including magazine advertisements and also possibly equipment such as bondage gear and uniforms. In the case of the Amsterdam window prostitutes and escorts, who run their own websites and take bookings that way, we effectively see sole traders with premises and a booking system.

All sole traders may make sporadic use of agents, such as taxi drivers or hotel staff who contact them on behalf of visitors, etc. Where an agent becomes permanent, as in the stereotypical notion of the 'pimp', we leave the world of the sole trader and enter the standard small firm situation. Interview studies of prostitutes [see e.g. the discussion in Edlund & Korn (2001) and various reports that can be found via the Prostitutes' Education Network at http://www.bayswan.org/penet.html] express surprise that the stereotypical controlling pimp, with a team of prostitutes, seems to be very much a minority form of supply structure. Some caution ought to be interpreted over the use of interviews to collect information on the supply chain, as we would expect anyone who is controlled by a threatening agent to be both less likely to reply and less likely to tell the truth.

One factor which promotes street prostitution is the frequent historical focus of defining the sale of sex as illegal via the use of a building dedicated to the trade. Openly tolerated and outright legal prostitution has often been the multiple choice of women all located in one building type, albeit sometimes disguised as a private club or masquerading/doubling as hotel staff. Outright bordellos do presently exist, such as in Nevada and in the 'sex farms' of the Dutch/Belgian border where the workers live on the premises. This is a phenomenon induced by spatial isolation. There is little economic incentive to have 'live-in' prostitutes in a large urban centre, but in rural regions segregation may be necessary to placate objectors. Segregation is often backed up with other restrictions, such as curfews and zonal bans on the social life of the prostitutes, although these are also to be found in areas where prostitutes do not live on premises regulated by the political authorities [see Reynolds (1981, ch. 4)].

Where illegality is enforced, prostitution often operates under the guise of another building-based trade which also offers economies of scope due to sharing costs across the legitimate activities. Depending on the time and culture such 'fronts' are to be found in bath houses, karaoke bars, bars, hotels and massage parlours where the prostitute can readily pose as an employee in some other line of work that is easily turned into a sexual transaction when freedom from the law seems guaranteed. The building-based worker then tends to move to employee status, although in a situation of illegality it is difficult for them to acquire the rights and entitlements of other trades.

The escort agency is essentially like a bordello with added flexibility on the matter of the site transaction, that is whether it is a hotel, the supplier's own home or the demander's own home. In the absence of dedicated premises this is strictly an agency akin in economic terms to a flat-letting agency or an employment agency which is taking a matching fee off the supplier. The escort agency is likely to evolve into a primarily internet-sourced supply structure or 'virtual bordello'. The benefits can be seen in a site like the '192' escort search website sorted by region of the UK (at http://www.192escorts.com). This gives age, description, numerous pictures, the price list and a number of customer reports. This is an umbrella site for individuals and escort agencies which have an off-line presence. In general, the latter still seem to be very small in terms of the number of employees. This seems to be a feature of this market in countries with varying shades of legal acceptance so that, as yet, there is no tendency to a 'McDonaldsization' of paid sex markets. Probably the largest number of individuals being employed by a single employer is likely to be found in the organized crime sector in countries with problems of transition to a market economy.

One reason for a small and unorganized scale of supply is the attitude of reluctant toleration. Even where sex services are fully legal they are (as with addictive drugs) not given the free market rein of regular commodities. Many countries, even those with illegality in force, have 'Yellow Page' telephone directories which teem with advertisements for escort agencies, but there is no more widespread advertising. Customers cannot be actively sought via television and radio, and promotional activities like discounts, off-peak pricing, special offers and so on do not seem to be in operation. Stock markets do not appear to quote such companies and hence they do not seem to be merging with firms in other industries where synergies and scope and scale economies might be anticipated. The largest degree of merger with other industries seems to be in some organized crime control of hotels which include gambling and prostitution on the premises.

In principle, the building-based, and internet-centred, sex workers could organize themselves as a worker co-operative or some type of profit-sharing collective, but there seems to be little sign of this as small but conventional hierarchical firm structures, or agency fee-taking, are in place. The problem of rights and lack of protection against employers in such a scenario has led to the appearance of voluntary organizations, which cover all sex workers including porn actors, in many countries, but these tend to be information and campaigning bodies only as they would find it difficult to aspire to the status of a trade union or professional association. The apex of suppliers' demands for rights in regulation can be found in the World Charter for Prostitutes' Rights which was published in Amsterdam in 1985 and is reprinted in Pheterson (1989). This asks for decriminalization of all uncoerced acts of prostitution and the application of standard business codes to third-party agents. Additional protection from third-party fee collectors is also asked for to prevent 'exploitation' of sex workers in terms of unfair trading. The document demands the removal of laws restricting the rights of prostitutes to travel, associate and the absence of rules on where they can live or conduct business. This is a fundamental rejection of 'red light districts' (RLDs) as a suitable form of market clustering. Aside from the abolition of the above hindrances, the charter asks for positive measures in the form of granting sex workers adequate unemployment insurance, health insurance and housing benefits and equivalent tax treatment to other workers.

Even wider measures than the above were proposed. One is to set up a committee to deal with appeals from prostitutes over violation of rights with working prostitutes being included on the committee. Finally, it is proposed that education should be geared towards the normalization of attitudes towards prostitutes implied by all of the above. That is, along with their sex education at school children would be taught that commercial trading in sex, up to full bodily intimacy, is as 'normal' as buying a loaf from the supermarket rather than baking it in your home oven.

WAGES OF SIN: HIGH OR NOT?

The phrase 'wages of sin' was of course not devised with reference to the earnings of prostitutes; indeed it referred to the punishment of death. The main theoretical economic paper on prostitution [Edlund & Korn (2001)] is keen to emphasize that prostitution is highly lucrative relative to the comparable pay that sex vendors could obtain elsewhere. This is shown in their Table 1 which collates a number of studies of prostitutes' earnings in various countries. There have always been co-existent observations on prostitution as a trap of poverty and yet, on the other hand, as a source of enormous earnings. In 1963 the British Prime Minister Harold Wilson had this to say, in a speech in the House of Commons, concerning the role of Christine Keeler in the Profumo scandal:

> There is something utterly nauseating about a system of society which pays a harlot 25 times as much as it pays its Prime Minister, 250 times as much as it pays its Members of Parliament and 500 times as much as it pays some of its ministers of religion. [Isaacs (1993, p. 204)]

All this from the first British Prime Minister to be formally trained in economics! Interestingly, this quote seems to point in the direction of considering the World Charter for Prostitutes' Rights in the light of the envy issues covered in Chapter 5 rather than condemning paid sex outright as a sin which can only ever be tolerated as a necessary evil.

Economic theory might suggest that the recent spread of promiscuity and the fall of stigma at entering prostitution, and paid sex work in general, might drive down any such premia,[1] but reports of massive wages continue. In 1993 an undergraduate philosophy student, at London University, was quoted as saying:

> The money you can earn is mind blowing. In one month working in an escort agency I earned £5,000 – enough to support myself through a year at university. I can't see why people are so shocked at the idea of students working in the sex industry . . . it takes up very little time and is a very high earner. [Isaacs (1993, p. 204)]

These may be the extremes of the very fortunate (in terms of looks and personal charm), where the same sort of economic rents accrue which were discussed in the case of 'superstars' in Chapter 5. Harold Wilson might just as well have objected to the high-paid movie actors of his day as to Christine Keeler if he wished to be ethically consistent. What of the lowest paid?: the street prostitutes in countries with a primarily illegal orientation and the window prostitutes in Amsterdam, the prime example of the conventional idea of a legal system. In 2001 the low end of street prostitution in many countries would be little more than 10–20 dollars for a 'basic' level of service,[2] and in some cases reports have even appeared fairly recently of full sex for about four dollars. The very low rates are of course potentially quite high wages in low-income countries where the alternative is no wages.

Amsterdam 'window' prices are reportedly, at present, about 35 dollars for a higher-quality prostitute. This is comparatively cheap for the consumer as it equates to not much more than a full-price compact disc in a European country and is much less than the cost of an intermediate microeconomics textbook. From the suppliers' side these may still however be high wages, even in high-income economies, if the individual faces very menial alternatives due to low stocks of human capital. Street prostitutes may be in the position, if they are single mothers, that any legal employment places them in a poverty trap where they are no better off for working due to lost benefits. In illegal regimes there is no loss from these prices via taxation. Further, the basic cost leaves scope for negotiating extras which may be elastic in terms of their prices, particularly when the customer is inexperienced. A seasoned sex vendor can judge the willingness to pay of the punter as we move from a basic market-set price to a bilateral monopoly negotiation where the asymmetry of the situation is such that the negotiating skills of the seller will tend to be higher, particularly where there is a high proportion of transient demanders. As the empirical evidence suggests that travelling away from home and being new to an area are significant determinants of participating in the demand for paid sex, then the scope for bargaining up transient custom seems potentially large. One must add the caveat that the prevalence of internet reports which even name specific women, and expose their tactics, is likely to undercut the supply-side bargaining power.

So, let us accept the view that prostitutes do earn much higher wages than they would in comparable occupations or industries.[3] How do we explain this? There is a vast number of specific reasons deriving from two sources, the standard Smithian compensating wage differential position and, in addition to this, features of the market that prevent full equilibration. The specific reasons may be as follows.

(i) Compensation for loss of position in the primary sex market of monogamous relationships including formal marriage. Even if being a prostitute does not bar a woman from marriage [as assumed in the extreme models of Edlund & Korn (2001)] it may still lead to a fall in the average 'quality' of partner that can be obtained, all other things being equal, due to the perception of stigma from the pool of potential partners.

(ii) Wage compensation may be needed to overcome entry barriers from other forms of social exclusion such as the restrictions on residence, the operation of curfews, etc.

(iii) Average incomes may be higher due to a differential skew of opportunities. That is 'productivity' differentials, between prostitutes may translate into higher wage differentials at the top end of this profession compared to other professions due to greater relevance of idiosyncratic human capital that is not so marked elsewhere. For example, in non-stigmatized service sector employment such as hairdressing the top-end workers may not command the same proportionate premia relative to mid-range workers.

(iv) Risks of assault, disease, arrest, punishment and so forth are higher than in other occupations which have similarly low entry-level requirements. In many countries, illegality is often structured in such a way that the risk falls on the seller not the buyer.

(v) Front loading in the wage profile. Success in this market is highly dependent on biological youth, as discussed earlier, and therefore the entrant needs higher pay in the early period as a form of informal pension scheme or insurance.

(vi) Boredom. Unless the worker has a high latent demand for sex *per se* they will surely require compensation for the sheer boredom and psychic effort of daily repetitive attempts to simulate excitement for customers.

(vii) Distaste. This occupation offers potential psychological and physical pain costs. The supplier may face clients whom they find deeply unpleasant in the abstract and/or also requests for services that are deeply unpleasant (or possibly physically painful).

(viii) Loss of recreational sexual pleasure. Following on from the last point, some anti-prostitution activists make the more pointed claim that involvement in paid sex leaves the worker with 'an impoverished sexual and emotional life' [Chapkis (1997, p. 77) quoting Hoigard and Finstad].

(ix) Anti-social and inconvenient hours. In pure labour market theory terms these would be grounds for higher fees.

(x) There seems no intrinsic reason why this market should reach a clearing equilibrium. Excess demand might create the textbook upward pressure on prices. It may further be the case that higher prices are a quality signal, in a 'noisy' non-equilibrating market. Quality here may mean good health but also the willingness to keep secrets of regular professional or business customers. The use of price as a quality signal might create the appearance of excess demand. High prices can be used to screen quality on the demand side also:

for example a 'high-class' Finnish call girl, in 1993, claimed [Chapkis (ibid., p. 96)] that men who pay more are likely to be healthier, less threatening and so on.

(xi) Taboos. Suppliers who feel themselves to be sinning would require compensation to enter the trade.

(xii) Agent fees. Comparable occupations may not involve so much additional cost paid to agents for matching services and/or hire of premises.

Some of the above factors are intimately linked to the degree of legality and tolerance of the market. It is not possible to predict a priori whether greater legal accommodation would push up the rate of pay as it would seem likely to expand both the supply and the demand. Unfortunately we have no real idea of the relevant supply or demand elasticities, although probably the major factor which might decrease supply would be an improvement in women's labour market opportunities elsewhere.

CONCLUSION: POLICY MEASURES

Prostitution is neither fully legal nor fully illegal in any country; it is simply tolerated to a greater or lesser degree. Where it is formally illegal and enforcement does take place it tends to fall on the suppliers, although some areas of the USA differ by confiscating the cars of clients, sending offenders to 'John School', where they are lectured to by ex-prostitutes and, in Minneapolis at least, there is even 'naming and shaming' in the form of placing the pictures of those convicted on the internet. No country has a full-scale integrated plan for the role of prostitution and its 'sex economy' in general, although those countries, like Cuba, that have an overt strategy of 'sex tourism' come the closest. Nevertheless the plan is simply a revenue-maximizing one rather than a welfare-maximizing one.

In most liberal/neo-liberal economies little interest has been shown, unlike the case with addictive consumption drugs, in the amount of tax revenue that could be claimed from formal control of the prostitution sector. Yet in the period of licensing and tolerance in the Middle Ages, a large fraction of papal income was derived from the legal brothels [Ryley-Scott (1996, p. 68)]. However since the emergence of capitalism we see that the moral balancing act of using the rhetoric of taxes as deterrents of 'sin' as a veil for revenue raising is not universally emergent, even when the underlying activity is well developed in the economy. An interesting sidelight on this issue is that many countries which have supposedly illegal prostitution *and* very strict punishments for trading in drugs seem, from the anecdotal evidence, to be much stricter in enforcing their anti-drugs policy.

The main policy issues that emanate from this market are then not financial

ones, rather those of health, particularly contagious diseases, and the exploitation and abuse of vulnerable entrants. The high degrees of protection sought in
the Charter discussed above run counter to the guiding principles of most
liberal market economies, which would see general microeconomic and
macroeconomic policies to be sufficient to prevent people from being
'exploited' in this or any other market. Undoubtedly, piecemeal strategies of
regulation (such as offering free condoms or needle exchanges to drug users)
have been driven by moral panics over health threats such as the older
venereal diseases and the contemporary threat of HIV/AIDS. More coherent
strategies have emerged in places, usually individual cities/towns, where there
is a historical tradition that usually springs from being a 'hot spot' due to
military, naval or trade activity bringing large inflows of males who might be
in the state described by Mandeville above.

A long-run coherent 'normalization' strategy would have both beneficial
and detrimental consequences. There may be gains in terms of better health,
tax revenues and the exclusion of unscrupulous third parties. It is not
axiomatic that undesirable third parties will be driven out as this depends on
how far the spontaneous semi-tolerated market has developed. If it has reached
the point where organized crime rules the roost then it may be prohibitively
costly to eradicate them or even impossible if there has been 'capture' of the
regulators by the use of bribes, etc. Harking back to Chapter 6, it should
however be pointed out that dishonest motivations only lead to dishonest
behaviour when the structure of the market control allows it. Spontaneously
evolved illegal systems or corrupted legal systems could still generate substantial internalization of the health risk externalities so long as consumers have
some power to monitor the quality or 'reputation' of the supply and there is
some competition in supply. As with drugs we must not lose sight of the fact
that it is not usually in the interest of the illegal business person to kill off their
customers.

One unintended negative by-product of having a well-organized regulated
system, with good working conditions, is that it may promote an excess flow
of misinformed and myopic workers (some of them illegal immigrants) from
low-income countries. Amongst other things this may lead to an expansion of
the illegal system alongside the regulated system as these workers need to be
absorbed somewhere. As suggested above, the mere presence of careful regulation does not eliminate the illegal market. For one thing, the consumer may
have great difficulty distinguishing between which suppliers are legal and
which illegal, that is assuming they would want to in the first place. If
consumers were to demand the production of health tests, for example, they
would face problems in detecting forgeries. In addition the psychology of
making this kind of purchase suggests that the buyer would screen out such
dissonant information.

ENDNOTES

1. Of course countervailing pressure from rising real incomes could drive the premium up, although it has to be admitted that there is no direct evidence on the income elasticity of demand for paid sex goods and services.
2. The basic package for a fixed price, around the world, seems to be rapid oral sex with a condom followed by intercourse with a condom in fairly generally accepted positions. Some countries, particularly with non-regulated systems, seem to exhibit duplicitous advertising in that, when the customer arrives, they find the oral sex was not included in the price after all.
3. Earnings will vary much more than prices in this industry due to the number of sales that are made being widely different between sellers. Someone who is more skilled in conserving the effort and risk put into each sale is clearly in a position to make much higher earnings.

11. Conclusion

The journey taken here has been made for two main purposes. Firstly, to explore the implications of the rational choice model, as used within the discipline of economics, with an eye on the degree to which economists are consistent in the readings they derive from it. Secondly, to analyse the nature of the acknowledged sins as both causes and effects in the context of the economy as the driver of institutions. Inevitably the second objective has given rise to eclectic traversing of the boundaries of neo-classical microeconomics. Three main areas of discourse from beyond economics have intruded themselves. In the order of probably increasing influence these are: linguistics, psychology and anthropology.

Explicit analysis of language has had relatively few airings in economics. In 1937, L.M. Fraser produced a now forgotten text on the meanings attached to words as used by economists. This kind of thing was revived by McCloskey (1985), who began something of a bandwagon of literature and economics writings, overwhelmingly focused on the use of rhetorical strategies to persuade readers of the correctness of one's argument. This has expanded to include various explorations of the intersection between economics and literature, as revealed in the collection edited by Woodmansee & Osteen (1999). Still, there is not much focus on the use of language, in economics, to convey gradations of moral meaning. As we saw in Chapter 6, the precise use of words by economists can be an important tool in branding, or rebranding, the sin level of an activity in the marketplace. It has to be admitted that economists are not always consistent in these matters when they gravitate towards the policy area. Harmful effects on third parties have, since Pigou, had the neutral term of 'externalities' attached to them. Without a division of externalities into morally objectionable (sins) and otherwise, the door is wide open for an objective cost–benefit analysis to condone all sorts of possibly strange welfare improvements (sun king cannibalism, pervasive heroin use, adultery and frequent murder) if the circumstances were right. The focus of microeconomic theory on marginal adjustments, by rational decision-makers, means that 'absolute' concepts (such as morality and justice) tend to become redefined out of existence unless some taboo is forcing economists to preserve them, which they sometimes do, subconsciously, by linguistic perversion and confusion. As Deirdre McCloskey sagely observed in a recent commentary (2001), economic models only really tell us that anything is possible. In the absence of explicit 'Hippocratic oath' style credos being imposed on professional economists, the unthinkable, unacceptable outcome moves into the realm of distributional judgements. Distributional judgements do not just concern the spread of monetary wealth amongst the population, but are also inherently connected with sin, i.e. not depriving certain people of things as was discussed in connection with the 'liberal' position stated by Hausman & McPherson (1993) in Chapter 7. In the matter of life and death, it is probably not extreme to claim that polluting multinationals are killing many people in the developing world and that heavily promoted alcohol products and motor vehicles are killing thousands of people on the roads of the world. These activities are fuelled by much lying, deception, envy, greed and so on. They are accepted as part of the price of progress because responsibility and intent are displaced and depersonalized. The same occurs with purely monetary wrong-doings like burglary and 'fiddling' at work. These spread because they are justified as not really harming specific individuals. Economics and its metaphors of the market are a vital part of the depersonalizing, responsibility-removing process as the blame is derogated to 'the system' for failing to coordinate with appropriate incentives, rather than individuals being to blame.

Somewhat inevitably I have had recourse to psychological inputs in the course of the text. This is, by now, not uncommon and seems to be an expanding activity even amongst mainstream economists. Psychology relates to sin in so far as the individual has to process decision-making through filters in their mind about what is right or wrong conduct. As the individual does not exist in a vacuum, it has proved useful to explore anthropological texts on the group element in such mental processing. Anthropologists show the relativity of any cultural situation and have provided rational explanations for many group codes that may, to us, seem illogical and irrational. The presence or absence of sin for specific actions falls into this category. At various points in Chapters 3 and 7 we have even, at times, suggested that magical thinking was not collectively irrational. Anthropological hindsight suggests that sin is not at all 'original', in the sense that there is no guarantee that primitive economies will spontaneously evolve any concepts of it as institutions. For example, Peter Freuchten's 1961 book on the Eskimos reports a tolerance of many callous and inconsiderate acts that we may consider sinful (even if reduced to taboos or simply 'wrongs' for us), which his residence partly altered. These customs and institutions were held in place by the parlous state of existence under which people lived.

So, let me conclude by returning to the subject of sin as a subject in itself rather than a vehicle for the inspection of the internal coherence of economic theory. Sin in general and specific sins, as enshrined in the seven deadly sins and the ten commandments of the Bible and the enormous list of prohibitions in the Torah, became prominent when organized religions emerged to take the place of mythological stories as ruling cultural belief systems. The reduction of multiple God schemata to a single deity facilitates this process. There is no simple one-to-one mapping between religion and economic progress. At certain times and places a strict line on sin is conducive to economic growth and development by serving useful functions like stimulating work effort and increasing or decreasing the savings rate. However, there is a more direct line of causation between economic progress and religion. The arrival of advanced capitalism threatens religion by providing alternatives, in both spiritual and material terms, along with a rising shadow price of time which militates against traditional religious observances. Hence established doctrines of religion, as economic organizations, are forced to respond or die. As explored in Chapter 3 such responses can be in either direction. New religious 'firms' will arise to meet gaps in the mix of product characteristics in terms of doctrine and practice. Existing firms will shift their product mix, in terms of more or less sin regulation, depending on where they are currently positioned along the continuum of religious products. As sin is the product which religious firms sell, then just as much as with ice-cream markets, many different varieties can be sustained.

Inevitably, many people will lapse from religious affiliation altogether and many more, with a nominal allegiance, will become lax in observance. So, the question then arises how these lost sheep stand in relation to sin as they have left the explicit market of sin regulation, that is organized religion, behind. Casual empiricism rapidly informs us that they do not all become rampant hedonists,[1] albeit ones with a rationally managed life of pleasure as discussed in the treatment of the 'rational addiction' model in Chapters 2 and 8. Something constrains such people from rising to the peak of pleasure that might be within their grasp. In the resolutely mainstream tradition within economics this question would be delegated to the therapeutic community with the implicit idea that only a negligible fraction of society will exhibit neuroses and personality disorders. Returning to Nietzsche, however, we may point out that what is socially deemed to be normal may well not be best for many individuals. Even where religion has become weakened in its overt influence, the ideas of sin live on in attenuated notions of misconduct. A primary level of attenuation is required for what was formerly a sin to become merely a taboo. It will acquire the status of simply being something one 'should not do' without the notion of an accompanying payback from the vengeful deity. At a further stage, taboos weaken when social punishments are not enforced regularly. Now, we reach the point where behaviour such as adultery, lying and so on might not be seen as sins but still cause disapproval.

This takes us into the difficulty of distinguishing between whether or not something *is* a sin. Many would now see a wide selection of what has been discussed in this book as not 'really' sins, but would still go on to say that these things are 'wrong'. But why is something wrong if it is not a sin? The status of wrongness derives from atavistic retention, in the subconscious, of actions once having been sinful and/or guilt from 'wrongness' being a useful institution for society to regulate. One then regresses further to ask why codes of guilt and wrongness are useful to societies. As mentioned above usefulness would seem to revolve around the desirability of stable economic growth. In the end society, or any other abstract institution, has no intrinsic reason to be rational *per se* as economic sociologists, like Talcott Parsons (1937), would emphasize. In terms of rational choice economics, information problems, co-ordination failures and so on may enforce welfare-reducing limitations on the citizens. Clearly, one of these may be 'too many' feelings of guilt coming from legacies of sinfulness.

If one were to approach this proposition from the standpoint of critiquing organized religion then the culprit would seem to be the legends of the Fall. Subtle continuance of the notion of fallen mankind, even in secularized economies, is enough to give us feelings of generalized sin even where we are not conscious of admitting to specific sinning. Abstract feelings of sinfulness are found in many existentialist novels and in the more seriously intentioned works of rock music composers. In a global sense the legend of the Fall may be a huge piece of negative capital which (see Chapter 2) individuals are disin-centivized to actively shift due to large costs of so doing and little scope for capturing the free-rider gains to others. Some people will still attempt this and, if one accepts the last sentence, then these people will naturally be the most tortured by the repression under which their choices are constrained.

As we draw to a close there is the danger of a small, quiet, modest conclusion derived from conventional microeconomic theory. That is, the felt notion of sin is a cause of X-inefficiency due to failures by individuals to attain their 'true' preferences and efficiently pursue them. If individuals are rational they will spot this lacuna and swiftly move to rectify the welfare loss. The more radical views of Marcuse and Lyotard, in Chapter 4, go deeper than this. They locate the source of the problem in the inevitability of individuals defeating their own interests by denying themselves pleasure whether or not they believe in powerful deities who may punish them.

Finally, I will finish within the mainstream of economists. As remarked at the outset, this study has eschewed any kind of global cost–benefit analysis of sin, although statistical evidence of various sorts has been drawn on. Still, if one was asked to calculate the importance of sin in the economy then we seem to find that some people will have to agree that it is quite large so long as we comply with the traditional notion that all of the seven deadly sins and the ten commandments are sins. McCloskey & Klamer (1995) (see Chapter 6) told us that 1/4 of GDP is persuasion. As a large part of this is lying and we have to add on further quotients for resources used in stealing and all the other sins discussed in the present work, then it seems that nearly all of GDP is sinful.

ENDNOTE

1. The word hedonic leads a diverse existence in economics. When the theory of utility-maximizing individuals was formalized in the nineteenth century it was often called a hedonic calculus, but it did not seek to advocate pleasure-seeking. In modern times the most frequent use of the word hedonic in economics is to describe the contribution that the characteristics of goods make to their price. For example, a hedonic pricing model for computers would include measures of their speed, facilities, etc. as the hedonic elements.

Bibliography

Akerlof, G. (1970), 'The market for lemons; quality uncertainty and the market mechanism', *Quarterly Journal of Economics*, **84**, 488–500.

Akerlof, G. (1984), 'A theory of social custom', in Akerlof, G. (ed.), *An Economic Theorist's Book of Tales*, Cambridge University Press, Cambridge.

Akerlof, G. (1991), 'Procrastination and obedience', *American Economic Review*, **81**(2), 1–19.

Akerlof, G. & Dickens, W.T. (1982), 'The economic consequences of cognitive dissonance', *American Economic Review*, **72**, 307–19.

Albery, N. (1992), *The Book of Visions. An Encyclopedia of Social Innovations*, Virgin Books, London.

Alchian, A. (1953), 'The meaning of utility measurement', *American Economic Review*, **43**(1), 26–50.

Andreoni, J. (2001), 'The economics of philanthrophy, in Smelser', N.J. & Baltes, P.B. (eds), *International Encyclopedia of the Social and Behavioral Sciences*, Elsevier, London.

Anon. (1997), 'Degrees in adultery', *Cherwell*, Trinity 1997, Issue 5.

Arens, W. (1979), *The Man-Eating Myth. Anthropology and Anthropophagy*, Oxford University Press, New York.

Arrow, K.J. (1986), 'Rationality of self and others in an economic system', in Hogarth, R.M. & Reder, M.W. (eds), *Rational Choice*, University of Chicago Press, Chicago and London.

ASH (1993), *Her Share of Misfortune: Women, smoking and low income*, An Expert Report of the ASH Working Group on Women and Smoking, London: Action on Smoking and Health.

ASH (1995), *Factsheet No. 1. Smoking Statistics*, October, London: Action on Smoking and Health.

Atkinson, A.B. & Skegg, J. (1973), 'Anti-smoking publicity and the demand for tobacco in the U.K.', *Manchester School*, **41**(3), 265–82.

Averett, S. & Hochman, H. (1994), 'Addictive behavior and public policy', *Pubic Finance*, **49** (suppl.), 244–58.

Axelrod, R. (1984), *The Evolution of Cooperation*, Basic Books, New York.

Ayres, C.E. (1962), *The Theory of Economic Progress*, Second Edition, Schocken Books, New York.

Azzi, C. & Ehrenberg, R. (1975), 'Household allocation of time and church attendance', *Journal of Political Economy*, **84**, 27–56.

Bacon, F. (1906), *The Essayes or Counsels Civil & Morall of Francis Bacon Lord Verulam*, J.M. Dent, London. Reprint of 1625 edition.

Baier, K. (1966), 'Responsibility and freedom', in De George, R.T. (ed.), *Ethics and Society*, Anchor: Doubleday, New York, pp. 49–84.

Baker, R.R. (1996), *Sperm Wars: infidelity, sexual conflict and other bedroom battles*, Fourth Estate, London.

Baker, R.R. & Bellis, M.A. (1995), *Human Sperm Competition*, Chapman and Hall, London.

Bannerjee, A. (1992), 'A simple model of herd behavior', *Quarterly Journal of Economics*, **107**, 797–818.

Baran, P.A. & Sweezy, P.M. (1966), *The Political Economy of Growth*, Monthly Review Press, New York.

Barash, D. (1979), *The Whisperings Within*, Harper and Row, New York.

Barthold, T.A. & Hochman, H.M. (1988), 'Addiction as extreme seeking', *Economic Inquiry*, **26**(1), 89–106.

Bastable, C.F. (1892), *Public Finance*, Macmillan, London.

Bayer, B.E. (2000), 'Seven investing sins', [*Rulebreaker*] July 14. Found on the web at: http://www.fool.com/portfolios/rulebreaker/2000/rulebreaker000714.htm

Becker, G.S. (1965), 'A theory of the allocation of time', *Economic Journal*, **75**, 493–517.

Becker, G.S. (1968), 'Crime and punishment: An economic approach', *Journal of Political Economy*, **76**(2), 169–217.

Becker, G.S. (1973), 'A theory of marriage: Part One', *Journal of Political Economy*, **81**(4) 813–46.

Becker, G.S. (1974), 'A theory of marriage: Part Two', *Journal of Political Economy*, **82**(2), S11–26.

Becker, G.S. (1991a), *A Treatise on the Family*, Harvard University Press, Cambridge.

Becker, G.S. (1991b), 'A note on restaurant pricing and other examples of social influences on price', *Journal of Political Economy*, **99**, 1109–16.

Becker, G.S. (1992), 'Habits, addictions and traditions', *Kyklos*, **45**(Fasc.), 327–46.

Becker, G.S. & Murphy, K. (1988), 'A theory of rational addiction', *Journal of Political Economy*, **96**(4), 675–700.

Becker, G.S. & Stigler, G.K. (1977), 'De Gustibus Non Est Disputandum', *Journal of Political Economy*, **67**(1), 76–90.

Becker, G.S., Michael, R.T. & Landes, E.M. (1977), 'An economic theory of marital instability', *Journal of Political Economy*, **85**(6), 1141–87.

Becker, G.S., Grossman, M. & Murphy, K. (1994), 'An Empirical analysis of cigarette addiction', *American Economic Review*, **84**(3), 396–418.

Becker, H.S. (1953), 'Becoming a marihuana user', *American Journal of Sociology*, **59**, 235–42.

Bedau, H.A. (1982), *The Death Penalty in America*, Third Edition, New York University Press.

Beecher, J. & Bienvenu, R. (1975), *The Utopian Vision of Charles Fourier. Selected Texts on Work, Love & Passionate Attraction*, Jonathan Cape, London.

Bergler, E. (1970), *The Psychology of Gambling*, International Universities Press, New York.

Bergstrom, A. & Bagnoli, M. (1993), 'Courtship as a waiting game', *Journal of Political Economy*, **101**(1), 185–203.

Bernheim, D. (1994), 'A theory of conformity', *Journal of Political Economy*, **102**, 841–77.

Bernstein, P.L. (1996), *Against the Gods*, John Wiley and Sons, New York.

Bierce, A. (1911), *The Devil's Dictionary*, Wordsworth Editions, London (1996 edition).

Bikhchandani, S., Hirshleifer, D. & Welch, I. (1992), 'A theory of fads, fashion, custom and cultural change in informational cascades', *Journal of Political Economy*, **100**(5), 992–1026.

Birenbaum-Carmeli, D. (1995), 'Smoking during pregnancy: Canadian policy in the context of medical and legal views', *International Journal of Sociology and Social Policy*, **15**(4/5), 1–19.

Blank, R.M., George, C.C. & London, R.A. (1996), 'State abortion rates. The impact of policies, providers, politics, demographics and economic environment', *Journal of Health Economics*, **15**(5), 513–54.

Boadway, R. & Bruce, N. (1984), *Welfare Economics*, Basil Blackwell, Oxford.

Bowers, W.J., Pierce, J.L. & McDevitt, J.L. (1984), *Legal Homicide: Death as Punishment in America 1864–1982*, Northwestern University Press.

Bowles, S. & Gintis, H. (1999), 'Is equality passé. Homo reciprocans and the future of egalitarian politics', *Boston Review*, **23**(6), 4–10.

Bowles, S., Gintis, H. & Osborne, M. (2001), 'Incentive-enhancing preferences: personality, behavior and earnings', *American Economic Review*, **91**(2), 155–8.

Breakwell, G.M. & Millward, L.J. (1997), 'Sexual self-concept and sexual risk-taking', *Journal of Adolescence*, **20**(1), 29–41.

Brennan, T.J. (1989), 'A methodological assessment of multiple utility frameworks', *Economics and Philosophy*, **5**, 189–208.

Bressler, F. (1983), *The Mystery of Georges Simenon: A Biography*, Beaufort Books, New York.

Bretteville-Jensen, A.L. (1999), 'Gender, heroin consumption and economic behaviour', *Health Economics*, **8**(5), 379–89.

Bretteville-Jensen, A.L. & Sutton, M. (1996), 'The income generating behaviour of injecting drug-users in Oslo', *Addiction*, **91**(1), 63–79.

Brittan, S. (2000), 'Review of: Frank, R.H. 1999. Luxury Fever: Why Money Fails to Satisfy in an Era of Success', *Times Literary Supplement*, 7 April.

Brown, P. & Tuzin, D. (eds) (1983), *The Enthnography of Cannibalism*, Society of Psychological Anthropology, Washington, DC.

Bruce, S. (1993), 'Religion and rational choice: A critique of economic explanations of religious behavior', *Sociology of Religion*, **54**(2), 193–205.

Buchanan, J.M. (1965), 'An economic theory of clubs', *Economica*, **32**(1), 1–14.

Buchanan, J.M. (1973), 'A defense of organised crime', in Rottenberg, S. (ed.), *The Economics of Crime and Punishment*, American Enterprise Institute, Washington, DC.

Buchanan, C. & Prior, E.W. (1984), 'Bureaucrats and babies: government supply of the regulation of genetic material', *Economic Record*, **60**, 222–30.

Bullock, A. & Trombley, S. (1999), *The New Fontana Dictionary of Modern Thought*, Third Edition, HarperCollins, London.

Burdett, K. & Coles, M.G. (1997), 'Marriage and class', *Quarterly Journal of Economics*, **112**(1), 141–68.

Buss, D. (1994), *The Evolution of Desire*, Basic Books, New York.

Buss, D.M. & Shackelford, T.K. (1997), 'Susceptibility to infidelity in the first year of marriage', *Journal of Research in Personality*, **31**, 193–221.

Byrnes, J.P., Miller, D.C. & Schafer, W.D. (1999), 'Gender differences in risk taking: A meta-analysis', *Psychological Bulletin*, **125**(3), 367–83.

Cabot, L. & Cowan, T. (1992), *Power of the Witch. A Witch's Guide To Her Craft*, Arkana Penguin Books, London.

Cairncross, F. (2001), 'A survey of illegal drugs', *The Economist*, 28 July. See also: http://www.economist.com/surveys/sources.cfm/20010728

Cameron, S. (1989a), 'On the welfare economics of capital punishment', *Australian Economic Papers*, **28**(53), 253–66.

Cameron, S. (1989b), 'An empirical analysis of the determinants of cigarette tax rates', *Journal of Public Finance and Public Choice/Economia Delle Scelte Pubbliche*, **7**(1–2), 46–54.

Cameron, S. (1993), The demand for capital punishment', *International Review of Law and Economics*, **13**, 47–59.

Cameron, S. (1994), 'A review of the econometric evidence on the effects of capital punishment', *Journal of Socio-Economics*, **23**(4), 197–214.

Cameron, S. (2000a), 'Heavy drinking: Risk, restraint and other determinants', *Journal of Interdisciplinary Economics*, **11**(3–4), 255–68.

Cameron, S. (2000b), 'Exit-voice and rational choice: The economics of partner out-sourcing', Unpublished manuscript.

Cameron, S. (2001), 'Some econometric evidence contradictory to the received wisdom on health and religion', *Risk, Decision and Policy*, **5**, 239–53.

Cameron, S. & Collins, A. (1997), 'Estimates of a hedonic ageing equation for partner search', *Kyklos*, **50**(3), 409–18.

Cameron, S. & Collins, A. (1999), 'The economics of dangerous liaisons: deliberate misrepresentation of preferences for entertainment', *Rivista Internazionale di Commerciali/International Review of Economics and Business*, **46**(2), 285–300.

Cameron, S. & Collins, A. (2000a), *Playing the Love Market: Dating, Romance and the Real World*, Free Association Books, London.

Cameron, S. & Collins, A. (2000b), 'Demanding Sex', Unpublished manuscript.

Cameron, S. & Ward, D. (2000), 'Abstinence, excess, success: Alcohol, cigarettes, wedlock and earnings', *Economic Issues*, **5**(2), 37–52.

Cameron, S. & Welford, R. (1992), 'The market for genetic material: Estimates of the income elasticity of the willingness to pay', *Journal of Social and Evolutionary Systems*, **15**(1), 87–94.

Cameron, S., Collins, A. & Thew, N. (1999), 'Prostitution services: An exploratory empirical analysis', *Applied Economics*, **31**, 1523–9.

Carter, J.R. & Irons, M. (1991), 'Are economists different, and if so, why?', *Journal of Economic Perspectives*, **5**(2), 171–7.

Carter, R. (1998), *Mapping the Mind*, Weidenfeld and Nicolson, London.

Cassone, A. & Marchese, C. (1999), 'The economics of religious indulgences', *Journal of Institutional and Theoretical Economics*, **155**(3), 429–42.

Chaloupka, F.J. (1992), 'Clean air laws, addiction and cigarette smoking', *Applied Economics*, **24**(2), 193–205.

Chaloupka, F.J., Grossman, M., Bickel, W.K. & Saffer, H. (eds) (1999), *The Economic Analysis of Substance Abuse: An Integration of Econometric and Behavioral Economic Research*, NBER, University of Chicago Press.

Chapkis, W. (1997), *Live Sex Acts: Women performing erotic labour*, Cassell, London.

Charles, R. & Maclaren, D. (1982), *The Social Teachings of Vatican II: Its Origins and Development. Catholic Social Ethics: an historical and comparative study*, Plater Publications, Oxford.

Chase, S. (1930), *The Tragedy of Waste*, Macmillan, New York.

Chase Econometrics (1977), *The Economic Impact of the Tobacco Industry on the United States Economy*.

Coase, R.H. (1960), 'The problem of social cost', *Journal of Law and Economics*, **3**(1), 1–44.

Coleman, J.S. (1987), 'Norms and social capital', in Radniitzky, G. & Bernholz, P. (eds), *Economic Imperialism. The Economic Approach Applied Outside The Field of Economics*, Paragon House, New York.

Collard, D. (1978), *Altruism and Economy*, Martin Robertson.

Collier, P. (2000), *Economic Causes of Civil Conflicts and their Implications for Policy*, World Bank, Washington, DC.

Collins, R. (1993), 'Emotional energy as the common denominator of rational action', *Rationality and Society*, **5**(2), 203–30.

Corti, Count (1931), *A History of Smoking*, Bracken Books, London (trans. by Paul England).

Coutoyannis, P. & Jones, A.M. (1999), 'Rationality, addiction and adjustment costs', Working Paper, University of York.

Cowling, K. (1982), *Monopoly Capitalism*, Macmillan, London.

Cunningham, S. (1999), *The Truth About Witchcraft Today*, Llewellyn Publications, Minnesota.

D'Amato, A. (1980), 'The Speluncean Explorers – Further Proceedings', 32 *Stanford Law Review*, **467**, Code A80a.

Daly, H. (ed.) (1973), *Towards a Steady-state Economy*, W.H. Freeman, San Francisco.

Daniel, K. (1995), 'The marriage premium', in Tomassi, M. & Ierulli, K. (eds), *The New Economics of Human Behaviour*, Cambridge University Press, Cambridge.

Davidson, A.B. & Ekelund, R.B. (1997), 'The medieval church and rents from marriage market regulations', *Journal of Economic Behavior and Organization*, **32**(2), 215–46.

Dawkins, R. (1976), *The Selfish Gene*, Oxford University Press, London.

De Gaston, J.F., Weed, S. & Jensen, L. (1996), 'Understanding gender differences in adolescent sexuality', *Adolescence*, **31**(121), 217–31.

De Givry, G. (1971), *Witchcraft, Magic and Alchemy*, Dover Publications, New York.

Dees, J.G. & Cramton, P.C. (1991), 'Shrewd bargaining on the moral frontier: towards a theory of morality in practice', *Business Ethics Quarterly*, **1**(2), 135–67.

DeJong, D., Forsythe, R., Lundholm, R. & Uecker, W. (1985), 'A laboratory investigation of the moral hazard problem in an agency relationship', *Journal of Accounting Research*, **23**(Suppl.), 81–120.

Dezhbakhsh, H., Rubin, P. & Shepherd, J.M. (2001), 'Does Capital Punishment have a Deterrent Effect? New Evidence from Post-Moratorium Panel Data', Working Papers 01–01, Department of Economics, Emory University.

Dicey, A.V. (1914), *Lectures on the Relation Between Law and Public Opinion in England*, Second Edition. (Edition used is 1962 Macmillan, London, with a preface by E.C.S. Wade.)

Dong, P. & Raffill, T.E. (1997), *China's Super Psychics*, Marlowe and Company, New York.

Douglas, M. (1970), 'Primitive rationing: A study in controlled exchange', in Firth, R. (ed.), *Themes in Economic Anthropology*, Tavistock, London, pp. 119–48.

Douglas, M. (1973), *Natural Symbols*, Penguin Books, Harmondsworth.

Douglas, M. (1990), 'Risk and justice', *Daedalus*, **119**(4), 1–16.

Douglas, M. & Isherwood, B. (1979), *The World of Goods: Towards an Anthropology of Consumption*, Allen Lane, London.

Drago, R. (1995), 'A simple model of guilt with an application to unstaffed roadside stands', *Review of Social Economy*, **53**(3), 368–92.

Dryden, W. (1998), *Overcoming Jealousy*, Sheldon Press, London.

Duck, S. (1998), *Human Relationships*, Third Edition, Sage, London.

Duesenberry, J.S. (1949), *Income, Saving and the Theory of Consumer Behavior*, Harvard University Press, Cambridge, MA.

Durex (1998), 'Global Sex Survey', available as downloadable pdf file from http:www.durex.com

Durkheim, E. (1915), *The Elementary Forms of the Religious Life*, Free Press, Glencoe, IL.

Durkheim, E. (1938), *The Rules of Sociological Method*, Catlin, G.E.G. (ed.), Free Press, Macmillan, New York.

Duska, R.F. (1993), 'To Whom It May Concern: unpublished letter to the editor of the *Harvard Business Review*', 1 July.

Earl, P.E. (1983), *The Economic Imagination*, Wheatsheaf, Brighton.

Earl, P.E. (1990), 'Economics and psychology: a survey', *Economic Journal*, **100**, 718–55.

Easterlin, R.A. (1995), 'Will raising income raise the happiness of all?', *Journal of Economic Behavior and Organization*, **27**, 35–48.

Edlund, L. & Korn, E. (2001), 'A theory of prostitution', Stockholm School of Economics, mimeograph.

Ehrenberg, R.G. (1977), 'Household allocation of time and religiosity: replication and extension', *Journal of Political Economy*, **85**(2), 415–23.

Elffers, H. (1999), 'Tax evasion', in Earl, P.E. & Kemp, S. (eds), *The Elgar Companion to Consumer Research and Economic Psychology*, Edward Elgar, Cheltenham, pp. 556–60.

Ellison, C.G. (1991), 'Religious involvement and subjective well-being', *Journal of Health and Social Behavior*, **32**(1), 80–99.

Elster, J. (1982), 'Sour grapes-utilitarianism and the genesis of wants' in Sen, A. & Williams, B. (eds), *Utilitarianism and Beyond*, Cambridge University Press, Cambridge, chapter 11.

Elster, J. (1993), 'Some unresolved problems in the theory of rational behaviour', *Acta Sociologica*, **36**(3), 179–90.

Elster, J. (1998), 'Emotions and economic theory', *Journal of Economic Literature*, **36**(1), 47–74.

Elster, J. (ed.) (1999), *Addiction: Entries and Exits*, Russell Sage Foundation, New York.

Ensminger, J. (1997), 'Transaction costs and Islam: Explaining conversion in Africa', *Journal of Institutional and Theoretical Economics*, **153**(1), 4–29.

Etzioni, A. (1987), 'Toward a Kantian socio-economics', *Review of Social Economy*, **45**(1), 37–47.

Fair, R. (1978), 'A theory of extramarital affairs', *Journal of Political Economy*, **86**(1), 45–61

Farb, P. & Armelagos, G. (1980), *Consuming Passions. The Anthropology of Eating*, Houghton Mifflin Company, Boston.

Farrar, J. & Farrar, S. (1996), *A Witches' Bible. The Complete Witches' Handbook*, Phoenix Publishing, Washington, DC.

Farrell, J. (1995), 'Talk is cheap', *American Economic Review*, **85**(2), 186–90.

Fels, R. (1971), 'The price of sin', in Townsend, H. (ed.), *Price Theory: Selected Readings*, Penguin, Harmondsworth.

Festinger, L. (1957), *A Theory of Cognitive Dissonance*, Stanford University Press, Stanford, CA.

Finke, R. & Stark, R. (1992), *The Churching of America 1776–1990: Winners and Losers in our Religious Economy*, Rutgers University Press, Newark, NJ.

Fisher, H. (1995), *Anatomy of Love. The Natural History of Monogamy, Adultery and Divorce*, Fawcett Books, New York.

Fitch, E (1999), *A Grimoire of Shadows. Witchcraft, Paganism & Magick*, Llewellyn Publications, St Paul, MN.

Forst, B., Filatov, V. & Klein, L.R. (1978), 'The deterrent effect of capital punishment: an assessment of the estimates', in Blumstein, A., Nagin, D. & Cohen, J. (eds), *Deterrence and Incapacitation: estimating the effect of criminal sanctions on crime rates*, National Academy of Sciences, Washington, DC.

Frank, R.H. (1985), *Choosing the Right Pond*, Oxford University Press.

Frank, R.H. (1988), *Passions Within Reason*, W.W. Norton, New York.

Frank, R.H. (1989), 'Frames of reference and the quality of life', *American Economic Review*, **79**(2), 80–85.

Frank, R.H. (1993), 'The strategic role of the emotions', *Rationality and Society*, **5**(2), 160–84.

Frank, R.H. (1999), *Luxury Fever: Why Money Fails to Satisfy in an Era of Success*, The Free Press.

Fraser, L.M. (1937), *Economic Thought and Language*, A&C Black Ltd, London.

Frazer, J. (1993), *The Golden Bough*, Wordsworth Reference Library Edition.

French, M.T. & Zarkin, G.A. (1995), 'Is moderate alcohol use related to wages? Evidence from four worksites', *Journal of Health Economics*, **14**, 319–44.

Freuchten, P. (1961), *Book of the Eskimos*, World Publishing Company, Cleveland and New York.

Frey, B.S. & Eichenberger, R. (1996), 'Marriage paradoxes', *Rationality and Society*, **8**(2), 187–206.

Friedman, M. (1953), 'The methodology of positive economics', in *Essays in Positive Economics*, Aldine, Chicago.

Friedman, M. (1972), 'Prohibition and Drugs', *Newsweek*, 1 May. Reproduced at: http:www.druglibrary.org/special/friedman/prohibition_and_drugs.htm

Friedman, M. (1972), 'Milton Friedman Responds', *Business and Society Review*, **5**, 5–16.

Friedman, M. (1991), 'Drugs as a Socialist Conspiracy', reproduced at: http://www.druglibrary.org/special/friedman/socialist.htm

Friedman, M. & Savage, L.J. (1948), 'The utility analysis of choices involving risk', *Journal of Political Economy*, **61**, 279–304.

Fromm, E. (1949), *Man for Himself*, Routledge and Kegan Paul, London.

Gagnon, J., Kolata, G., Michael, R.T. & Laumann, E.O. (1994a), *Sex in America: A Definitive Survey*, Time Warner, New York.

Gagnon, J., Michael, R.T., Michaels, S. & Laumann, E.O. (1994b), *The Social Organisation of Sexuality*, University of Chicago Press, Chicago.

Galbraith, J.K. (1958), *The Affluent Society*, Riverside Press, Cambridge, MA.

Gale, D. & Shapley, L. (1962), 'College admissions and the stability of marriage', *American Mathematical Monthly*, **69**(1), 9–15.

Gardner, M. (2000), *Did Adam and Eve Have Navels?*, W.W. Norton & Company, New York and London.

Gathorne-Hardy, J. (1993), *The Rise and Fall of the British Nanny*, Weidenfeld, London.

Geoghegan, V. (1981), *Reason and Eros: The Social Theory of Herbert Marcuse*, Pluto Press, London.

George, D. (1993), 'Does the market create preferred preferences?' *Review of Social Economy*, **51**(3), 323–46.

Gerencher, K. (1998), 'The Economics of Sloth: Professor charts the costs of procrastination, self control'. Found on the web at: http://aolpf.market-watch.com/source/glq/aolpf/archive/20000614/news/current/personal.asp

Gibbbard, A. (1973), 'Manipulation of voting schemes: a general result', *Econometrica*, **41**, 587–601.

Gifford, A. Jr (1999), 'Being and time: On the nature and the evolution of institutions', *Journal of Bioeconomics*, **1**(1), 127–49.

Gilad, B., Kaish, S. & Loeb, P.D. (1987), 'Cognitive dissonance and utility maximization', *Journal of Economic Behavior and Organization*, **8**(1), 61–73.

Glaser, D. (1977), 'The realities of homicide versus the assumptions of economists in assessing capital punishment', *Journal of Behavioral Economics*, **6**, 243–68.

Glover, J. (1977), *Causing Death and Saving Lives*, Penguin Books, Harmondsworth.

Goldstein, A. (1994), *Addiction: From Biology to Drug Policy*, W.H. Freeman, New York.

Goodwin, C.D. (1988), 'The heterogeneity of economists' discourse: philosopher, priest and hired gun', in Klamer, A., McCloskey, D. & Solow, R.M. (eds), *The Consequences of Economic Rhetoric*, Cambridge University Press, Cambridge.

Granovetter, M. (1979), 'Threshold models of collective behavior', *American Journal of Sociology*, **83**, 1420–43.

Griffin, V. (1999), *The Mistress*, Bloomsbury Publishing, London.

Grossbard-Shechtman, A. (1982), 'A theory of marriage formality', *Economic Development and Cultural Change*, **30**, 813–30.

Grossbard-Shechtman, A.S. (1984), 'A theory of the allocation of time in markets for labour and marriage', *Economic Journal*, **94**, 863–82.

Grossbard-Shechtman, A.S. (1995), 'Marriage market models', in Tomassi, M. & Ierulli, K. (eds), *The New Economics of Human Behaviour*, Cambridge University Press, Cambridge, pp. 92–112.

Grossman, M. (1995), 'The economic approach to addictive behaviour', in Tomassi, M. & Ierulli, K. (eds), *The New Economics of Human Behaviour*, Cambridge University Press, Cambridge, pp. 157–71.

Gruber, J. (2001), 'Tobacco at the crossroads: the past and future of smoking regulation in the United States', *Journal of Economic Perspectives*, **15**(2), 193–212.

Hall, B.B. & Bold, F. (1998), 'Product variety in religious markets', *Review of Social Economy*, **56**(1), 1–19.

Halper, J. (1988), *Quiet Desperation: The Truth About Successful Men*, Warner, New York.

Hamberg, E. & Peterson, T. (1994), 'The religious market: denominational competition and religious participation in contemporary Sweden', *Journal of the Scientific Study of Religion*, **33**, 205–16.

Hammermesh, D. & Biddle, S. (1994), 'Beauty and the labour market', *American Economic Review*, **84**(5), 1174–95.

Hammermesh, D. & Soss, N. (1974), 'An economic theory of suicide', *Journal of Political Economy*, **82**(1), 83–98.

Harner, M. (1977), 'The ecological basis for Aztec sacrifice', *American Ethnologist*, **4**, 117–35.

Harrison, G.W. & McCabe, K.A. (1996), 'Stability and preference distortion in resource matching. An experimental study of the marriage problem', in

Isaac, R.M. (ed.), *Research and Experimental Economics*, Vol. 8, JAI Press, Greenwich, CT.

Harth, P. (ed.) (1970), *The Fable of the Bees*, Bernard Mandeville, Chivers-Penguin Library Edition, Bath.

Hausman, D. & McPherson, M. (1993), 'Taking ethics seriously: economics and contemporary moral philosophy', *Journal of Economic Literature*, **31**(2), 671–731.

Heien, D. (1996), 'The relationship between alcohol consumption and earnings', *Journal of Studies on Alcohol*, **57**(5), 536–42.

Heiner, R.A. (1983), 'The origins of predictable behavior', *American Economic Review*, **73**, 560–95.

Hine, P. (1995), *Condensed Chaos*, New Falcon Publications, Tempe, AZ.

Hinnells, J.R. (ed.) (1991), *Who's Who of Religions*, Macmillan, London.

Hirsch, F. (1976), *The Social Limits to Growth*, Harvard University Press, Cambridge, MA.

Hirschman, A.O. (1970), *Exit, Voice and Loyalty: Response to Decline in Firms, Organizations and States*, Harvard University Press, Cambridge, MA.

Hirshleifer, D. (1995), 'The blind leading the blind: social influence, fads, and informational cascades', in Tommasi, M. & Ierulli, K. (eds), *The New Economics of Human Behavior*, Cambridge University Press, Cambridge.

Hoffler, R.A. & Witte, A.D. (1979), 'Benefit–cost analysis of the sentencing decision: The case of homicide', in Gray, C.M. (ed.), *The Costs of Crime*, Sage Criminal Justice System Annuals, Vol. 12, Beverly Hills and London.

Hogg, G. (1961), *Cannibalism and Human Sacrifice*, Pan Books, London.

Hogg, J. (1997), *The Private Memoirs of a Justified Sinner*, Wordsworth Classics, Ware, Herts (originally published 1824).

Holt, C.A. & Laury, S.K. (1998), 'Theoretical explanations of treatment effects in voluntary contributions experiments', in Plott, C.R. & Smith, V.L. (eds), *Handbook of Experimental Economics Results*, Elsevier Press, New York.

Honderich, T. (ed.) (1995), *The Oxford Companion to Philosophy*, Oxford University Press, Oxford and New York.

Hotelling, H. (1929), 'Stability in competition', *Economic Journal*, **39**(1), 41–57.

Houthakker, H. & Taylor, L.D. (1970), *Consumer Demand in the United States: Analyses and Projections*, Second Edition, Harvard University Press, Cambridge, MA.

Howitt, D. & Cumberbatch, G. (1990), *Pornography: Its Impacts and Influences, a Review of the Available Research Evidence on the Effects of Pornography*, Home Office Research and Planning Unit, HMSO, London.

Iannacone, L.R. (1984), 'Consumption capital and habit formation with an application to religious participation', University of Chicago, Ph.D. dissertation.

Innacone, L.R. (1992), 'Sacrifice and stigma: reducing free riding in cults, communes and other collectives', *Journal of Political Economy*, **100**(2), 271–97.

Innacone, L.R. (1995), 'Household production, economic behavior and the economics of religion', in Tomassi, M. & Ierulli, K. (eds), *The New Economics of Human Behaviour*, Cambridge University Press, Cambridge, pp. 172–87.

Innacone, L. (1998), 'Introduction to the economics of religion', *Journal of Economic Literature*, **36**(3), 1465–95.

Isaacs, A. (ed.) (1993), *Cassell Dictionary of Sex Quotations*, Cassell, London.

Jacobs, J. (1966), *The Fables of Aesop*, Schocken Books, New York (reprint of 1894 edition).

Jacobson, B. (1986), *The Ladykillers*, Pluto Press, London.

James, W. (1902), *The Varieties of Religious Experience. A Study in Human Nature*, Longmans Green, New York. [Edition used is in Coles, R. (ed.) (1997), *Selected Writings: William James*, Book-of-the-Month Club, New York.]

Jennings, M.M. & Entine, J. (1998), 'Business with a soul: A reexamination of what counts in business ethics', *Hamline (Minnesota) Journal of Law and Public Policy*, Fall.

Jevons, W.S. (1910), *Money and the Mechanism of Exchange*, Kegan Paul, Trench, Trubner & Co. Ltd, London.

Jones, A.M. (1999), 'Adjustment costs, withdrawal and cigarette consumption', *Journal of Health Economics*, **18**, 125–37.

Jones, S.R.G. (1984), *The Economics of Conformism*, Basil Blackwell, Oxford.

Kahneman, D., Knetsch, J.J. & Thaler, R. (1986), 'Fairness as a constraint on profit seeking: entitlements in the market', *American Economic Review*, **76**, 728–41.

Kandori, M. (1992), 'Social norms and community enforcement', *Review of Economic Studies*, **59**(1), 63–80.

Kaplan, R.M., Pierce, J.P., Gilpin, E.A., Johnson, M. & Bal, D.G. (1993), 'Stages of smoking cessation: the 1990 California Tobacco Survey', *Tobacco Control*, **2**(2), 139–44.

Karney, B.R. & Bradbury, T.N. (1995), 'The longitudinal course of marital quality and stability: a review of theory, methods and research', *Psychological Bulletin*, **118**, 3–34.

Kendell, R.E., de Romanie, M. & Ritson, E.B. (1983), 'Effects of economic changes on Scottish drinking habits', *British Journal of Addiction*, **78**, 365–79.

Kenkel, D. (1993), 'Drinking, driving and deterrence: the effectiveness and social costs of alternative policies', *Journal of Law and Economics*, **36**, 877–913.

Keynes, J.M. (1936), *The General Theory of Employment, Interest and Money*, Macmillan, London.

Kindleberger, C.P. (1978), *Manias, Panics and Crashes*, Basic Books, New York.

Kirsch, J. (1997), *The Harlot by the Side of the Road. Forbidden Tales of the Bible*, Rider, London.

Kirzner, I. (1973), *Competition and Entrepreneurship*, The University of Chicago Press, Chicago and London.

Knight, F.H. (1922), *Risk, Uncertainty and Profit*, Houghton Mifflin, Boston and New York.

Kraft, C.H. (1992), *Defeating Dark Angels. Breaking Demonic Oppression in the Believer's Life*, Servant Publications, Ann Arbor, MI.

Krafft-Ebing, R. Von (1997), *Psychopathia Sexualis*, Velvet Publications, London (originally published in 1897).

Kreps, D.L. & Wilson, R. (1982), 'Reputation and information', *Journal of Economic Theory*, **27**, 253–79.

Kuran, T. (1995), 'Islamic economics and the Islamic subeconomy', *Journal of Economic Perspectives*, **9**(4), 155–73.

Kuran, T. (1997), 'Islam and underdevelopment: An old puzzle revisited', *Journal of Institutional and Theoretical Economics*, **153**(1), 41–71.

La Gaipa, J.J. (1982), 'Rituals of disengagement', in Duck, S. (ed.), *Personal Relationships 4: Dissolving Personal Relationships*, Academic Press, London.

Laiou, A.E. (ed.) (1993), *Consent and Coercion to Sex and Marriage in Ancient and Medieval Societies*, Dumbarton Oaks, Washington, DC.

Lancaster, K.O. (1971), *Consumer Demand: A New Approach*, Columbia University Press, New York.

LaVey, A.Z. (1989), *The Satanic Witch*, Feral House, Vernice, CA.

Lea, S.E.G., Walker, C.M. & Webley, P. (1992), 'An interview study of the origins of problem debt', University of Exeter, Department of Psychology: Economic Psychology Research Group, Internal Report Number 92/106.

Ledyard, J.O. (1995), 'Public goods: A survey of experimental research', in Roth, A. & Kagel, J. (eds), *A Handbook of Experimental Economics*, Princeton University Press, Princeton, NJ, pp. 111–94.

Leibenstein, H. (1950), 'Bandwagon, snob and Veblen effects in the theory of consumers' demand', *Quarterly Journal of Economics*, **64**(2), 183–201.

Leibenstein, H. (1996), 'Allocative efficiency vs. "X-efficiency" ', *American Economic Review*, **57**, 392–415.

Leibenstein. H. (1978), 'X-inefficiency exists: A reply to an exorcist', *American Economic Review*, **69**(1), 203–11.

Leigh, J. (1995), 'Smoking, self-selection and absenteeism', *Quarterly Review of Economics and Finance*, **35**(4), 365–86.

Lester, D. & Yang, B. (1994), *Economic Perspectives on Suicide*, AMS, New York.

Levin, J.S. (1994), 'Religion and health. Is there an association: is it valid and is it causal', *Social Science and Medicine*, **38**(11), 1475–82.

Levin, J.S & Vanderpool, H.Y. (1987), 'Is frequent religious attendance really conducive to better health? Towards an epistemology of religion', *Social Science and Medicine*, **24**(7), 589–600.

Levine, D. (1997), 'More bad news for smokers? The effect of smoking on earnings', *Industrial and Labor Relations Review*, **50**(3), 493–509.

Levitt, S.D. & Venkatesh, S. (1998), 'An Economic Analysis of a Drug-Selling Gang's Finances', NBER Working Paper No. 6592, June.

Levy, D. (1988), 'Utility enhancing consumption constraints', *Economics and Philosophy*, **4**(1), 69–88.

Lipsey, R.G. & Rosenbluth, G. (1971), 'A contribution to the new theory of demand: a rehabilitation of the Giffen good', *Canadian Journal of Economics*, **4**(2), 131–63.

Long, S.H. & Settle, R.F. (1977), 'Household allocation of time and church attendance: some additional evidence', *Journal of Political Economy*, **85**(2), 409–31.

Low, S. (1911), *Masters of Literature. De Quincey*, Bell and Sons Ltd, London.

Lyotard, J. (1993), *Libidinal Economy*, Indiana University Press, Bloomington (transl. by I.H. Grant).

Machina, M. (1989), 'Choice under uncertainty: problems solved and unsolved', in Hey, J. (ed.), *Current Issues in Microeconomics*, Macmillan, London, pp. 12–46.

Machlup, T. (1969), 'Positive and normative economics: an analysis of the ideas', in Heilbroner, R.L. (ed.), *Economic Means and Social Ends*, Prentice-Hall, Englewood Cliffs, NJ, chapter 6.

MacIntyre, A. (1984), 'Does applied ethics rest on a mistake?', *The Monist*, **67**(4), 499–512.

MacIntyre, A. (1988), *Whose Justice? Which Rationality?* University of Notre Dame Press, Notre Dame, IN.

Mahony, J. & Waller, D. (1992), 'Art therapy in the treatment of alcohol and drug abuse', in Waller, D. & Gilroy, A. (eds), *Art Therapy: A Handbook*, Open University Press, pp. 173–88.

Mailath, G. (1998), 'Do people play Nash equilibrium?', *Journal of Economic Literature*, **36**(3), 1347–74.

Maital, S. (1988), 'Novelty, comfort and pleasure: inside the utility-function black box', in Albanese, P.O. (ed.), *Psychological Foundations of Economic Behavior*, Praeger, New York, pp. 1–30.

Mandela, N. (1993), 'Message from Mr. Nelson Mandela to mark the 5th World No-Tobacco Day (1992)', *Tobacco Control*, **2**(2), 99.

Manski, C.F. (2000), 'Economic analysis of social interactions', *Journal of Economic Perspectives*, **14**(3), 115–36.

Marcuse, H. (1955), *Eros and Civilization*, Beacon Press, Boston.

Mars, G. (1982), *Cheats At Work. An Anthropology of Workplace Crime*, George Allen & Unwin, London.

Martyn, D. (1999), 'Sade's ethical economies', in Woodmansee, M. & Osteen, M. (eds), *The New Economic Criticism*, Routledge, London and New York, pp. 258–76.

Maynard, A. & Wagstaff, K. (1988), 'The economic aspects of the illicit drug market and drug enforcement policies in the U.K.', *Home Office Research Study 95*.

McCain, R. (1990a), 'Humanistic economics again', *Forum For Social Economics*, **19**(2), 78–87.

McCain, R. (1990b), 'Impulse filtering: A new model of freely willed economic choice', *Review of Social Economy*, **48**(2), 125–34.

McClelland, D.C. (1961), *The Achieving Society*, Van Nostrand, Princeton, NJ.

McCloskey, D. (1985), *The Rhetoric of Economics*, University of Wisconsin Press, Madison.

McCloskey, D. (2001), 'Other things equal: mottoes for science: Intedete late in gubernando: and Qui scis?', *Eastern Economic Journal*, **27**(2), 209–10.

McCloskey, D. & Klamer, A. (1995), 'One quarter of GDP is persuasion', *American Economic Review*, **85**(2), 191–5.

McKee, D.L. & Sesnowitz, M.L. (1976), 'Welfare economic aspects of capital punishment', *American Journal of Economics and Sociology*, **35**(1), 41–7.

McKee, D.L. & Sesnowitz, M.L. (1977), 'On the death penalty and emotionalism. A reply to Reynolds', *American Journal of Economics and Sociology*, **36**(1), 110–111.

Medoff, M.H. (1988), 'An economic analysis of the demand for abortions', *Economic Inquiry*, **26**, 353–9.

Miele, F. (1996), 'The (im)moral animal: A quick & dirty guide to evolutionary psychology & the nature of human nature', *The Skeptic*, **4**(1), 42–9.

Millon, T. et al. (2000), *Personality Disorders in Modern Life*, John Wiley.

Molho, I. (1997), *The Economics of Information: Lying and Cheating in Organisations*, Basil Blackwell, Oxford.

Moore, G.E. (1912), *Ethics*, The Clarendon Press, Oxford.

Nelson, R.R. & Winter, S.G. (1982), *An Evolutionary Theory of Economic Behavior and Capabilities*, Harvard University Press, Cambridge, MA.

Neuman, S. (1986), 'Religious observance within a human capital framework', *Applied Economics*, **18**(11), 1193–202.

Neumark, D. & Postlewaite, A. (1998), 'Relative income concerns and the rise in married women's employment rate', *Journal of Public Economics*, **70**(1), 157–83.

News of the World (1998), 'Are you ready for an affair?', Sunday Magazine, 30 August.

Newhouse, J.P. (1970), 'Theory of the non-profit hospital', *American Economic Review*, **60**(1), 64–75.

Ng, Y.-K. (1983), *Welfare Economics*, Revised Edition, Macmillan, London and Basingstoke.

Nietzsche, F. (1990), *Twilight of the Idols/The Anti-Christ*, Penguin, Harmondsworth (the *Anti-Christ* was originally published in 1895).

Norman, M. (1998), 'Getting Serious About Adultery: Who Does It and Why They Risk It', *New York Times*, 4 July.

Occult Census (1989), Sorcerer's Apprentice Press, Leeds.

O'Guinn, T.C. & Shrum, L.J. (1990), 'The psychology of normative economic beliefs: Mass-mediated processes and effects in consumer socialization', in Lea, S.E.G., Webley, P. & Young, B.M. (eds), *Applied Economic Psychology in the 1990s*, Washington Singer Press, pp. 716–30.

Orphanides, A. & Zevros, D. (1995), 'Rational addiction with learning and regret', *Journal of Political Economy*, **103**, 739–58.

Ortiz de Montellano, B.R. (1978), 'Aztec cannibalism: an ecological necessity', *Science*, **200** (May 12), 611–17.

Oswald, A. (1983), 'Altruism, jealously and the theory of optimal non-linear taxation', *Journal of Public Economics*, **20**(1), 77–88.

O'Toole, K. (1998), *Pornocopia*, Serpent's Tail, London.

Pacula, R.L. (1997), 'Women and substance use: are women less susceptible to addiction?, *American Economic Review*, **87**(2), 454–9.

Parisi, F. (2000), 'Spontaneous emergence of law: Customary law', in Bouckaert, B. & De Geest, G. (eds), *Encyclopedia of Law and Economics, Vol. V. The Economics of Crime and Litigation*, Edward Elgar, Cheltenham, pp. 603–30.

Parker, R. (2001), 'Baseball's best are justified in trying to increase their salaries', *The Detroit News*, February 28.

Parsons, T. (1937), *The Structure of Social Action*, Free Press, Glencoe, IL.

Peacock, J.L. (1975), *Consciousness and Change*, Basil Blackwell, Oxford.

Pearson, G. (1983), *Hooligan: A History of Respectable Fears*, Schocken Books, New York.

Peck, M.S. (1983), *People of the Lie*, Simon and Schuster, New York.

Pheterson, G. (ed.) (1989), *A Vindication of the Rights of Whores*, Seal Press, Seattle.

Pierce, J.P., Fiore, M.C., Novotny, T.E., Hatziandrew, E.J. & Davis, R.M. (1989), 'Trends in cigarette smoking in the United States: educational differences are increasing', *Journal of the American Medical Association*, **261**, 56–60.

Popper, K.R. (1959), *The Logic of Scientific Discovery*, Routledge (translation of 1935 edition).

Posner, R.A. (1992), *Sex and Reason*, Harvard University Press, Cambridge, MA.

Posner, R.A. & Rasmussen, E.B. (1999), 'Creating and enforcing norms with special references to sanctions', *International Review of Laws and Economics*, **19**(3), 369–82.

Presley, J.R. & Sessions, J.G. (1994), 'Islamic economics: The emergence of a new paradigm', *Economic Journal*, **104**(424), 584–96.

Prostitutes' Education Network. PENET: http://www.bayswan.org/penet.html

Pryor, F. (1990), 'A Buddhist economic system – in principal: The way of the law is profitable', *American Journal of Economics and Sociology*, **49**(3), 339–49.

Pryor, F. (1991), 'A Buddhist economic system – in practice', *American Journal of Economics and Sociology*, **50**(1), 17–32.

Radin, M.J. (1996), *Contested Commodities*, Harvard University Press, Cambridge, MA and London.

Rasmussen, E. (2001), *Games and Information*, Third Edition, Basil Blackwell, Oxford.

Ray, J.L. (1982), 'Attitudes to the death penalty in South Africa with some international comparisons', *Journal of Social Psychology*, **116**, 287–8.

Reder, M. (1979), 'The place of ethics in the theory of production', in Boskin, M. (ed.), *Economics and Human Welfare: Essays in Honour of Tibor Scitovsky*, Academic Press, New York, pp. 133–46.

Rees, R. (1985), 'Cheating in a duopoly supergame', *Journal of Industrial Economics*, **32**(4), 369–87.

Reibstein, J. & Richards, R. (1993), *Sexual Arrangements: Monogamy, Marriage and Affairs*, Mandarin, London.

Reynolds, F.E. & Clifford, R.T. (1980), 'Sangha, society and the struggle for national identity: Burma and Thailand, in Reynolds, F.E. & Ludwig, T. (eds), *Transitions and Transformations in the History of Religions*, Brill, Leiden, pp. 56–94.

Reynolds, H. (1981), *Cops and Dollars: The Economics of Criminal Law and Justice*, C.C. Thomas, Springfield, IL.

Reynolds, M.O. (1977), 'On welfare economics of capital punishment', *American Journal of Economics and Sociology*, **36**, 105–9.

Rives Child, J. (1989), *Casanova: A New Perspective*, Constable, London.

Room, A. (1996), *Brewer's Dictionary of Phrase and Fable*, Fifteenth Edition, Cassell, London.

Rosario, V.A. (1997), *The Erotic Imagination. French Histories of Perversity*, Oxford University Press, New York.

Rose-Ackermann, S. (1999), *Corruption and Government*, Cambridge University Press, Cambridge.

Rosen, S. (1981), 'The economics of superstars', *American Economic Review*, **71**(5), 845–57.

Ross, E.A. (1907), *Sin and Society: An Analysis of Latter-Day Iniquity*, Houghton Mifflin, Boston.

Royal Commission on Capital Punishment 1949–1953. Report (1953), HMSO, London, Cmmd 8932.

Russell, J.B. (1980), *A History of Witchcraft: Sorcerers, Heretics and Pagans*, Thames and Hudson, London.

Ryan, W.F. (1999), *The Bathhouse at Midnight: Magic in Russia*, Pennsylvania State University Press, University Park, PA.

Ryley-Scott, G. (1996), *The History of Prostitution*, Senate, London.

Saffer, H. & Chaloupka, F.J. (1999), 'Demographic differentials in the demand for alcohol and illicit drugs', in Chaloupka, F.J., Grossman, M., Bickel, W.K. & Saffer, H. (eds), *The Economic Analysis of Substance Use and Abuse*, NBER, University of Chicago Press, Chicago and London, chapter 7.

Sandler, T. & Tschirhart, J. (1980), 'The economic theory of clubs: an evaluative survey', *Journal of Economic Literature*, **18**(4), 1481–521.

Satterthwaite, M.A. (1975), 'Strategy-proofness and Arrow's conditions', *Journal of Economic Theory*, **10**, 187–217.

Sawhill, I.V. (1998), 'Teen Pregnancy Prevention: Welfare Reform's Missing Component', *Brookings Policy Brief No. 38*, November. Available at: http://www.brookings.edu

Sawkins, J.W., Seaman, P.T. & Williams, H.C.S. (1997), 'Church attendance in Great Britain: An ordered logic approach', *Applied Economics*, **29**, 125–34.

Schelling, T. (1971), 'What is the business of organised crime?', *The Journal of Public Law*, **20**(1), 71–84.

Schelling, T. (1984), 'Self command in practice, in policy, and in a theory of rational choice', *American Economic Review*, **74**(2), 1–11.

Schmidtchen, D. & Mayer, D. (1997), 'Established clergy, friars and the Pope, Some institutional economics of the Medieval Church', *Journal of Institutional and Theoretical Economics*, **153**(1), 129–49.

Schneider, F. & Enstel, D. (2000), 'Shadow Economies Around the World: Size, Causes and Consequences', International Monetary Fund Working Paper, January.

Schumacher, E.F. (1968), 'Buddhist economics', *Resurgence*, **1**(11). [Reprinted in Daly, H. (ed.), *Towards A Steady-State Economy*, W.H. Freeman and Company, San Francisco.]

Schumpeter, J.A. (1934), *The Theory of Economic Development*, Harvard University Press, Cambridge, MA.

Schutz, A. (1943), 'The problem of rationality in the social world', *Economica*, **10**, 130–49.

Scitovsky, T. (1976), *The Joyless Economy*, Oxford University Press, Oxford.

Scitovsky, T. (1986), *Human Desire and Economic Satisfaction*, Wheatsheaf, Brighton.

Scott, Sir Walter (2001), *Letters on Demonology and Witchcraft*, Wordsworth Editions in association with the Folklore Society.

Seddon, R. (ed.) (1993), 'Understanding the human being', *Selected Readings of Rudolf Steiner*, Rudolf Steiner Press, Bristol.

Sellin, T. (1959), *The Death Penalty*, American Law Institute, Philadelphia.

Sen, A.K. (1970), 'The impossibility of a Paretian liberal', *Journal of Political Economy*, **78**, 152–7.

Sen, A.K. (1976/7), 'Rational fools: A critique of the behavioural foundations of economic theory', *Philosophy and Public Affairs*, **6**, 317–44.

Shackelford, T.K. & Buss, D.M. (1997), 'Marital satisfaction in evolutionary psychological perspective', in Sternberg, R.J. & Hojjat, M. (eds), *Satisfaction in Close Relationships*, Guilford, New York, pp. 7–25.

Shavell, S. (1987), 'A model of optimal incapacitation', *American Economic Review*, **77**(2), 107–10.

Shi, D.E. (1985), *The Simple Life: Plain Living and High Thinking in American Culture*, Oxford University Press, New York.

Shiller, R.J. (1995), 'Conversation, information, and herd behavior', *American Economic Review*, **85**(2), 181–5.

Sidgwick, H. (1919), *Outlines of the History of Ethics for English Readers*, Macmillan, London.

Skinner, J. & Slemrod, J. (1985), 'An economic perspective on tax evasion', *National Tax Journal*, **38**(3), 345–53.

Smart, J.J.C. (1961), 'Free will, praise and blame', *Mind*, **70**(279), 291–306.

Smith, A. (1759), *The Theory of Moral Sentiments*, 1976 Liberty Classics Edition, West, E.G. (ed.), Indianapolis.

Smith, I. (1993), 'The economics of church decline in Scotland', *International Journal of Social Economics*, **20**(12), 27–36.

Smith, I. (1999), 'The economics of the Apocalypse: Modelling the Biblical book of Revelation', *Journal of Institutional and Theoretical Economics*, **155**(3), 443–57.

Smith, M.E. (1996), *The Aztecs*, Basil Blackwell, Oxford.

Stanford, P. (1996), *The Devil: A Biography*, Henry Holt and Company, New York.

Stark, A. (1993), 'What's the matter with business ethics', *Harvard Business Review*, (May–June), 38–48.

Stark, R. & Innacone, L.R. (1994), 'A supply-side reinterpretation of the "secularisation" of Europe', *Journal for the Scientific Study of Religion*, **33**, 230–52.

Statman, D. (1997), 'Hypocrisy and self-deception', *Philosophical Psychology*, **10**(1), 57–75.

Stevenson, R. (1997), *Winning the War On Drugs*, Institute of Economic Affairs, London (second impression).

Stigler, G.J. (1970), 'The optimum enforcement of laws', *Journal of Political Economy*, **78**, 626–36.

Sullivan, D.H. (1985), 'Simultaneous determination of church contributions and church attendance', *Economic Inquiry*, **23**(2), 309–20.

Sumner, H. (1906), *Folkways*, Dover Publications, New York.

Suranovic, S.M., Goldfarb, R.S. & Leonard, T.C. (1999), 'An economic theory of cigarette addiction', *Journal of Health Economics*, **18**(1), 1–29.

Swanda, J.R. (1990), 'Goodwill, going concern, stocks and flows: A prescription for moral analysis', *Journal of Business Ethics*, **9**(9), 751–60.

Symons, D. (1979), *The Evolution of Human Sexuality*, Oxford University Press, Oxford.

Taylor, T. (1996), *The Prehistory of Sex: Four Million Years of Culture*, Fourth Estate, London.

Thaler, R. & Shefrin, H.M. (1988), 'An economic theory of self control', *Journal of Political Economy*, **89**, 392–406.

That's Life (magazine) (2001), as reported in 'A Nation of Fibbers' on p. 161 of ITV Teletext Services (UK) September 2, 2001.

Thomas, K. (1997), *Religion and the Decline of Magic*, Weidenfeld & Nicolson, London.

Todd, P.M. (1997), 'Searching for the next best mate', in Conte, R., Hegelsmann, R. & Terna, P. (eds), *Simulating Social Phenomena*, Springer-Verlag, Berlin.

Tomer, J. (1996), 'Good habits and bad habits: a new age socio-economic model of preference formation', *Journal of Socio-Economics*, **25**(6), 619–38.

Tomer, J. (1998), 'Addictions are not rational: a socio-economic model of addictive behavior', Paper presented at the SASE Conference, Madison, WI.

Troilo, G. (1999), 'Collecting', in Earl, P.E. & Kemp, S. (eds), *The Elgar Companion to Consumer Research and Economic Psychology*, Edward Elgar, Cheltenham, pp. 88–92.

Tullock, G. (1966), 'Information without profit', reprinted in Lamberton, D. (ed.), *Economics of Information and Knowledge*, Penguin, Harmondsworth, 1971.

Twomey, P.J. (1999), 'Habit', in Earl, P.E. & Kemp, S. (eds), *The Elgar Companion to Consumer Research and Economic Psychology*, Edward Elgar, Cheltenham, pp. 270–75.

Usher, D. (1986), 'Police, punishment and public goods', *Public Finance*, **41**(1), 96–115.

Van Raaij, F. (1990), 'The effect of marketing communications on the initiation of juvenile smoking', in Lea, S.E.G., Webley, P. & Young, B.M. (eds),

Applied Economic Psychology in the 1990s, Washington Singer Press, pp. 152–98.

Vaughan, P. (1998), *The Monogamy Myth*, Vaughan and Vaughan, Revised Edition.

Vernon, M.D. (1969), *Human Motivation*, Cambridge University Press, Cambridge.

Viscusi, W.K. (1992), *Smoking: Making the Risky Decision*, Oxford University Press, New York.

Waldfogel, J. (1998), 'Understanding the "family gap" in pay for women with children', *Journal of Economic Perspectives*, **12**(1), 137–56.

Webb, N. & Whybrow, R. (1982), *The Gallup Report*, Sphere Books, London.

Webley, P. (1999), 'Children's Saving', in Earl, P.E. & Kemp, S. (eds), *The Elgar Companion to Consumer Research and Economic Psychology*, Edward Elgar, Cheltenham, pp. 72–4.

Weinstein, N.D. (1980), 'Unrealistic optimism about future life events', *Journal of Personality and Social Psychology*, **39**(5), 806–20.

Weiss, Y. & Willis, R.J. (1985), 'Children as collective goods and divorce settlements', *Journal of Labor Economics*, **3**(2), 268–92.

Weisskopf, W.A. (1965), 'Economic growth versus existential balance', *Ethics*, **75**(2) [reprinted in Daly, H. (ed.) (1973), *Towards a Steady-state economy*, W.H. Freeman & Co., San Francisco].

Wellings, K., Field, J., Johnson, A.M. & Wadsworth, J. (1994), *Sexual Behaviour in Britain*, Penguin Books, Harmondsworth.

Williamson, O.E. (1975), *Markets and Hierarchies: Analysis and Antitrust Implications*, The Free Press, New York.

Williamson, O.E. (1976), 'The economics of international organisation: Exit and voice in relation to markets and hierarchies', *American Economic Review*, **66**(2), 369–77.

Wilson, E.O. (1975), *Sociobiology: The New Synthesis*, Harvard University Press, Cambridge, MA.

Winston, G.C. (1980), 'Addiction and backsliding: a theory of compulsive consumption', *Journal of Economic Behavior and Organization*, **1**, 295–324.

Woodmansee, M. & Osteen, M. (eds) (1999), *The New Economic Criticism*, Routledge, London and New York.

World Bank (1993), *World Development Report: Investing in Health*, Washington, DC.

World Sex Guide. http://www.worldsexguide.org/

Wright, R. (1994), *The Moral Animal: The New Science of Evolutionary Psychology*, Vintage, New York.

Yalom, M. (1997), *A History of the Breast*, HarperCollins, London.

Young, P. (1992), 'The economics of convention', *Journal of Economic Perspectives*, **10**(1), 105–22.

Youngson, R. & Schott, I. (1996), *Medical Blunders. Amazing True Stories of Mad, Bad and Dangerous Doctors*, Robinson, London.

Yousefi, M., McCormick, K. & Abizadeh, S. (1995), 'Islamic banking and Friedman's rule', *Review of Social Economy*, **53**(1), 65–87.

Zadek, S. (1993), 'The practice of Buddhist economics: another view', *American Journal of Economics and Sociology*, **52**(4), 433–44.

Zaleski, P.A. & Zech, P.E. (1995), 'The effect of religious market competition on church giving', *Review of Social Economy*, **53**(3), 350–67.

Zarkin, G.A., French, M.T., Mroz, T. & Bray, J.W. (1998), 'Alcohol use and wages: new results from the National Household Survey on Drug Abuse', *Journal of Health Economics*, **17**(1), 53–68.

Zeisel, H. & Gallup, A.M. (1989), 'Death penalty sentiment in the United States', *Journal of Quantitative Criminology*, **5**(3), 285–96.

Index